Other Books and Series by Jeff Bowen

Applications for Enrollment of Chickasaw Newborn Act of 1905
Volumes I thru VII

Cherokee Intermarried White 1906 Volume I thru X

Applications for Enrollment of Creek Newborn Act of 1905 Volume I, II, III & IV

Visit our website at **www.nativestudy.com** to learn more about these and other books and series by Jeff Bowen

APPLICATIONS FOR ENROLLMENT OF CREEK NEWBORN ACT OF 1905

VOLUME V

TRANSCRIBED BY
JEFF BOWEN

NATIVE STUDY
Gallipolis, Ohio
USA

Other Books and Series by Jeff Bowen

1901-1907 Native American Census Seneca, Eastern Shawnee, Miami, Modoc, Ottawa, Peoria, Quapaw, and Wyandotte Indians (Under Seneca School, Indian Territory)

1932 Census of The Standing Rock Sioux Reservation with Births And Deaths 1924-1932

Census of The Blackfeet, Montana, 1897-1901 Expanded Edition

Eastern Cherokee by Blood, 1906-1910, Volumes I thru XIII

Choctaw of Mississippi Indian Census 1929-1932 with Births and Deaths 1924-1931   Volume I
Choctaw of Mississippi Indian Census 1933, 1934 & 1937, Supplemental Rolls to 1934 & 1935 with Births and Deaths 1932-1938, and Marriages 1936-1938 Volume II

Eastern Cherokee Census Cherokee, North Carolina 1930-1939
Census 1930-1931 with Births And Deaths 1924-1931 Taken By Agent L. W. Page Volume I
Eastern Cherokee Census Cherokee, North Carolina 1930-1939
Census 1932-1933 with Births And Deaths 1930-1932 Taken By Agent R. L. Spalsbury   Volume II
Eastern Cherokee Census Cherokee, North Carolina 1930-1939
Census 1934-1937 with Births and Deaths 1925-1938 and Marriages 1936 & 1938 Taken by Agents R. L. Spalsbury And Harold W. Foght Volume III

Seminole of Florida Indian Census, 1930-1940 with Birth and Death Records, 1930-1938

Texas Cherokees 1820-1839 A Document For Litigation 1921

Choctaw By Blood Enrollment Cards 1898-1914 Volumes I thru XVII

Starr Roll 1894 (Cherokee Payment Rolls) Districts: Canadian, Cooweescoowee, and Delaware Volume One
Starr Roll 1894 (Cherokee Payment Rolls) Districts: Flint, Going Snake, and Illinois   Volume Two
Starr Roll 1894 (Cherokee Payment Rolls) Districts: Saline, Sequoyah, and Tahlequah; Including Orphan Roll   Volume Three

Cherokee Intruder Cases Dockets of Hearings 1901-1909 Volumes I & II

Indian Wills, 1911-1921 Records of the Bureau of Indian Affairs
Books One thru Seven;
Native American Wills & Probate Records 1911-1921

Other Books and Series by Jeff Bowen

Turtle Mountain Reservation Chippewa Indians 1932 Census with Births & Deaths, 1924-1932

Chickasaw By Blood Enrollment Cards 1898-1914 Volume I thru V

Cherokee Descendants East An Index to the Guion Miller Applications Volume I
Cherokee Descendants West An Index to the Guion Miller Applications Volume II (A-M)
Cherokee Descendants West An Index to the Guion Miller Applications Volume III (N-Z)

Applications for Enrollment of Seminole Newborn Freedmen, Act of 1905

Eastern Cherokee Census, Cherokee, North Carolina, 1915-1922, Taken by Agent James E. Henderson
    Volume I (1915-1916)
    Volume II (1917-1918)
    Volume III (1919-1920)
    Volume IV (1921-1922)

Complete Delaware Roll of 1898

Eastern Cherokee Census, Cherokee, North Carolina, 1923-1929, Taken by Agent James E. Henderson
    Volume I (1923-1924)
    Volume II (1925-1926)
    Volume III (1927-1929)

Applications for Enrollment of Seminole Newborn Act of 1905 Volumes I & II

North Carolina Eastern Cherokee Indian Census 1898-1899, 1904, 1906, 1909-1912, 1914 Revised and Expanded Edition

1932 Hopi and Navajo Native American Census with Birth & Death Rolls (1925-1931) Volume 1 - Hopi
1932 Hopi and Navajo Native American Census with Birth & Death Rolls (1930-1932) Volume 2 - Navajo

Western Navajo Reservation Navajo, Hopi and Paiute 1933 Census with Birth & Death Rolls 1925-1933

Cherokee Citizenship Commission Dockets 1880-1884 and 1887-1889 Volumes I thru V

Copyright © 2011
by Jeff Bowen

ALL RIGHTS RESERVED
No part of this publication may be reproduced
or used in any form or manner whatsoever
without previous written permission from the
copyright holder or publisher.

Originally published:
Baltimore, Maryland
2011

Reprinted by:

Native Study LLC
Gallipolis, OH
www.nativestudy.com
2020

Library of Congress Control Number: 2020917992

ISBN: 978-1-64968-084-6

Made in the United States of America.

This series is dedicated to the descendants of the Creek newborn listed in these applications.

DEPARTMENT OF THE INTERIOR.

Commissioner to the Five Civilized Tribes.

NOTICE.

Opening of Land Office at Wewoka,
IN THE SEMINOLE NATION, INDIAN TERRITORY.

Notice is hereby given that on Monday, September 4, 1905, the Commissioner to the Five Civilized Tribes will establish a land office at Wewoka, in the Seminole Nation, Indian Territory, for the purpose of allowing citizens and freedmen of the Seminole Nation to select allotments of land for their minor children enrolled under the Act of Congress approved March 3, 1905 (33 Stat. L 1060), and for the further purpose of allowing citizens and freedmen of the Seminole Nation, whose allotments are incomplete, to select additional land in order to bring the value of their allotments up to the standard of $309.09, as nearly as may be practicable.

Each child whose enrollment in accordance with the Act of March 3, 1905, has been duly approved by the Secretary of the Interior, is entitled to receive an alllotment of forty acres without regard to the character or value of the land selected.

Selection of allotments for minor children must be made by their citizen or freedmen parents or by a duly appointed guardian, or curator, or by a duly appointed administrator.

TAMS BIXBY,
Commissioner.

Muskogee, Indian Territory,
July 29, 1905.

This particular notice makes mention of the Act of 1905. The Creek and Seminole were closely related tribes. Both tribes' notices were like similar in nature.

DEPARTMENT OF THE INTERIOR,
Commission to the Five Civilized Tribes.

Closing of Citizenship Rolls

OF THE MUSKOGEE OR CREEK NATION.

WHEREAS, on June 13, 1904, the Secretary of the Interior, under the authority in him vested by the provisions of the act of Congress approved March 3, 1901, (31 Stat., 1058) ordered that September 1, 1904, be and the same is hereby fixed as the time when the rolls of the Muskogee or Creek Nation shall be closed:

Notice is hereby given that the Commission to the Five Civilized Tribes will, at its office in Muskogee, Indian Territory, up to and inclusive of September 1, 1904, receive applications for the enrollment of citizens and freedmen of the Muskogee or Creek Nation, and that after that date the application of no person whomsoever for enrollment as a citizen or freedman of said nation will be received by the Commission.

Commission to the Five Civilized Tribes,
TAMS BIXBY, Chairman,
T. B. NEEDLES,
C. R. BRECKINRIDGE,
Commissioners.

Muskogee, Indian Territory,
June 25, 1904.

A notice like this was printed in newspapers and posted throughout Indian Territory.

INTRODUCTION

This series concerns Applications for Enrollment of Creek Newborn, National Archive film M-1301 (Act of 1905), as described in the National Archives publication *American Indians*. It falls under the heading Applications for Enrollment of the Commission to the Five Civilized Tribes, 1898-1914, M-1301 and is transcribed from microfilm rolls 414-419. This shows the application forms filled out by individuals applying for enrollment in the Five Civilized Tribes under the Dawes Commission. These applications contain additional information that wasn't abstracted to the census cards that you find in series M-1186. This particular roll (Creek by Birth) contains its own series of numbers separate from M-1186. To find each party's roll number you would have to reference M-1186. On July 25, 1898, there was an Indian Territory Division created in the Office of the Department of Interior. This division was created because of the increased work caused by what was called the Curtis Act, named after Senator Charles Curtis. Basically, this law stated that the tribal rolls needed to be descriptive and pointed out that each tribal roll was without description and had to be redone. At this point there was such a struggle among the Creeks to accept that the Government was going to change their way of life, again, that their leaders were refusing to cooperate in handing over their census information. The Commission had found that enrolling the Creeks was a difficult task not only because the Creek feared what was coming but also because their tribal structure was consistent with being a confederacy with forty-four different bands whose tribesmen lived in different towns of which each had a king that was supposed to keep track of their citizenry. The Commission reported that there was very little evidence of any census that existed and what there was had been kept carelessly. There were attempts and tribal conflicts along the way, but the Curtis Act would make it so they had to do it again no matter what effort from the past. In 1899, Agent Wesley Smith educated Washington to the fact that it was difficult to verify Creek eligibility. The acts passed by the Creeks themselves concerning enrollment since 1893 had been strewn amongst the archives of the Creek Council in Muskogee, I.T., and there was no provision ever approved for the printing of the those enrollments. There was confusion and difficulty let alone the fact that surnames were practically unknown among the Creek. But there was no confusion on March 9, 1905, when the Commission stated they would come to seven towns in the Creek Nation and accept applications that had to be made on a standardized blank form and contain a notarized affidavit from the mother and the attending doctor or midwife. A few by mail, but most of them were offered to a field party led by Commissioner Needles. The Commission took in applications for 2,410 children by the deadline of midnight, May 2, 1905.

This series contains applications and correspondence from 1,171 of those claimants. Realizing there were over 2,400 applicants originally, it is understood that not all were accepted. Also included are names of doctors, lawyers, mid-wives, and others who attended to the Creek Nation before and during this time in history.

Jeff Bowen
Gallipolis, Ohio
NativeStudy.com

Applications for Enrollment of Creek Newborn
Act of 1905   Volume V

N.C. 339.

DEPARTMENT OF THE INTERIOR,
COMMISSIONER TO THE FIVE CIVILIZED TRIBES,
Near Checotah, Indian Territory, February 8, 1907.

      In the matter of the application for the enrollment of John Coonhead, deceased, as a citizen by blood of the Creek Nation.

      LOTTY BEAR, being duly sworn, by J. McDermott, a notary public, testified as follows through Jesse McDermott, official interpreter.

BY THE COMMISSIONER:

Q What is your name? A Lotty Carr is my name now but it was Lotty Bear.
Q What is your age? A About 35.
Q What is your postoffice address? A Checotah.
Q Are you a citizen of the Creek Nation? A Yes.
Q Do you know Susannah Coonhead? A Yes.
Q Do you know a child of hers by the name of John Coonhead? A Yes.
Q Do you know when John was born? A Three years ago last April.
Q You were the midwife were you not? A Yes, the baby was born at my house.
Q Is the child living at the present time? A I heard that the child has died since the mother took him with her over near Hanna, I.T. I do not know when he died.
Q Do you know the father of that child? A Wiley Coonhead is the father.
Q Were Susannah and Wiley Coonhead lawfully married prior to the birth of the child? A Yes, Wiley was sent to prison is what caused her to be living with me at the time the child was born.
Q Do you know under what name she is enrolled? A Susannah Jackson.
Q Do you know the name of her mother? A No, I do not as her mother was a Cherokee and lived over in the neighborhood of Ft. Gibson.
Q Do you know the name of her father? A Thlatiske is the nickname that he had and that is the only name I knew him by. He was one of the brothers of Joe Jackson.
Q To which Creek Indian town does she belong? A Hillabee Canadian. She might be on the Kechopatakee town. Her father lived on Elk Creek.
Q Do you know where her allotment is located? A I am told that it is located between Checotah and Muskogee. I have some letters here for her and have written to her a number of times but she refuses to answer me.

      I, Jesse McDermott, on oath state that the above and foregoing is a full and true transcript of my notes as taken in said cause on said date.

                                                 Jesse McDermott

Applications for Enrollment of Creek Newborn
Act of 1905   Volume V

Subscribed and sworn to before me this 6th day of February 1907.

My commission expires Jany 22nd 1911   J.D. Faulkner
                                                                                    Notary Public.

                                                                                                F.H.W.
N.C. 339.   A.G.
DEPARTMENT OF THE INTERIOR,
COMMISSIONER TO THE FIVE CIVILIZED TRIBES.

In the matter of the application for the enrollment of John Coonhead, deceased, as a citizen by blood of the Creek Nation.

DECISION.

The record in this case shows that on March 22, 1905, an application was filed in affidavit form for the enrollment of John Coonhead as a citizen by blood of the Creek Nation. Further proceedings were had February 6, 1907.

The evidence in this case and the records in the possession of this office show that the applicant, John Coonhead, was the child of Willie Coonhead and Susanna Coonhead. The given name of the said father of the applicant appears in the original application as Wiley but the evidence and the records of this office show that Wiley Coonhead and Willie Coonhead are one and the same person, whose name appears as Willie Coonhead in a partial schedule of citizens by blood of the Creek Nation, approved by the Secretary of the Interior March 28, 1902, opposite roll No. 7985.

The name of the mother of the applicant appears in the original application as Susana[sic] Coonhead who is identified from the records of this office and the evidence in this case as Susanna Jackson in a partial schedule of citizens by blood of the Creek Nation approved by the Secretary of the Interior March 13, 1902, opposite roll No. 381. It is therefore considered that the given name of the said mother is Susanna.

The evidence further shows that the applicant, John Coonhead, was born April 8, 1903 and was still living March 4, 1905.

It is, therefore, ordered and adjudged that said John Coonhead, deceased, is entitled to be enrolled as a citizen by blood of the Creek Nation, under the provisions of the Act of Congress approved March 3, 1905 (33 Stat., 1048), and the application for his enrollment as such is accordingly granted.

                                                                    Tams Bixby Commissioner.
Muskogee, Indian Territory.
FEB 23 1907

Applications for Enrollment of Creek Newborn
Act of 1905   Volume V

BIRTH AFFIDAVIT.

DEPARTMENT OF THE INTERIOR.
COMMISSION TO THE FIVE CIVILIZED TRIBES.

    IN RE APPLICATION FOR ENROLLMENT, as a citizen of the Creek Nation, of John Coonhead , born on the 8th day of April , 1903

Name of Father: Wiley Coonhead	a citizen of the Creek	Nation.
Name of Mother: Susana Coonhead	a citizen of the Creek	Nation.

                      Postoffice   Checotah, Ind. Ter.

AFFIDAVIT OF MOTHER.

UNITED STATES OF AMERICA, Indian Territory,
   Western   DISTRICT.

    I, Susana Coonhead , on oath state that I am 24 years of age and a citizen by blood , of the Creek Nation; that I am the lawful wife of Wiley Coonhead , who is a citizen, by blood of the Creek Nation; that a male child was born to me on the 8th day of April , 1903 , that said child has been named John Coonhead , and was living March 4, 1905.

                                                  her
Witnesses To Mark: Susana x Coonhead
  { F.A. McIntosh   mark
    Daniel N. Bard

    Subscribed and sworn to before me this 20th day of March , 1905.

My commission expires July 3rd 1906.   Charles Buford
                                                    Notary Public.

AFFIDAVIT OF ATTENDING PHYSICIAN OR MID-WIFE.

UNITED STATES OF AMERICA, Indian Territory,
   Western   DISTRICT.

    I, Lotty Bear , a mid-wife , on oath state that I attended on Mrs. Susana Coonhead , wife of Wiley Coonhead on the 8th day of April , 1903 ; that there was born to her on said date a male child; that said child was living March 4, 1905, and is said to have been named John Coonhead

                                                  her
                                              Lotty x Bear
Witnesses To Mark: mark
  { Daniel N. Bard
    F.A. McIntosh

Applications for Enrollment of Creek Newborn
Act of 1905   Volume V

Subscribed and sworn to before me this 20th day of March, 1905.

My commission expires July 3rd 1906.   Charles Buford
                                                                                Notary Public.

(The above Birth Affidavit given again.)

HGH

COMMISSIONERS:
TAMS BIXBY,
THOMAS B. NEEDLES,
C.R. BRECKINBRIDGE.

DEPARTMENT OF THE INTERIOR,
COMMISSIONER TO THE FIVE CIVILIZED TRIBES.

REFER IN REPLY TO THE FOLLOWING:

Cr NC-339.

WM. O. BEALL
Secretary

ADDRESS ONLY THE
COMMISSION TO THE FIVE CIVILIZED TRIBES

Muskogee, Indian Territory, June 12, 1905.

Susanna Coonhead,
        Checotah, Indian Territory.

Dear Madam:

In the matter of the application for the enrollment of your minor child, John Coonhead, as a citizen of the Creek Nation, you are advised that the Commission cannot identify you on its rolls.

You are requested to furnish the Commission with your maiden name, the names of your parents, the Creek Indian Town to which you claim to belong, your roll number as same appears on your deeds to land in the Creek Nation, and any other information which will help identify you as a citizen of said Nation.

Respectfully,

Tams Bixby
        Chairman.

NC. 339.

Muskogee, Indian Territory, July 15, 1905.

Wiley Coonhead,
        Checotah, Indian Territory.

Dear Sir:

Applications for Enrollment of Creek Newborn
Act of 1905   Volume V

In the matter of the application for the enrollment of your minor child, John Coonhead, as a citizen of the Creek Nation, you are advised that without further information, it is impossible for this office to identify Susanna Coonhead, the mother of said child, as a citizen of the Creek Nation.

You are requested to furnish this office with her maiden name, the names of her parents, the Creek Indian Town to which she belongs, and if possible the numbers which appear on her deeds to land in the Creek Nation, and any other information that will help identify her as a citizen of the Creek Nation.

Respectfully,

Commissioner.

N.C. 339

Muskogee, Indian Territory, August 3, 1905.

Susanna Coonhead,
　　Care Willie Coonhead,
　　　　Checotah, Indian Territory.

Dear Madam:

March 22, 1905, there was filed in this office your affidavit relative to the birth of your minor child John Coonhead.

This office is unable to identify you on its rolls of citizens of the Creek Nation and you are requested to state your maiden name, the names of your parents, the Creek Indian Town to which you belong, and, if possible, the numbers which appear on your deeds to land in the Creek Nation.

Respectfully,

Commissioner.

NC 339.

Muskogee, Indian Territory, January 12, 1907.

Daniel Bard,
　　Checotah, Indian Territory.

Dear Sir:

In the matter of the application for the enrollment of John Coonhead, child of Wiley and Susanna Coonhead, you are advised that this office cannot identify the latter

Applications for Enrollment of Creek Newborn
Act of 1905   Volume V

on its rolls of citizens of the Creek Nation, and you are requested to furnish this office within five days her maiden name, the names of her parents, and her roll number as same appears on her allotment certificates or deeds to land in the Creek Nation.

Respectfully,

Commissioner.

REFER IN REPLY TO THE FOLLOWING:

NC 339,

DEPARTMENT OF THE INTERIOR,
COMMISSIONER TO THE FIVE CIVILIZED TRIBES.

Muskogee, Indian Territory, January 12, 1907.

Susanna Coonhead,
    c/o Wiley Coonhead,
        Checotah, Indian Territory.

Dear Madam:

    This office is unable to identify you on its rolls of citizens of the Creek Nation, and you are requested to write within five days stating your maiden name, the names of your parents, the Creek Indian town to which you belong, and, if possible, your roll number as same appears on your allotment certificates or deeds to land in the Creek Nation, in order that the right to enrollment as a citizen of the Creek Nation of your minor child, John Coonhead, may be adjudicated.

Respectfully,

Tams Bixby
Commissioner.

NC 339.

Muskogee, Indian Territory, March 18, 1907.

Susanna Coonhead,
    c/o Wiley Coonhead,
        Checotah, Indian Territory.

Dear Madam:

    You are hereby advised that the Secretary of the Interior under date of March 4, 1907, approved the enrollment of your minor child, John Coonhead, as a citizen by blood of the Creek Nation, and that the name of said child appears upon the roll of new born

Applications for Enrollment of Creek Newborn
Act of 1905 Volume V

citizens by blood of the Creek Nation, enrolled under the act of Congress approved March 3, 1905, as number 1284.

This child is now entitled to allotment, and application therefor should be made without delay at the Creek Land Office, Muskogee, Indian Territory.

Respectfully,

Commissioner.

BIRTH AFFIDAVIT.

DEPARTMENT OF THE INTERIOR.
COMMISSION TO THE FIVE CIVILIZED TRIBES.

IN RE APPLICATION FOR ENROLLMENT, as a citizen of the Creek Nation, of Bessie Scott, born on the 12 day of July, 1901

Name of Father:	Turner Scott	a citizen of the	Creek	Nation.
Name of Mother:	Lucinda Scott	a citizen of the	Creek	Nation.

Postoffice   Dustin Ind Ter

AFFIDAVIT OF MOTHER.

UNITED STATES OF AMERICA, Indian Territory,
Western   DISTRICT.

I, Lucinda Scott, on oath state that I am about 30 years of age and a citizen by blood, of the Creek Nation; that I ~~am~~ was the lawful wife of Turner Scott, who is a citizen, by blood of the Creek Nation; that a female child was born to me on 12" day of July, 1901, that said child has been named Bessie Scott, and was living March 4, 1905. That no one attended on me as midwife or physician at the birth of the child.

            her
          Lucinda x Scott
Witnesses To Mark: mark
 { Alex Posey
   D.C. Skaggs

Subscribed and sworn to before me this 20" day of March, 1905.

          Drennan C Skaggs
           Notary Public.

Applications for Enrollment of Creek Newborn
Act of 1905   Volume V

BIRTH AFFIDAVIT.

DEPARTMENT OF THE INTERIOR.
COMMISSION TO THE FIVE CIVILIZED TRIBES.

IN RE APPLICATION FOR ENROLLMENT, as a citizen of the Creek Nation, of Pleasant Scott, born on the 22 day of July , 1901

Name of Father:	Turner Scott	a citizen of the Creek	Nation.
Name of Mother:	Lucinda Scott	a citizen of the Creek	Nation.

Postoffice   Watsonville I.T.

AFFIDAVIT OF MOTHER.

UNITED STATES OF AMERICA, Indian Territory,
   Western   DISTRICT.

I, Lucinda Scott , on oath state that I am 26 years of age and a citizen by blood, of the Creek Nation; that I am the unlawful wife of Turner Scott , who is a citizen, by blood of the Creek Nation; that a female child was born to me on 22 day of July , 1901 , that said child has been named Pleasant Scott , and is now living.

                          her
                      Lucinda x Scott
Witnesses To Mark: mark
   JD Berry
   Charles Coachman

Subscribed and sworn to before me this 9 day of September , 1901.

                              William T Martin
                              Notary Public.

(The above Birth Affidavit of Bessie Scott given again.)

AFFIDAVIT OF DISINTERESTED WITNESS.

UNITED STATES OF AMERICA.
Western DISTRICT,   SS
INDIAN TERRITORY.

We, the undersigned, on oath state that we are personally acquainted with Lucinda Scott who was the wife of Turner Scott; that there was born to her a female child

Applications for Enrollment of Creek Newborn
Act of 1905 Volume V

on or about the 12" day of July, 1901; that the said child has been named Bessie Scott, and was living March 4, 1905, and is now living.

    We further state that we have no interest in this case.

Witnesses:

J McDermott   Charley Wesley

J. W. Clements   her
                                  Matilda x Wesley
                                        mark

    Subscribed and sworn to before me this 22 day, November, 1906.

My Commission
Expires July 25' 1907   J McDermott
                                        Notary Public.

Cr.
NC 340

                                 Muskogee, Indian Territory, June 8, 1905.

Lucinda Scott,
    Dustin, Indian Territory.

Dear Madam:

    In the matter of the application for the enrollment of your minor child, Bessie Scott, as a citizen of the Creek Nation, you are advised that the Commission requires the affidavits of two disinterested witnesses relative to its birth.

    For this purpose, there are herewith enclosed two blank forms of birth affidavit. In having same executed, care should be taken to see that all blanks are properly filled, all names written in full and in the event that the person signing the affidavit is unable to write, signatures by mark must be attested by two witnesses.

                              Respectfully,

2 BA   Chairman.

Applications for Enrollment of Creek Newborn
Act of 1905 Volume V

NC 340.

Muskogee, Indian Territory, July 27, 1905.

Turner Scott,
    Dustin, Indian Territory.

Dear Sir:

    In the matter of the application for the enrollment of your minor child, Bessie Scott, as a citizen by blood of the Creek Nation, you are advised that this office requires the affidavits of two disinterested witnesses relative to its birth.

    For this purpose, there are herewith enclosed two blank forms of birth affidavit. In having same executed, care should be taken to see that all blanks are properly filled, all names written in full and in the event that the person signing the affidavit is unable to write, signatures by mark must be attested by two witnesses.

    This matter should receive your prompt attention.

    Respectfully,

    Commissioner.

REFER IN REPLY TO THE FOLLOWING:
B.A.N.E.-80

**DEPARTMENT OF THE INTERIOR,
COMMISSIONER TO THE FIVE CIVILIZED TRIBES.**

Muskogee, Indian Territory, January 24, 1906.

Lucinda Scott,
    Care of Turner Scott,
        Dustin, Indian Territory.

Dear Madam:

    In the matter of the application for the enrollment of your minor child, Pleasant Scott, born July 22, 1901, you are advised that this office requires proof of death of said child.
    There is herewith inclosed[sic] blank form of birth affidavit, and you are requested to execute same before an officer authorized to administer oaths and return it to this office in the inclosed[sic] envelope.

    In the event that said child is not dead this office requires your affidavit and the affidavit of the mid-wife in attendance at its birth, stating the name of the child, the

Applications for Enrollment of Creek Newborn
Act of 1905   Volume V

names of its parents, the date of its birth, and whether or not it was living March 4, 1905 March 4, 1905.

This matter should receive your prompt attention.

Respectfully,
Wm O. Beall
Acting Commissioner.

[Handwritten at bottom of above letter]

The child referred to is <u>Not</u> <u>Dead</u> you will Please correct form and oblige.

Lucind[sic] Scott

NC 340.

Muskogee, Indian Territory, March 1, 1907.

Lucinda Scott,
   c/o Turner Scott,
      Dustin, Indian Territory.

Dear Madam:

    You are hereby advised that on February 15, 1907, the Secretary of the Interior approved the enrollment of your minor child, Bessie Scott, as a citizen by blood of the Creek Nation, and that the name of said child appears upon the roll of New Born citizens of the Creek Nation, enrolled Act of Congress approved March 3rd, 1905, as number 1135.

    The child is now entitled to allotment, and application therefor should be made without delay at the Creek Land Office, Muskogee, Indian Territory.

Respectfully,
Commissioner.

Applications for Enrollment of Creek Newborn
Act of 1905   Volume V

BIRTH AFFIDAVIT.

DEPARTMENT OF THE INTERIOR.
COMMISSION TO THE FIVE CIVILIZED TRIBES.

IN RE APPLICATION FOR ENROLLMENT, as a citizen of the Creek Nation, of Fanny Ellis, born on the 10 day of December, 1904

Name of Father: Sargent Ellis   a citizen of the   Creek   Nation.
Name of Mother: Annie Ellis   a citizen of the   Creek   Nation.
                        Postoffice   Paden, Indian Territory

AFFIDAVIT OF MOTHER.

UNITED STATES OF AMERICA, Indian Territory,
   Western   DISTRICT.

I, Annie Ellis, on oath state that I am about 25 years of age and a citizen by blood, of the Creek Nation; that I am the lawful wife of Sargent Ellis, who is a citizen, by blood of the Creek Nation; that a female child was born to me on 10" day of December, 1904, that said child has been named Fanny Ellis, and was living March 4, 1905.

                                    Annie Ellis
Witnesses To Mark:

Subscribed and sworn to before me this 14" day of March, 1905.

                                    Drennan C Skaggs
                                        Notary Public.

AFFIDAVIT OF ATTENDING PHYSICIAN OR MID-WIFE.

UNITED STATES OF AMERICA, Indian Territory,
   Western   DISTRICT.

I, Wally Ellis, a midwife, on oath state that I attended on Mrs. Annie Ellis, wife of Sargent Ellis on the 10" day of December, 1904; that there was born to her on said date a female child; that said child was living March 4, 1905, and is said to have been named Fanny Ellis
                                        her
                                    Wally x Ellis
Witnesses To Mark: mark
   Alex Posey
   D C Skaggs

Applications for Enrollment of Creek Newborn
Act of 1905   Volume V

Subscribed and sworn to before me this 14" day of March, 1905.

Drennan C Skaggs
Notary Public.

BIRTH AFFIDAVIT.

DEPARTMENT OF THE INTERIOR.
COMMISSION TO THE FIVE CIVILIZED TRIBES.

IN RE APPLICATION FOR ENROLLMENT, as a citizen of the Creek Nation, of Mary Ellis, born on the 13 day of March, 1903

| Name of Father: | Sargent Ellis | a citizen of the | Creek | Nation. |
| Name of Mother: | Annie Ellis | a citizen of the | Creek | Nation. |

Postoffice   Paden, Indian Territory

AFFIDAVIT OF MOTHER.

UNITED STATES OF AMERICA, Indian Territory,
Western   DISTRICT.

I, Annie Ellis, on oath state that I am about 25 years of age and a citizen by blood, of the Creek Nation; that I am the lawful wife of Sargent Ellis, who is a citizen, by blood of the Creek Nation; that a female child was born to me on 13" day of March, 1903, that said child has been named Mary Ellis, and was living March 4, 1905.

Annie Ellis

Witnesses To Mark:
{

Subscribed and sworn to before me this 14 day of March, 1905.

Drennan C Skaggs
Notary Public.

AFFIDAVIT OF ATTENDING PHYSICIAN OR MID-WIFE.

UNITED STATES OF AMERICA, Indian Territory,
Western   DISTRICT.

I, Wally Ellis, a midwife, on oath state that I attended on Mrs. Annie Ellis, wife of Sargent Ellis on the 13 day of March, 1903; that there was born to her on

Applications for Enrollment of Creek Newborn
Act of 1905   Volume V

said date a female child; that said child was living March 4, 1905, and is said to have been named Mary Ellis

            her
         Wally x Ellis
Witnesses To Mark: mark
 { Alex Posey
  D C Skaggs

  Subscribed and sworn to before me this 14" day of March, 1905.

          Drennan C Skaggs
          Notary Public.

N.C. 341.   F.H.W.
                         AG
DEPARTMENT OF THE INTERIOR,
COMMISSIONER TO THE FIVE CIVILIZED TRIBES.

  In the matter of the applications for the enrollment of Mary Ellis and Fanny Ellis as citizens by blood of the Creek Nation.

DECISION.

  The record in this case shows that on March 23, 1905, applications were made, in affidavit form, for the enrollment of Mary Ellis and Fanny Ellis as citizens by blood of the Creek Nation. A statement without date signed by mark, by "Wiley" as midwife and witnessed by Anne Ellis, a letter bearing date of October 10, 1906, a copy of a letter dated November 9, 1906, and letters dated November 10 and 12, 1906, are attached to and made part of the record herein.
  The evidence in this case shows that the applicants are the children of Sargent Ellis and Anne Ellis but the reports of this office fail to show that either the father or the mother of said applicants is a duly enrolled citizen of the Creek Nation, or that applications have been made for their enrollment as such.
  It is therefore, ordered and adjudged that there is no authority of law for the enrollment of Mary Ellis and Fanny Ellis as citizens by blood of the Creek Nation and the applications for their enrollment as such are accordingly denied.

                  Tams Bixby
                  Commissioner.
Muskogee, Indian Territory.
JAN 29 1907

Applications for Enrollment of Creek Newborn
Act of 1905   Volume V

Cr. NC 341.

Muskogee, Indian Territory, June 8, 1905.

Annie Ellis,
    Paden, Indian Territory.

Dear Madam:

    In the matter of the application for the enrollment of your minor children, Mary and Fannie Ellis, as citizens of the Creek Nation, you are advised that the Commission is unable to identify you, or the father of said children, on its rolls.

    You are requested to advise the Commission as to any other name by which the father of said children is known; also you maiden name, the names of your parents, the Creek Indian Town to which you claim to belong, and if possible, the roll number which appears on your deeds to land in the Creek Nation, which will help to identify you as a citizen of said Nation.

                      Respectfully,

                              Chairman.

United States of America?
Indian Territory,
Western Judicial District.

Dawes Commission,
    Muskogee,

Dear Sir:

    The mother and father of Mary and Fannie Ellis have their allotments in the Shawnee nation. Sargis Ellis, the father of the above mentioned children is an own relative of Dabe[sic] Ellis who has an allotment here in the Creek Nation. Dave and Sargis Ellis are own brothers and Sargis Ellis is the father of the above mentioned children.

    This is to certify that I "Wiley" was the midwife at the birth of the above mentioned children and they was born in the Creek Nation, and I further certify that Dave and Sargis Ellis are relatives.

Anne Ellis,   "Wiley" Her Mark, Midwife.
Mother of the above mentioned children.

Applications for Enrollment of Creek Newborn
Act of 1905 Volume V

NC 341.

Muskogee, Indian Territory, January 31, 1907.

The Honorable,
    The Secretary of the Interior.

Sir:

    There is herewith transmitted the record of proceedings in the matter of the application for the enrollment of the record of proceedings in the matter of the application for the enrollment of Mary Ellis and Fanny Ellis, as citizens by blood of the Creek nation, including the decision of the Commissioner, dated January 29, 1907.

                  Respectfully,

Through the
Commissioner of Indian Affairs,

EK-3.   Commissioner.

NC 341.

Muskogee, Indian Territory, January 31, 1907.

M. L. Mott,
    Attorney for Creek Nation,
        Muskogee, Indian Territory.

Sir:

    There is herewith enclosed one copy of the decision of the Commissioner to the Five Civilized Tribes in the matter of the application for the enrollment of Mary Ellis and Fanny Ellis, as citizens by blood of the Creek Nation.

    The decision, with a copy of the proceedings had in the case, is this day transmitted to the Secretary of the Interior for his review and decision. The final decision of the Secretary will be made known to you as soon as the Commissioner is informed of t the Secretary of the Interior for his review and decision. The final decision of the Secretary will be made known to you as soon as the Commissioner is informed of the same.

                    Respectfully,

                                                Commissioner.

EK-2.

Applications for Enrollment of Creek Newborn
Act of 1905 Volume V

NC 341.

Muskogee, Indian Territory, January 31, 1907.

Annie Ellis,
    C/o Sargent Ellis,
        Paden, Indian Territory.

Dear Madam:

    There is herewith enclosed one copy of the decision of the Commissioner to the Five Civilized Tribes in the matter of the application for the enrollment of your minor children, Mary Ellis and Fanny Ellis, as citizens by blood of the Creek Nation, denying said application.

    The decision, with a copy of the proceedings had in the case, is this day transmitted to the Secretary of the Interior for his review and decision. The final decision of the Secretary will be made known to you as soon as the Commissioner is informed of the same.

        Respectfully,

Register.   Commissioner.

EK-1.

DEPARTMENT OF THE INTERIOR.   KLM OK
WASHINGTON February 25, 1907

I T D 4272-1907
LRS
Direct

Commissioner to the Five Civilized Tribes,
    Muskogee, Indian Territory.

Sir:

    January 31, 1907, you transmitted the record in the matter of the application for the enrollment of Mary Ellis and Fanny Ellis, as citizens by blood of the Creek Nation, together with your decision of January 29, 1907, denying the application.

    Reporting February 19, 1907 (Land 11095-1907), the Indian Office recommends that your decision be approved.

A copy of its letter is enclosed.

    Your decision is hereby affirmed.

Applications for Enrollment of Creek Newborn
Act of 1905   Volume V

Office.
The papers in the case and a carbon copy hereof have been sent to the Indian

Respectfully,

Jesse E. Wilson
Assistant Secretary

1 inc and 2 inc for Ind Of

Refer in reply to the following
Land 11095-1907

DEPARTMENT OF THE INTERIOR,
OFFICE OF INDIAN AFFAIRS,
COPY   WASHINGTON. February 19, 1907.

The Honorable
    The Secretary of the Interior.

Sir:

I have the honor to transmit herewith a communication from the Commissioner to the Five Civilized Tribes, dated January 31 1907, enclosing the record of proceedings in the matter of the application for the enrollment of Mary Ellis and Fanny Ellis, as citizens by blood of the Creek Nation, including the Commissioner's decision of January 29, 1907.

It is shown by the record herein that applications were made in affidavit form on March 23, 1905, for the enrollment of Marry[sic] Ellis and Fanny Ellis as citizens by blood of the Creek Nation.

The record further shows that the applicants are children of Sargent Ellis and Anne (or Annie) Ellis, but the records in the office of the Commissioner fail to show that either the father or mother of the applicants is a duly enrolled citizen of the Creek Nation, or that applications have been made for the enrollment as such. The record further shows that both the parents are enrolled citizens of the absentee Shawnee tribe of Indians and are allottees of the Shawnee Reservation, Shawnee Okla. The Office is therefore of the opinion that the decision of the Commissioner to the Five Civilized Tribes, denying the application for the enrollment of Mary Ellis and Fanny Ellis as citizens by blood of the Creek Nation is correct, and it is recommended that it be affirmed.

Very respectfully,
C F Larrabee
Acting Commissioner

EWE SD

Applications for Enrollment of Creek Newborn
Act of 1905   Volume V

N C 341

JHW

Muskogee, Indian Territory, March 7, 1907.

Annie Ellis,
    c/o Sargent Ellis,
        Paden, Indian Territory.

Dear Madam:--

    You are hereby advised that under date of February 25, 1907, the Secretary of the Interior affirmed the decision of the Commissioner to the Five Civilized Tribes, denying the application for the enrollment of your minor children, Mary and Fannie Ellis, as citizens by blood of the Creek Nation.

    Respectfully,

    Commissioner.

BIRTH AFFIDAVIT.

DEPARTMENT OF THE INTERIOR.
COMMISSION TO THE FIVE CIVILIZED TRIBES.

(Child present)

    IN RE APPLICATION FOR ENROLLMENT, as a citizen of the CREEK Nation, of Raymond Deere, born on the 5" day of Dec, 1902

Name of Father: Thompson Deere   a citizen of the   Creek   Nation.
Name of Mother: Lucy "   a citizen of the   Creek   Nation.

    Postoffice   Senora, I.T.

AFFIDAVIT OF MOTHER.

UNITED STATES OF AMERICA, Indian Territory,
    WESTERN   DISTRICT.

    I, Lucy Deere, on oath state that I am 26 years of age and a citizen by blood, of the Creek Nation; that I am the lawful wife of Thompson Deere, who is a citizen, by blood of the Creek Nation; that a male child was born to me on 5" day of Dec, 1902, that said child has been named Raymond Deere, and is now living. the midwife is now dead

    Lucy Deere

Applications for Enrollment of Creek Newborn
Act of 1905 Volume V

Witnesses To Mark:

    Subscribed and sworn to before me this 24" day of Mar , 1905.

                                J. McDermott
                                Notary Public.

AFFIDAVIT OF ATTENDING PHYSICIAN OR MID-WIFE.

UNITED STATES OF AMERICA, Indian Territory,
    WESTERN   DISTRICT.

    I, Thompson Deere , a (blank) , on oath state that I attended on Mrs. Lucy Deere , wife of Mine on the 5 day of Dec. , 1902 : that there was born to her on said date a male child; that said child is now living and is said to have been named Raymond Deere

                                Thompson Deere

Witnesses To Mark:

    Subscribed and sworn to before me this 24" day of Mar , 1905.

                                J. McDermott
                                Notary Public.

BIRTH AFFIDAVIT.
DEPARTMENT OF THE INTERIOR.
COMMISSION TO THE FIVE CIVILIZED TRIBES.

    IN RE APPLICATION FOR ENROLLMENT, as a citizen of the Creek Nation, of Raymond Deere , born on the 5 day of Dec. , 1902

Name of Father: Thompson Deere   a citizen of the   Creek   Nation.
(Illegible) #1
Name of Mother: Lucy Deere   a citizen of the   Creek   Nation.
Tulledega
                            Postoffice   Senora, I.T.

Applications for Enrollment of Creek Newborn
Act of 1905 Volume V

Acquaintance
AFFIDAVIT OF ~~ATTENDING PHYSICIAN OR MID-WIFE~~.

UNITED STATES OF AMERICA, Indian Territory,
  Western   DISTRICT.

                    acquainted with
~~I~~ We, the undersigned, ~~, a (blank)~~, on oath state that ~~I~~ we ~~attended on~~ Mrs. Lucy Deere , wife of Thompson Deere ~~on the (blank) day of (blank) , 1 ;~~ that there was born to her on said date a male child; that said child was living March 4, 1905, and is said to have been named Raymond Deere

             Daniel Starr

Witnesses To Mark: Thomas Thompson

{ Subscribed and sworn to before me this 8" day of July, 1905.

             Drennan C Skaggs
              Notary Public.

                  N-C 342

      Muskogee, Indian Territory, June 8, 1905.

Lucy Deere,
  Senora, Indian Territory.

Dear Madam:

    In the matter of the application for the enrollment of your minor child, Raymond Deere, as a citizen of the Creek Nation, you are advised that the Commission requires the affidavits of two disinterested witnesses relative to the birth of its[sic] child.

    For this purpose, there are herewith enclosed two blank forms of birth affidavit. In having those executed, care should be taken to see that all blanks are properly filled, all names written in full and in the event that the person signing an affidavit is unable to write, signatures by mark must be attested by two witnesses.

           Respectfully,

2 BA   Chairman.

Applications for Enrollment of Creek Newborn
Act of 1905   Volume V

N.C. 343

DEPARTMENT OF THE INTERIOR,
COMMISSIONER TO THE FIVE CIVILIZED TRIBES.
Muskogee, Indian Territory, August 7, 1905.

In the matter of the application for the enrollment of Mardie Unah as a citizen by blood of the Creek Nation.

Nicey Unah, being duly sworn, testified as follows:

Through Jesse McDermott Official Interpreter.

By Commissioner.

Q What is your name? A Nicey Unah.
Q What is your post office address? A Morse.
Q What is your age? A About twenty three
Q Are you a citizen of the Creek Nation? A Yes, sir
Q What is the name of your father? A Ahfonoka, he is dead.
Q What is the name of your mother? A Hoktoche, she is living.
Q At Morse? A Yes, sir
Q To what Creek Indian town do you belong? A Nuyoke
Q What were the names of your brothers and sisters? A Simmer, Sayochee, Cheparney, Malley
Q Have you a brother named Farnoske? A He is dead, he was my brother though.
Q You are sure you had a brother named Farnoske? A Yes, sir
Q Have you a new born child? A Yes, sir
Q Is that it there? A Yes, sir
Q What is its name? A Mardie
Q What is your name now? A Since I am married to this man my name if Nicey Unussee
Q When was this child born? A The child is only five months old It was born on the 26th February last.
Q Are you sure of that date? A Yes, sir
Q You made out an affidavit before Mr. Skaggs a notary public for the commission on the 14th of March, 1905, how old was the child then? A I don't know for sure but I think it was about three weeks old

Barnosee Unnussee being sworn testified as follows,

Through Jesse McDermott Official Interpreter.

Q What is your name? A Barnosee Unnussee.
Q That is the way you are finally enrolled? A Yes, sir
Q What is the name of your father? [sic] Unussee
Q What is the name of your mother? A Harney

Applications for Enrollment of Creek Newborn
Act of 1905   Volume V

Q To what Indian town do you belong? A Ofuskee, Deep Fork
Q How old are you? A I am about twenty three.
Q What is your post office address? A My present address is Morse
Q Are you the father of that boy there? A Yes, sir
Q What's his name? A Mardie Unussee
Q Your wife made out an affidavit stating his name was Mardie Unah, she made a mistake did she? A Yes, sir
Q When was this child born? A February 26th
Q Can you explain how it was she made out an affidavit stating the childs[sic] name was Mardie Unah? A When I was going to school the teacher adopted a new name and called me Barney Unah therefore she signed the affidavit that way
Q Her name really as your wife is Unussee? A Yes, sir
Q Do you remember when she went before the notary public in March? A Yes, sir
Q About how old was this child then? A About three weeks.

Anna Garrigues, on oath states that the above and foregoing is a true and correct copy of her stenographic notes as taken in said cause on said date.

Anna Garrigues

Subscribed and sworn to before
me this 8th day of July 1905.   Edw C Griesel
                                         Notary Public.

BIRTH AFFIDAVIT.

DEPARTMENT OF THE INTERIOR.
COMMISSION TO THE FIVE CIVILIZED TRIBES.

IN RE APPLICATION FOR ENROLLMENT, as a citizen of the Creek Nation, of Mardie Unah , born on the 26 day of Feb , 1905

Name of Father:	Barney Unah	a citizen of the	Creek	Nation.
Name of Mother:	Nicey Unah	a citizen of the	Creek	Nation.

Postoffice   Morse, I.T.

Acquaintance

AFFIDAVIT OF MOTHER.

UNITED STATES OF AMERICA, Indian Territory,
       Western   DISTRICT.

I, B.T. Anderson , on oath state that I am *(blank)* years of age and a citizen by *(blank)*, of the United States Nation; that I am the lawful wife of personally acquainted

Applications for Enrollment of Creek Newborn
Act of 1905   Volume V

with Nicey Unah , who is a citizen, by blood of the Creek Nation; that a male child was born to ~~me~~ her on or about 26 day of Feb , 1905 , that said child has been named Mardie Unah, and was living March 4, 1905.

                                                            Bennie T Anderson

Witnesses To Mark:

      Subscribed and sworn to before me this 22 day of June , 1905.

My Commission Expires March 5th, 1908.   C. C. Eskridge
                                                                Notary Public.

BIRTH AFFIDAVIT.
DEPARTMENT OF THE INTERIOR.
COMMISSION TO THE FIVE CIVILIZED TRIBES.

IN RE APPLICATION FOR ENROLLMENT, as a citizen of the Creek Nation, of Mardie Unah , born on the 26 day of Feb , 1905

Name of Father: Barney Unah   a citizen of the   Creek   Nation.
Name of Mother: Nicey Unah   a citizen of the   Creek   Nation.

                                    Postoffice   Morse, I.T.

AFFIDAVIT OF MOTHER.

UNITED STATES OF AMERICA, Indian Territory, }
    Western   DISTRICT.

      I, Benton Callahan , on oath state that I am *(blank)* ~~years of age and~~ a citizen by blood , of the Creek Nation; that I am ~~the lawful wife of~~ personally acquainted with Nicey Unah , who is a citizen, by blood of the Creek Nation; that a Male child was born to ~~me~~ her on or about the 26 day of Feb , 1905 , that said child has been named Mardie Unah, and was living March 4, 1905.

                                                Benton Callahan

Witnesses To Mark:

      Subscribed and sworn to before me this 22 day of June , 1905.

My Commission Expires March 5th, 1908.   C. C. Eskridge
                                                               Notary Public.

Applications for Enrollment of Creek Newborn
Act of 1905 Volume V

BIRTH AFFIDAVIT.

DEPARTMENT OF THE INTERIOR.
COMMISSION TO THE FIVE CIVILIZED TRIBES.

IN RE APPLICATION FOR ENROLLMENT, as a citizen of the Creek Nation, of Mardie Unah, born on the 26 day of February, 1905

Name of Father:	Barney Unah	a citizen of the	Creek	Nation.
Name of Mother:	Nicey Unah	a citizen of the	Creek	Nation.

Postoffice   Morse, Indian Territory

AFFIDAVIT OF MOTHER.

UNITED STATES OF AMERICA, Indian Territory,
      Western   DISTRICT.

I, Nicey Unah, on oath state that I am about 20 years of age and a citizen by blood, of the Creek Nation; that I am the lawful wife of Barney Unah, who is a citizen, by blood of the Creek Nation; that a male child was born to me on 26 day of February, 1905, that said child has been named Mardie Unah, and was living March 4, 1905. That no one attended on me as midwife or physician at the time the child was born

                              her
                         Nicey x Unah
Witnesses To Mark: mark
{ Alex Posey
{ DC Skaggs

Subscribed and sworn to before me this 14" day of March, 1905.

                    Drennan C Skaggs
                    Notary Public.

NC 343.

Muskogee, Indian Territory, May 31, 1905.

Mardie Unah,
      Morse, Indian Territory.

Dear Madam:

There are herewith enclosed two blank forms of birth affidavit which you are requested to have signed by two disinterested witnesses, and in executing same care

Applications for Enrollment of Creek Newborn
Act of 1905   Volume V

should be exercised to see that all blanks are properly filled, all names written in full and in the event that either of the persons signing the affidavits is unable to write, signatures by mark must be attested by two witnesses. Each affidavit must be executed before a Notary Public and the notarial seal and signature of the officer must be attached to each separate affidavit.

The Commission is unable to identify either you or the father of said child, and you are requested to furnish the Commission with any other names by which you and he are known, the names of your parents, the Creek Indian Towns to which you belong, and if possible, the numbers which appear on your deeds to land in the Creek Nation.

                            Respectfully,
                                    Com in Char
LM-2BA   ~~Chairman~~.

NC-343

                    Muskogee, Indian Territory, July 27, 1905.

Barney Unah,
    Morse, Indian Territory.

Dear Sir:

In the matter of the application for the enrollment of your minor child, Mardie Unah, as a citizen by blood of the Creek Nation, you are advised that this office cannot identify you or Nicey Unah, the mother of said child, as a citizen of said Nation.

You are requested to state the names of yourself and said Nicey Unah as same appear on the final roll of citizens of the Creek Nation, the names of your parents, the Creek Indian Towns to which each of you belongs, and, if possible, the roll numbers as same appear on your and your wife's deeds to lands in the Creek Nation, which will help identify both of you as citizens thereof.

                            Respectfully,

                                    Commissioner.

Applications for Enrollment of Creek Newborn
Act of 1905   Volume V

Cr NC-344

Muskogee, Indian Territory, June 8, 1905.

Winey Anderson,
    Morse, Indian Territory.

Dear Madam:

In the matter of the application for the enrollment of your minor children, Bessie and Wicey Anderson, as citizens of the Creek Nation, the Commission is unable to identify you on its rolls.

You are requested to furnish the Commission with your maiden name, the names of your parents, the Creek Indian Town to which you claim to belong, and, if possible, the roll number which appears on your deeds to land in the Creek Nation, which will help to identify you as a citizen of said Nation.

You are also requested to furnish the Commission with the affidavits to two disinterested witnesses relative to the birth of your said minor children, Bessie and Wisey Anderson. For this purpose, there are herewith enclosed two blank forms of birth affidavit. In having same executed, care should be taken to see that all blanks are properly filled, all names written in full and in the event that the person signing an affidavit is unable to write, signatures by mark must be attested by two witnesses.

                Respectfully,

                              Chairman.

2 B A

BIRTH AFFIDAVIT.

DEPARTMENT OF THE INTERIOR.
COMMISSION TO THE FIVE CIVILIZED TRIBES.

IN RE APPLICATION FOR ENROLLMENT, as a citizen of the Creek Nation, of Wisey Anderson, born on the 13th day of Sept, 1904

Name of Father: Bennie Anderson   a citizen of the   U.S.   Nation.
Name of Mother: Winey Anderson   a citizen of the   Creek   Nation.

                Postoffice   Morse, I.T.

Applications for Enrollment of Creek Newborn
Act of 1905 Volume V

disinterested acquaintance
AFFIDAVIT OF ~~MOTHER~~.

UNITED STATES OF AMERICA, Indian Territory,
   Western DISTRICT.

I, Benton Callahan, on oath state that I am *(blank)* ~~years of age and~~ a citizen by blood, of the Creek Nation; that I am ~~the lawful wife of~~ personally acquainted with Winey Anderson, who is a citizen, by blood of the Creek Nation; that a female child was born to ~~me~~ her on or about the 13 day of September, 1904, that said child has been named Wisey Anderson, and was living March 4, 1905.

                                        Benton Callahan

Witnesses To Mark:
{
{

Subscribed and sworn to before me this 22 day of June, 1905.

My Commission Expires March 5th, 1908.   C. C. Eskridge
                                                 Notary Public.

BIRTH AFFIDAVIT.

DEPARTMENT OF THE INTERIOR.
COMMISSION TO THE FIVE CIVILIZED TRIBES.

IN RE APPLICATION FOR ENROLLMENT, as a citizen of the Creek Nation, of Wisey Anderson, born on the 13th day of Sept, 1904

Name of Father: Bennie Anderson   a citizen of the United States Nation.
Name of Mother: Winey Anderson   a citizen of the   Creek   Nation.

              Postoffice   Morse, Indian Territory

AFFIDAVIT OF MOTHER.

UNITED STATES OF AMERICA, Indian Territory,
   Western DISTRICT.

I, Winey Anderson, on oath state that I am about 27 years of age and a citizen by blood, of the Creek Nation; that I am the lawful wife of Bennie Anderson, who is a citizen, ~~by (blank)~~ of the United States Nation; that a female child was born to me on 13 day of September, 1904, that said child has been named Wisey Anderson, and was living March 4, 1905. That no one attended on me as midwife or physician at the time the child was born

Applications for Enrollment of Creek Newborn
Act of 1905   Volume V

Witnesses To Mark:
{ Alex Posey
  DC Skaggs

her
Winey x Anderson
mark

Subscribed and sworn to before me this 14" day of March, 1905.

Drennan C Skaggs
Notary Public.

BIRTH AFFIDAVIT.

DEPARTMENT OF THE INTERIOR.
COMMISSION TO THE FIVE CIVILIZED TRIBES.

IN RE APPLICATION FOR ENROLLMENT, as a citizen of the Creek Nation, of Wisey Anderson, born on the 13" day of Sept, 1904

Name of Father:	Bennie Anderson	a citizen of the	U.S.	Nation.
Name of Mother:	Winey Anderson	a citizen of the	Creek	Nation.

Postoffice   Morse, I.T.

disinterested acquaintance

AFFIDAVIT OF ~~MOTHER~~.

UNITED STATES OF AMERICA, Indian Territory,
   Western   DISTRICT.

I, Parnosy Unah, on oath state that I am *(blank)* ~~years of age and~~ a citizen by blood, of the Creek Nation; that I am ~~the lawful wife of~~ personally acquainted with Winey Anderson, who is a citizen, by blood of the Creek Nation; that a female child was born to ~~me~~ her on or about the 13 day of September, 1904, that said child has been named Wisey Anderson, and was living March 4, 1905.

~~Be~~   Parnosy Unah

Witnesses To Mark:
{

Subscribed and sworn to before me this 22 day of June, 1905.

My Commission Expires March 5th, 1908.

C. C. Eskridge
Notary Public.

Applications for Enrollment of Creek Newborn
Act of 1905   Volume V

BIRTH AFFIDAVIT.

DEPARTMENT OF THE INTERIOR.
COMMISSION TO THE FIVE CIVILIZED TRIBES.

IN RE APPLICATION FOR ENROLLMENT, as a citizen of the Creek Nation, of Bessie Anderson, born on the 7th day of OCT, 1902

Name of Father:	Bennie Anderson	a citizen of the	U.S.	Nation.
Name of Mother:	Winey Anderson	a citizen of the	Creek	Nation.

Postoffice   Morse, I.T.

disinterested acquaintance
AFFIDAVIT OF ~~MOTHER~~.

UNITED STATES OF AMERICA, Indian Territory,
Western   DISTRICT.

I, Benton Callahan, on oath state that I am *(blank)* years of age and a citizen by blood, of the Creek Nation; that I am ~~the lawful wife of~~ personally acquainted with Winey Anderson, who is a citizen, by blood of the Creek Nation; that a female child was born to ~~me~~ her on or about the 7th day of October, 1902, that said child has been named Bessie Anderson, and was living March 4, 1905.

Benton Callahan

Witnesses To Mark:

Subscribed and sworn to before me this 22 day of June, 1905.

My Commission Expires March 5th, 1908.   C. C. Eskridge
Notary Public.

BIRTH AFFIDAVIT.

DEPARTMENT OF THE INTERIOR.
COMMISSION TO THE FIVE CIVILIZED TRIBES.

IN RE APPLICATION FOR ENROLLMENT, as a citizen of the Creek Nation, of Bessie Anderson, born on the 7th day of Oct, 1902

Name of Father:	Bennie Anderson	a citizen of the	U.S.	Nation.
Name of Mother:	Winey Anderson	a citizen of the	Creek	Nation.

Postoffice   Morse, I.T.

Applications for Enrollment of Creek Newborn
Act of 1905   Volume V

disinterested acquaintance
AFFIDAVIT OF ~~MOTHER~~.

UNITED STATES OF AMERICA, Indian Territory, }
    Western   DISTRICT.

    I, Parnosy Unah , on oath state that I am *(blank)* ~~years of age and~~ a citizen by blood , of the Creek Nation; that I am ~~the lawful wife of~~ personally acquainted with Winey Anderson , who is a citizen, by blood of the Creek Nation; that a female child was born to ~~me~~ her on or about the 7" day of October , 1902 , that said child has been named Bessie Anderson , and was living March 4, 1905.

                                Parnosy Unah

Witnesses To Mark:
{

    Subscribed and sworn to before me this 22 day of June , 1905.

My Commission Expires March 5th, 1908.   C. C. Eskridge
                                            Notary Public.

BIRTH AFFIDAVIT.
DEPARTMENT OF THE INTERIOR.
COMMISSION TO THE FIVE CIVILIZED TRIBES.

    IN RE APPLICATION FOR ENROLLMENT, as a citizen of the Creek Nation, of Bessie Anderson , born on the 7 day of October , 1902

Name of Father: Bennie Anderson   a citizen of the United States Nation.
Name of Mother: Winey Anderson   a citizen of the Creek Nation.

                              Postoffice   Morse, Indian Territory

---

AFFIDAVIT OF MOTHER.

UNITED STATES OF AMERICA, Indian Territory, }
    Western   DISTRICT.

    I, Winey Anderson , on oath state that I am about 27 years of age and a citizen by blood , of the Creek Nation; that I am the lawful wife of Bennie Anderson , who is a citizen, ~~by~~ *(blank)* of the United States Nation; that a female child was born to me on 7 day of October , 1902 , that said child has been named Bessie Anderson , and was living March 4, 1905. That no one attended on me as midwife or physician at the time the child was born

Applications for Enrollment of Creek Newborn
Act of 1905   Volume V

                                 her
Witnesses To Mark: Winey x Anderson
 { Alex Posey   mark
  DC Skaggs

   Subscribed and sworn to before me this 14" day of March, 1905.

                            Drennan C Skaggs
                              Notary Public.

BIRTH AFFIDAVIT.

DEPARTMENT OF THE INTERIOR.
COMMISSION TO THE FIVE CIVILIZED TRIBES.

IN RE APPLICATION FOR ENROLLMENT, as a citizen of the Creek Nation, of Wilhe Jackson Henry, born on the 23 day of December, 1904

Name of Father: W.A. Henry   a citizen of the United States Nation.
Name of Mother: Lula Henry   a citizen of the Creek Nation.
                        Postoffice   Dustin I.T.

AFFIDAVIT OF MOTHER.

UNITED STATES OF AMERICA, Indian Territory,
   Western   **DISTRICT.**

   I, Lula Henry, on oath state that I am 24 years of age and a citizen by blood, of the Creek Nation; that I am the lawful wife of W.A. Henry, who is a citizen, by blood of the United States Nation; that a boy child was born to me on 23 day of December, 1904, that said child has been named Wilhe Jackson Henry, and is now living.
                             Lula Henry
Witnesses To Mark:

   Subscribed and sworn to before me this 18th day of March, 1905.

                            E.E. Lewis
                            Notary Public.

Applications for Enrollment of Creek Newborn
Act of 1905   Volume V

AFFIDAVIT OF ATTENDING PHYSICIAN OR MID-WIFE.

UNITED STATES OF AMERICA, Indian Territory,　}
　　Western　　　DISTRICT.

   I, Mrs S. J. Roberts , a midwife , on oath state that I attended on Mrs. Lula Henry , wife of W. A. Henry on the 23 day of December , 1904 ; that there was born to her on said date a boy child; that said child is now living and is said to have been named Wilhe Jackson Henry

                her
Witnesses To Mark: Mrs. S J x Roberts
 { J S Henry   mark
   E.E. Lewis

 Subscribed and sworn to before me this 18th day of March , 1905.

         E E Lewis
           Notary Public.

BIRTH AFFIDAVIT.

DEPARTMENT OF THE INTERIOR.
COMMISSION TO THE FIVE CIVILIZED TRIBES.

 IN RE APPLICATION FOR ENROLLMENT, as a citizen of the Creek Nation, of Eugene Rolley Henry , born on the 7 day of February , 1902

Name of Father: W.A. Henry   a citizen of the United States Nation.
Name of Mother: Lula Henry   a citizen of the   Creek   Nation.

       Postoffice Dustin, I.T.

AFFIDAVIT OF MOTHER.

UNITED STATES OF AMERICA, Indian Territory, }
 Western   DISTRICT.

 I, Lula Henry , on oath state that I am 24 years of age and a citizen by blood , of the Creek Nation; that I am the lawful wife of W.A. Henry , who is a citizen, by blood of the United States Nation; that a boy child was born to me on 7 day of February , 1902 , that said child has been named Eugene Rolley Henry , and is now living.

         Lula Henry
Witnesses To Mark:
 {

Applications for Enrollment of Creek Newborn
Act of 1905   Volume V

Subscribed and sworn to before me this 18th day of March, 1905.

        E.E. Lewis
          Notary Public.

AFFIDAVIT OF ATTENDING PHYSICIAN OR MID-WIFE.

UNITED STATES OF AMERICA, Indian Territory,
  Western DISTRICT.

I, Mrs Amanda Smith, a midwife, on oath state that I attended on Mrs. Lula Henry, wife of W. A. Henry on the 7 day of February, 1902 ; that there was born to her on said date a boy child; that said child is now living and is said to have been named Eugene Rolley Henry

        Mr[sic] Amanda Smith

Witnesses To Mark:

Subscribed and sworn to before me this 20th day of March, 1905.

My Com. Exp. July 1" 1906   A. ?. Skelton
           Notary Public.

            NC. 346.

      Muskogee, Indian Territory, July 14, 1905.

Commissioner to the Five Civilized Tribes,
  Seminole Enrollment Division,
    Muskogee, Indian Territory.

Gentlemen:

  March 23, 1905, application was made to the Commission to the Five Civilized Tribes for the enrollment of Nellie Bell, born May 20, 1903, as a citizen by blood of the Creek Nation. It is stated in said application that the father of said child is Joseph Bell, a citizen of the Seminole Nation, and that the mother is Lizzie Marshall, a citizen of the Creek Nation.

  You are requested to inform the Creek Enrollment Division as to whether application has been made for the enrollment of said Nellie Bell, as a citizen of the Seminole Nation, and if so, what disposition has been made of the same.

Applications for Enrollment of Creek Newborn
Act of 1905   Volume V

Respectfully,

Commissioner.

DEPARTMENT OF THE INTERIOR.
COMMISSION TO THE FIVE CIVILIZED TRIBES.

Muskogee, Indian Territory, July 18, 1905.

Chief Clerk,
    Creek Enrollment Division.

Dear Sir:

    Receipt is acknowledged of your letter of July 14, 1905 (NC-346) stating that an application was made to the Commission to the Five Civilized Tribes for the enrollment of Nellie Bell, born May 20, 1903, child of Joseph Bell, a citizen of the Seminole Nation, and Lizzie Marshall, a citizen of the Creek Nation, as a citizen by blood of the Creek Nation and requesting to be informed as to whether an application has been made for the enrollment of said child as a citizen of the Seminole Nation.

    In reply to your letter you are advised that it does not appear from an examination of the records of this office that any application was made to the Commission to the Five Civilized Tribes for the enrollment of said Nellie Bell as a citizen of the Seminole Nation.

Respectfully,

Tams Bixby   Commissioner.

NC-346.

Muskogee, Indian Territory, July 29, 1905.

Josie Bell,
    Irene, Indian Territory.

Dear Sir:

    In the matter of the application for the enrollment of your minor daughter, Nellie Bell, as a citizen by blood of the Creek Nation there are on file the affidavits of yourself and wife only as to the birth of said child.

    This office will require the affidavit of the attending physician or midwife at the birth of said child or, in case there was no attending physician or midwife, the

Applications for Enrollment of Creek Newborn
Act of 1905   Volume V

affidavits of two disinterested parties who know when said child was born, the name of her parents and whether or not she was living March 4, 1905.

    A blank for proof of birth which has been partially filled out is inclosed[sic] herewith and you are requested to have the same properly executed and return to this office in the inclosed[sic] envelope. Be careful to see that the signatures of the affiants are identical with the names as they appear in the body of the affidavits. In case any signature is by mark it must be attested by two disinterested witnesses. Care should also be taken to see that the notary public before whom the affidavits are sworn to affixes his name and seal to each affidavit.

    Respectfully,

    Commissioner.

CTD-8.
Env.

NC 346.

Muskogee, Indian Territory, November 12, 1906.

Chief Clerk,
    Seminole Enrollment Division,
        General Office.

Dear Sir:

    You are hereby advised that the name of Nellie Bell, born May 20, 1903, to Josie Bell, an alleged citizen of the Seminole Nation, and Lizzie Marshall, a citizen by blood of the Creek Nation, is contained in a schedule of New Born citizens of the Creek Nation, approved by the Secretary of the Interior September 27, 1905, opposite Roll No. 369.

    Respectfully,

    Commissioner.

BIRTH AFFIDAVIT.

DEPARTMENT OF THE INTERIOR.
COMMISSION TO THE FIVE CIVILIZED TRIBES.

IN RE APPLICATION FOR ENROLLMENT, as a citizen of the Creek Nation, of Nellie Belle, born on the 20 day of May, 1903

Name of Father: Joseph Belle   a citizen of the   Seminole Nation.
Name of Mother: Lizzie Marshall (nee) Belle   a citizen of the   Creek   Nation.

Applications for Enrollment of Creek Newborn
Act of 1905 Volume V

Postoffice   Irene Ind. Ter.

AFFIDAVIT OF MOTHER.

UNITED STATES OF AMERICA, Indian Territory, }
Western   DISTRICT.

I, Lizzie Marshall (nee) Belle , on oath state that I am 20 years of age and a citizen by blood , of the Creek Nation; that I am the lawful wife of Joseph Belle , who is a citizen, by blood of the Seminole Nation; that a female child was born to me on 20 day of May , 1903 , that said child has been named Nellie Belle , and was living March 4, 1905.

                                                 her
Witnesses To Mark: Lizzie Marshall (nee) x Bell e
                                                 mark
{ Tupper Dunn
{ Josie Bell

Subscribed and sworn to before me this 20 day of March , 1905.

My Com. Exp. Aug 19-1908   Tupper Dunn
                                            Notary Public.

AFFIDAVIT OF ATTENDING PHYSICIAN OR MID-WIFE.

UNITED STATES OF AMERICA, Indian Territory, }
Western   DISTRICT.

I, Josie Bell , a midwife , on oath state that I attended on Mrs. Lizzie Marshall nee Belle , wife of mine on the 20 day of May , 1903 ; that there was born to her on said date a female child; that said child was living March 4, 1905, and is said to have been named Nellie Bell

                                                 Josie Bell
Witnesses To Mark:
{

Subscribed and sworn to before me this 20 day of March , 1905.

My Com. Exp. Aug 19-1908   Tupper Dunn
                                            Notary Public.

Applications for Enrollment of Creek Newborn
Act of 1905   Volume V

BIRTH AFFIDAVIT.

DEPARTMENT OF THE INTERIOR.
COMMISSION TO THE FIVE CIVILIZED TRIBES.

IN RE APPLICATION FOR ENROLLMENT, as a citizen of the Creek Nation, of Nellie Bell, born on the 20th day of May, 1903

Name of Father: Joseph Bell	a citizen of the Seminole Nation.
Name of Mother: Lizzie Marshall Bell	a citizen of the Creek Nation.

Postoffice   Irene I.T.

AFFIDAVIT OF MOTHER.

UNITED STATES OF AMERICA, Indian Territory,
Western   DISTRICT.

I, Lizzie Marshall Belle, on oath state that I am 20 years of age and a citizen by blood, of the Creek Nation; that I am the lawful wife of Josie Bell, who is a citizen, by blood of the Seminole Nation; that a female child was born to me on 20th day of May, 1903, that said child has been named Nellie Bell, and was living March 4, 1905.

                                                her
                             Lizzie Marshall Bell x
Witnesses To Mark: mark
   { H G Malot
    J.M. Turner

Subscribed and sworn to before me this 19 day of August, 1905.

                              H G Malot
                                  Notary Public.
                                  my Com Exp 2 July 1906

AFFIDAVIT OF ATTENDING PHYSICIAN OR MID-WIFE.

UNITED STATES OF AMERICA, Indian Territory,
Western   DISTRICT.

I, Rhoda Fixico, a midwife, on oath state that I attended on Mrs. Lizzie Marshall Belle, wife of Josie Bell on the 20th day of May, 1903; that there was born to her on said date a female child; that said child was living March 4, 1905, and is said to have been named Nellie Bell

                                        her
                                Rhoda x Fixico
                                    mark

Applications for Enrollment of Creek Newborn
Act of 1905   Volume V

Witnesses To Mark:
 { H G Malot
 { J.M. Turner

Subscribed and sworn to before me this 19 day of August, 1905.

H G Malot
Notary Public.
my Com Exp 2 July 1906

BIRTH AFFIDAVIT.

Department of the Interior,
COMMISSION TO THE FIVE CIVILIZED TRIBES.

IN RE Application for Enrollment, as a citizen of the Creek Nation, of Ruthia Ellen Helton, born on the 11th day of September, 1903

		non-citizen
Name of Father:	William B. Helton	a ^ ~~citizen~~ of the Creek Nation.
Name of Father:	Nellie Helton	a citizen of the Creek Nation.

Post Office: Sapulpa, Ind. Ter.

(3-22-05 child appears) HGH

AFFIDAVIT OF MOTHER.

UNITED STATES OF AMERICA, ⎫
  INDIAN TERRITORY,   ⎬
  Western   District.   ⎭

I, Mrs. Nellie Helton , on oath state that I am 30 years of age and a citizen by blood , of the Creek Nation; that I am the lawful wife of William B. Helton , who is a non citizen citizen[sic], by blood of the Creek Nation; that a Female child was born to me on 11th day of September A.D. , 1903, that said child has been named Ruthia Ellen Helton , and is now living.

Nellie Helton

Subscribed and sworn to before me this 21st day of March A.D., 1905.

My Commission expires July 11, 1906.   F.L. Mars
                                              Notary Public.

39

Applications for Enrollment of Creek Newborn
Act of 1905 Volume V

AFFIDAVIT OF ATTENDING PHYSICIAN OR MID-WIFE.

UNITED STATES OF AMERICA,
    INDIAN TERRITORY,
  Western   District.

I, Dr. Harry O. Lyford , a Physician , on oath state that I attended on Mrs. Nellie Helton , wife of William B. Helton on the 11th day of September , 1903 ; that there was born to her on said date a female child; that said child is now living and is said to have been named Ruthia Ellen Helton

                            Dr. Harry O. Lyford
Subscribed and sworn to before me this 21st day of March A.D, 1905.

My Commission expires July 11, 1906.   F.L. Mars
                                    Notary Public.

BIRTH AFFIDAVIT.

Department of the Interior,
COMMISSION TO THE FIVE CIVILIZED TRIBES.

IN RE Application for Enrollment, as a citizen of the Creek Nation, of Romie Robert Helton , born on the 11th day of September , 1903

                                    non-citizen
Name of Father: William B. Helton   a ^ ~~citizen~~ of the Creek   Nation.
Name of Father: Nellie Helton   a citizen of the   Creek   Nation.

                      Post Office: Sapulpa, I.T.

(3-22-05 child appears) HGH
                    AFFIDAVIT OF MOTHER.

UNITED STATES OF AMERICA,
    INDIAN TERRITORY,
  Western   District.

I, Mrs. Nellie Helton , on oath state that I am 30 years of age and a citizen by blood , of the Creek Nation; that I am the lawful wife of William B. Helton , who is a non citizen citizen[sic], by blood of the Creek Nation; that a male child was born to me on 11th day of September A.D. , 1903, that said child has been named Romie Robert Helton , and is now living.

                                         Nellie Helton

Applications for Enrollment of Creek Newborn
Act of 1905   Volume V

Subscribed and sworn to before me this 21st day of March A.D, 1905.

My Commission expires July 11, 1906.   F.L. Mars
                                         Notary Public.

AFFIDAVIT OF ATTENDING PHYSICIAN OR MID-WIFE.

UNITED STATES OF AMERICA,   ⎫
   INDIAN TERRITORY,   ⎬
  Western   District.   ⎭

I, Dr. Harry O. Lyford , a Physician , on oath state that I attended on Mrs. Nellie Helton , wife of William B. Helton on the 11th day of September A.D., 1903; that there was born to her on said date a female child; that said child is now living and is said to have been named Romie Robert Helton

Dr. Harry O. Lyford

Subscribed and sworn to before me this 21st day of March A.D, 1905.

My Commission expires July 11, 1906.   F.L. Mars
                                         Notary Public.

N.C. 348. (2455-B)

DEPARTMENT OF THE INTERIOR,
COMMISSIONER TO THE FIVE CIVILIZED TRIBES.
Castle, I.T., November 17, 1905.

In the matter of the application for the enrollment of Lousanna Tiger as a citizen by blood of the Creek Nation.

LOUISA TIGER, being duly sworn, testified as follows:

Through Alex Posey Official Interpreter:

BY THE COMMISSIONER:
Q What is your name? A Louisa Tiger.
Q How old are you? A About twenty-two.
Q What is your post office address? A Castle.
Q Are you a citizen of the Creek Nation? A Yes, sir.
Q To what town do you belong? A Arbeka North Fork.
Q Are you known by any other name than Louisa Tiger? A I am also known as Louisa Miller.

Applications for Enrollment of Creek Newborn
Act of 1905   Volume V

Q Who were your parents? A Sam Miller and Lizzie Miller. My father belongs to Hillabee Town and my mother to Arbeka North Fork.
Q Have you a child named Lousanna? A Yes, sir.
Q Who is the child's father? A Thomas Tiger.
Q To what town does he belong? A Fish Pond.
Q Is he your lawful husband? A He was my husband but he has deserted me. He has been gone ever since last Spring.
Q Your proper name then is Louisa Tiger? A Yes, sir.
Q When was your child, Lousanna, born? A July 30, 1904.
Q Who attended on you at the birth of the child? A My mother, Lizzie Miller.
Q Is your husband known by any other name than Thomas Tiger? A He is known among the Indians as Sawakee. His father if Heneha Chupco and his mother is Senegee.
Q To what town does Heneha Chupco belong? W Wewoka.
Q To what town does Senegee belong? A Fish Pond.

---oooOOOooo---

I, D. C. Skaggs, on oath state that the above and foregoing is a full and true transcript of my stenographic notes as taken in said cause on said date.

D.C. Skaggs

Subscribed and sworn to before me this 4 day of Jan. 1906.

Alex Posey
Notary Public.

NC-348.

Muskogee, Indian Territory, August 3, 1905.

Louisa Tiger,
    c/o Thomas Tiger,
        Castle, Indian Territory.

Dear Madam:

On March 25, 1905 you filed with the Commission to the Five Civilized Tribes an application for the enrollment of your infant daughter Lousanna Tiger and submitted your affidavit and the affidavit of Lizzie Miller, midwife, as to the birth of said child on July 30, 1904.

It is noted that you signed your name to the affidavit executed by yourself as "Louisa Miller, nee Tiger" stating in your affidavit that you are now the lawful wife of Thomas Tiger. It therefore appears that your name is Louisa Tiger. The notary public before whom the affidavits were sworn to neglected to affix his seal to the affidavit of the said Lizzie Miller.

Applications for Enrollment of Creek Newborn
Act of 1905   Volume V

For the purpose of correcting the discrepancies in the affidavits heretofore filed there is inclosed[sic] herewith blank proof of birth which has been partially filled out and you are requested to appear before a notary public with Lizzie Miller, the attending midwife at the birth of your child Lousanna Tiger, and execute the same.

Be careful to see that the notary public, before whom the affidavits are sworn to, attaches his name and seal to each affidavit. In case any signature is by mark it must be attached by two disinterested witnesses.

In the matter of the application for the enrollment of your , as a citizen of the Creek Nation identification of Thomas Tiger, the father of said child, upon the final roll of citizens by blood of the Creek nation you are requested to immediately inform this office as to the names of his parents and other members of his family and if possible to give his final roll number as the same appears on his allotment certificates and deed.

Respectfully,

CTD-16.
Env.

Commissioner.

BIRTH AFFIDAVIT.

DEPARTMENT OF THE INTERIOR.
COMMISSION TO THE FIVE CIVILIZED TRIBES.

IN RE APPLICATION FOR ENROLLMENT, as a citizen of the Creek Nation, of Lousanna Tiger , born on the 30 day of July , 1904

Name of Father: Thomas Tiger   a citizen of the   Creek   Nation.
Name of Mother: Louisa Tiger   a citizen of the   Creek   Nation.

Postoffice   Castle, Ind. Terr.

AFFIDAVIT OF MOTHER.

UNITED STATES OF AMERICA, Indian Territory,
    Western   DISTRICT.

I, Louisa Tiger , on oath state that I am about 22 years of age and a citizen by blood , of the Creek Nation; that I am the lawful wife of Thomas Tiger , who is a citizen, by blood of the Creek Nation; that a female child was born to me on 30 day of July , 1904 , that said child has been named Lousanna Tiger , and was living March 4, 1905.

                                            her
                                Louisa x Tiger
                                  mark

Applications for Enrollment of Creek Newborn
Act of 1905   Volume V

Witnesses To Mark:
- DC Skaggs
- Alex Posey

Subscribed and sworn to before me this 17 day of November, 1905.

                        Drennan C Skaggs
                        Notary Public.

AFFIDAVIT OF ATTENDING PHYSICIAN OR MID-WIFE.

UNITED STATES OF AMERICA, Indian Territory,
    Western   DISTRICT.

I, Lizzie Miller , a mid-wife , on oath state that I attended on Mrs. Louisa Tiger, wife of Thomas Tiger on the 30 day of July , 1904 ; that there was born to her on said date a female child; that said child was living March 4, 1905, and is said to have been named Lousanna Tiger

                              her
                      Lizzie x Miller
                          mark

Witnesses To Mark:
- DC Skaggs
- Alex Posey

Subscribed and sworn to before me this 17 day of November, 1905.

                        Drennan C Skaggs
                        Notary Public.

DEPARTMENT OF THE INTERIOR,
COMMISSION TO THE FIVE CIVILIZED TRIBES.
ON TRAIN OUT OF PADEN, I.T.
MAY 1, 1905.

In the matter of the application for new born children concerning Whose enrollment no affidavits could be obtained in time.

Fuller Knight, being duly sworn, testified as follows: Through Alex Posey, Official Interpreter.

Examination by the Commission.
Q What is your name? A Fuller Knight.
Q How old are you? A About 30.
Q What is your post office address? A Boley, I.T. I am a citizen of the Creek Nation of Arbeka Town. I know of a child named <u>Losanna Tiger</u>, the child of Thomas Tiger of

Applications for Enrollment of Creek Newborn
Act of 1905 Volume V

Fish Pond Town, and Louisa Tiger of Arbeka. This child will be a year old next July and is now living. Her post office is Boley. I am no kin just think they have not made application for this child.

    Henry G. Hains, being duly sworn, on his oath, states that above and foregoing is a true and correct transcript of his stenographic notes as taken in said cause on said date.

Henry G. Hains

Subscribed and sworn to before me this 10th day of May, 1905.

Drennan C Skaggs
Notary Public.

BIRTH AFFIDAVIT.

DEPARTMENT OF THE INTERIOR.
COMMISSION TO THE FIVE CIVILIZED TRIBES.

IN RE APPLICATION FOR ENROLLMENT, as a citizen of the Creek Nation, of Lousanna Tiger, born on the 30 day of July, 1904

Name of Father: Thomas Tiger   a citizen of the   Creek   Nation.
Name of Mother: Lousa[sic] Miller (nee)Tiger   a citizen of the   Creek   Nation.

Postoffice   Castle, I.T.

AFFIDAVIT OF MOTHER.

UNITED STATES OF AMERICA, Indian Territory, }
    Western   DISTRICT.

    I, Lousa Miller (nee) Tiger, on oath state that I am 20 years of age and a citizen by blood, of the Creek Nation; that I am the lawful wife of Thomas Tiger, who is a citizen, by blood of the Creek Nation; that a female child was born to me on 30 day of July, 1904, that said child has been named Lousanna Tiger, and was living March 4, 1905.

Louisa Miller nee Tiger

Witnesses To Mark:
  { HG Malot
    Tupper Dunn

    Subscribed and sworn to before me this 20 day of March, 1905.

My com exp. Aug 19-1908   Tupper Dunn
Notary Public.

Applications for Enrollment of Creek Newborn
Act of 1905   Volume V

AFFIDAVIT OF ATTENDING PHYSICIAN OR MID-WIFE.

UNITED STATES OF AMERICA, Indian Territory,
    Western   DISTRICT.

I, Lizzie Miller , a mid-wife , on oath state that I attended on Mrs. Louisa Miller (nee) Tiger, wife of Thomas Tiger on the 30 day of July , 1904 ; that there was born to her on said date a *(blank)* child; that said child was living March 4, 1905, and is said to have been named Lousanna Tiger

           her
         Lizzie x Miller
          mark

Witnesses To Mark:
  { HG Malot
  { Tupper Dunn

Subscribed and sworn to before me this 20 day of March , 1905.

My com exp. Aug 19-1908   Tupper Dunn
              Notary Public.

BIRTH AFFIDAVIT.

DEPARTMENT OF THE INTERIOR.
COMMISSION TO THE FIVE CIVILIZED TRIBES.

IN RE APPLICATION FOR ENROLLMENT, as a citizen of the Creek Nation, of Tchinina Henry , born on the 17th day of February , 1905

Name of Father: Hugh Henry   a citizen of the   Creek   Nation.
Name of Mother: Mintie Henry   a citizen of the   *(blank)*   Nation.

        Postoffice   Henryetta Ind. Ter.

AFFIDAVIT OF MOTHER.

UNITED STATES OF AMERICA, Indian Territory,
    Western   DISTRICT.

I, Mintie Henry , on oath state that I am 38 years of age and a citizen by *(blank)* , of the *(blank)* Nation; that I am the lawful wife of Hugh Henry , who is a citizen, by blood of the Creek Nation; that a Female child was born to me on 17th

Applications for Enrollment of Creek Newborn
Act of 1905   Volume V

day of February, 1905, that said child has been named Tchinina Henry, and was living March 4, 1905.

her
Mintie x Henry
mark

Witnesses To Mark:
{ Bille C. Scharnagel
{ John *(Illegible)*

Subscribed and sworn to before me this 20th day of March, 1905.

Olin W. Meacham
Notary Public.

My Com Expires Aug 30 1906

AFFIDAVIT OF ATTENDING PHYSICIAN OR MID-WIFE.

UNITED STATES OF AMERICA, Indian Territory,
   Western   DISTRICT.

I, Charles E. Scharnagel, a Physician, on oath state that I attended on Mrs. Mintie Henry, wife of Hugh Henry on the 17th day of February, 1905; that there was born to her on said date a Female child; that said child was living March 4, 1905, and is said to have been named Tchinina Henry

Charles E. Scharnagel M.D.

Witnesses To Mark:
{

Subscribed and sworn to before me this 20th day of February[sic], 1905.

Olin W. Meacham
Notary Public.

My Com Expires Aug 30 1906

(Lela Butcher)   C350

Muskogee, Indian Territory, December 13, 1905.

William F. Stoddard,
   Morse, Indian Territory.

Dear Sir:

Applications for Enrollment of Creek Newborn
Act of 1905   Volume V

In your letter of July 12, 1905, you state that Norfer and Musser Butcher have two children, Cheparney and Mildred.

You are advised that there is on file in this office an application for the enrollment of Lela Butcher, child of above persons and that it does not appear from the records that any application has been made for the enrollment of children by the name of Cheparney and Mildred Butcher.

In the matter of the application for the enrollment of Lela Butcher and in order to investigate the matter of the alleged application for said Mildred and Cheparney, you are requested to cause said Norfer and Musser Butcher to appear at the office of the Commissioner to the Five Civilized Tribes, at an early date for the purpose of being examined under oath.

Respectfully,

Acting Commissioner.

Cr NC-350

Muskogee, Indian Territory, June 8, 1905.

Nafa Butcher,
    Morse, Indian Territory.

Dear Sir:

In the matter of the application for the enrollment of your minor child, Lela Butcher, as a citizen of the Creek Nation, you are advised that the Commission requires the affidavits of the mother and the midwife or physician in attendance at its birth.

For this purpose, there is herewith enclosed a blank form of birth affidavit. In executing same, care should be taken to see that all blanks are properly filled, all names written in full, and in the event that either of the persons signing the affidavit is unable to write, signatures by mark must be attested by two witnesses.

Respectfully,

Chairman.

I B A

Applications for Enrollment of Creek Newborn
Act of 1905 Volume V

NC 350.

Muskogee, Indian Territory, June 22, 1905.

Mussy Butcher,
    Morse, Indian Territory.

Dear Madam:

    In the matter of the application for the enrollment of your minor child, Lela Butcher, as a citizen of the Creek Nation, you are advised that the Commission is not satisfied with the affidavits on file.

    You will be allowed ten days from date hereof within which to appear before the Commission at its office in Muskogee, Indian Territory, with the midwife who was in attendance at the birth of said child, for the purpose of being examined under oath.

Respectfully,

Chairman.

NC-350.

Muskogee, Indian Territory, July 29, 1905.

Norfer Butcher,
    Morse, Indian Territory.

Dear Sir:

    In the matter of the application for the enrollment of your daughter Lela Butcher there are on file at this office your affidavit stating that said child was born July 20, 1902 and that there was no physician or midwife in attendance at the birth of said child, and also the affidavits of Missie Butcher, your wife, and Afonoska, an alleged midwife, as to the birth of said child on July 4, 1902.

    You are requested to immediately furnish this office with the joint affidavit of yourself and wife stating the correct date of the birth of said child.

    It will also be necessary for you to file, in the matter of the enrollment of said child, the affidavits of two disinterested parties who are acquainted with the said Lela Butcher, know when she was born, the names of her parents and whether or not she was living March 4, 1905.

    You are also requested to incorporate in the joint affidavit of yourself and wife, above referred to, a statement explaining why the said Afonoska stated in her affidavit that she was the attending midwife at the birth of your said daughter when in fact, as you

Applications for Enrollment of Creek Newborn
Act of 1905   Volume V

stated in your affidavit, there was no attending physician or midwife at the birth of said child.

          Respectfully.

                Commissioner.

B C
Env.

          (Copy)
  Creek Nation.   Morse, Ind. Ter. July 12, 1905.

Commission to the Five Civilized Tribes,
  Muskogee, Ind. Ter.

Gentlemen:

  In regard to the matter of Norfer Butcher making application to enroll his two children Cheparny & Millie, I will say that he, the said Norfer Butcher is a father of these two children and Mussey Butcher is the mother of the children. Norfer Butcher belongs to Nuyaka Town, and Mussey Butcher belongs to Okfuskee Town (Deep Fork). All the information I can think of is this written above.

         Very respectfully,

            (signed) Wm. F. Stoddard

BIRTH AFFIDAVIT.

DEPARTMENT OF THE INTERIOR.
COMMISSION TO THE FIVE CIVILIZED TRIBES.

IN RE APPLICATION FOR ENROLLMENT, as a citizen of the Creek Nation, of Lela Butcher, born on the 4 day of July, 1902

Name of Father:	Nofa Butcher	a citizen of the	Creek	Nation.
Name of Mother:	Mussie Butcher	a citizen of the	Creek	Nation.

        Postoffice Morse I.T.

Applications for Enrollment of Creek Newborn
Act of 1905   Volume V

AFFIDAVIT OF MOTHER.

UNITED STATES OF AMERICA, Indian Territory, ⎫
   Western   DISTRICT.   ⎬
                                                  ⎭

      I, Mussie Butcher , on oath state that I am 26 years of age and a citizen by blood , of the Creek Nation; that I am the lawful wife of Nofa Butcher , who is a citizen, by blood of the Creek Nation; that a female child was born to me on 4 day of July , 1902 , that said child has been named Lela Butcher , and was living March 4, 1905.

                                                                       her
                                                       Mussie x Butcher
Witnesses To Mark: mark
  ⎧ Sam Wildan
  ⎩ *(Name Illegible)*
Subscribed and sworn to before me this 13 day of July, 1905.

    My Commission Expires March 5th, 1908.   C.C. Eskridge
                                                                     Notary Public.

AFFIDAVIT OF ATTENDING PHYSICIAN OR MID-WIFE.

UNITED STATES OF AMERICA, Indian Territory, ⎫
   Western   DISTRICT. ⎬
                                               ⎭

      I, Afonoska , a Mid wife , on oath state that I attended on Mrs. Mussie Butcher, wife of Nofa Butcher on the 4 day of July , 1902 ; that there was born to her on said date a female child; that said child was living March 4, 1905, and is said to have been named Lela Butcher

                                                                 Her
                                                      Afonoska x
Witnesses To Mark: mark
  ⎧ Benton Callahan
  ⎩ Barney Unah

Subscribed and sworn to before me this 13 day of July, 1905.

    My Commission Expires March 5th, 1908.   C.C. Eskridge
                                                                    Notary Public.

BIRTH AFFIDAVIT.
DEPARTMENT OF THE INTERIOR.
COMMISSION TO THE FIVE CIVILIZED TRIBES.

      IN RE APPLICATION FOR ENROLLMENT, as a citizen of the Creek Nation, of Lela Butcher, born on the 20 day of July , 1902

Applications for Enrollment of Creek Newborn
Act of 1905   Volume V

Name of Father: Nafa Butcher   a citizen of the   Creek   Nation.
Name of Mother: Mussey Butcher   a citizen of the   Creek   Nation.

Postoffice   Morse Indian Territory

AFFIDAVIT OF ~~MOTHER~~. Father

UNITED STATES OF AMERICA, Indian Territory,
Western   DISTRICT.

I, Nafa Butcher, on oath state that I am about 33 years of age and a citizen by blood of the Nation; that I am the lawful ~~wife~~ husband of Mussey Butcher, who is a citizen, by blood of the Creek Nation; that a female child was born to me on 20 day of July, 1902, that said child has been named Lela Butcher, and was living March 4, 1905.

                                his
                    Nafa x Butcher
Witnesses To Mark: mark
   Alex Posey
   DC Skaggs

Subscribed and sworn to before me this 14 day of March, 1905.

                               Drennan C Skaggs
                                   Notary Public.

NC 351

DEPARTMENT OF THE INTERIOR,
COMMISSIONER TO THE FIVE CIVILIZED TRIBES,
Paden, Indian Territory, October 2, 1906.

In the matter of the application for the enrollment of Carr Raymond (Warrior) Johnson as a citizen by blood of the Creek Nation.

MINNIE JOHNSON, being duly sworn, by J. McDermott, a Notary Public, testified as follows through Billie Mahady, a sworn Shawnee interpreter:

BY COMMISSIONER

Q What is your name? A Minnie Johnson.
Q What is your age? A About 31.
Q What is your postoffice address? A Paden.
Q Are you a Creek citizen? A No, I am a Shawnee Indian.
Q What degree of Shawnee blood do you claim to have? A I am part Creek and part Shawnee is all I know.

Applications for Enrollment of Creek Newborn
Act of 1905 Volume V

Q Have you selected your allotment of land in the Shawnee Nation? A Yes, I took my land over there.
Q Do you know Sam Warrior? A Yes.
Q Do you know whether or not he has any other name besides Sam Warrior? A He has two names, sometimes they call him Norbie. That is his Indian name.
Q Do you know whether or not he is a blood Creek Indian? A He is fullblood Euchee.
Q Did you have a child by Sam Warrior or Norbe as he is sometimes called? A Yes.
Q Were you lawfully married to him when you had this child by him? A I was married to him according to Indian custom.
Q What is the name of the child? A We call him Carr Raymond Warrior and Carr Raymond Johnson.
Q Under which of the names do you desire him enrolled? A Carr Raymond Johnson.
Q When was Carr Raymond born? A March 15, 1904.
Q Is he living? A Yes, here he is.
Q Does the father of the child contribute anything toward the support of the child? A No. I keep the child myself.
Q Does he live with you now? A He lives west of Shawnee near Norman.
Q If it should be found that your child, Carr Raymond, is entitled to be enrolled in both the Creek and Shawnee Nation, in which do you elect to have him enrolled and take his allotment of land distributions of money? A In the Creek Nation.

---oooOOOooo---

I, Jesse McDermott, on oath state that the above and foregoing is a full and true transcript of my notes as taken in said cause on said date.

Jesse McDermott

Subscribed and sworn to before me this 10th day of December, 1906.

Alex Posey
Notary Public.

(The above affidavit was given again.)

NC 351.

Muskogee, Indian Territory, May 31, 1905.

Minnie Johnson,
    Paden, Indian Territory.

Dear Madam:

Applications for Enrollment of Creek Newborn
Act of 1905 Volume V

In the matter of the application for the enrollment of your minor child, Carr Raymond Warrior, you are advised that the Commission is unable to identify the father of said child, Sam Warrior, on its rolls.

You are requested to inform this office as to any other name as to which Sam Warrior may be known, the names of his parents, the Creek Indian Town to which he belong[sic], and if possible, the numbers which appear on his deeds to land in the Creek Nation.

Respectfully,

Chairman.

New Born
Creek-351.

Muskogee, Indian Territory, August 2, 1905.

James F. Randlett,
    Col. U.S.A., U. S. Indian Agent
        Anadarko, Oklahoma Territory.

Dear Sir:

On March 14, 1905, an application was made to the Commission to the Five Civilized Tribes for the enrollment of Carr Raymond Warrior, born March 15, 1904, as a citizen by blood of the Creek Nation. It is stated in said application that the father of said child is Sam Warrior, who is identified as Norbe, number 9824 upon the final roll of citizens by blood of the Creek Nation, and that the mother of said child is Minnie Johnson, about thirty years of age, a citizen by blood of the Shawnee tribe of Indians.

You are requested to advise this office as to whether or not the said Carr Raymond Warrior has been enrolled by your agency as a citizen of the Shawnee tribe of Indians and whether or not she has received a share of the tribal property as such citizen.

Respectfully,

Commissioner.

NC-351.

Muskogee, Indian Territory, August 2, 1905.

Minnie Johnson,
    Paden, Indian Territory.

Applications for Enrollment of Creek Newborn
Act of 1905 Volume V

Dear Madam:

In the matter of the application for the enrollment of your son Carr Raymond Warrior, born March 15, 1904, as a citizen by blood of the Creek Nation it will be necessary for you to furnish this office with the affidavits of two disinterested persons who are acquainted with said child, know when he was born, the names of his parents and whether or not said child was living March 4, 1905.

If you were married to Sam Warrior, whom you state is the father of said child it will be necessary for you to furnish evidence of your marriage to him which may consist either of the original or a certified copy of your marriage license and certificate.

You are also requested to furnish this office with the affidavit of Sam Warrior as to the birth of said child.

Please give this matter your prompt attention.

                Respectfully,

                          Commissioner.

                DEPARTMENT OF THE INTERIOR,
                INDIAN SCHOOL SERVICE,
                      U.S. Indian Agency,
                          Shawnee, Okla. Aug. 8, 1905.

Hon. Tams Bixby,
    Commissioner,
        Muskogee, Ind. Ter.

Dear Sir:

Answering your letter of the 2nd instant to Col. Jas. F. Randlett at Anadarko, Okla. and by him referred to me for proper reply, the same having refernce[sic] to one Carr Raymond Warrior, son of Minnie Johnson of this agency and Sam Warrior of your agency, I have to state that said Carr Raymond Warrior has never been allotted at this agency nor has he received a share of nay tribal property at this agency.

                Very respectfully,

                        (Signed) Frank. A. Thackery,
                        Supt. & Spcl. Disbg. Agent.

Applications for Enrollment of Creek Newborn
Act of 1905   Volume V

N.C. 351.

Paden, Indian Territory, October 13, 1906.

Commissioner to the Five Civilized Tribes,
   Muskogee, Indian Territory.

Dear Sir:

There are herewith enclosed the affidavits of the mother and midwife in the matter of the application for the enrollment of your Carr Raymond Johnson as a citizen by blood of the Creek Nation. The original affidavit on file shows the name of the child as Carr Raymond Warrior. Testimony relative to the change of name has been secured.

                Respectfully,

                          (No name given.)

NC 351.

                Muskogee, Indian Territory, March 1, 1907.

Minnie Johnson,
   c/o Sam Warrior,
      Paden, Indian Territory.

Dear Madam:

You are hereby advised that on February 15, 1907, the Secretary of the Interior approved the enrollment of your minor child, Carr Raymond Johnson, as a citizen by blood of the Creek Nation, and that the name of the said child appears upon the roll of New Born citizens by blood of the Creek Nation, enrolled Act of Congress approved March 3, 1905, as number 1136.

The child is now entitled to allotment, and application therefor should be made without delay at the Creek Land Office, Muskogee, Indian Territory.

                Respectfully,

                          Commissioner.

Applications for Enrollment of Creek Newborn
Act of 1905 Volume V

BIRTH AFFIDAVIT.

DEPARTMENT OF THE INTERIOR.
COMMISSION TO THE FIVE CIVILIZED TRIBES.

IN RE APPLICATION FOR ENROLLMENT, as a citizen of the Creek Nation, of Carr Raymond Warrior, born on the 15 day of March, 1904

Name of Father:	Sam Warrior	a citizen of the	Creek	Nation.
Name of Mother:	Minnie Johnson	a citizen of the	Shawnee	Nation.

Postoffice   Paden, Indian Territory

AFFIDAVIT OF MOTHER.

UNITED STATES OF AMERICA, Indian Territory,
Western DISTRICT.

I, Minnie Johnson, on oath state that I am about 30 years of age and a citizen by blood, of the Shawnee Nation; that I am the lawful wife of Sam Warrior, who is a citizen, by blood of the Creek Nation; that a male child was born to me on 15 day of March, 1904, that said child has been named Carr Raymond Warrior, and was living March 4, 1905. That no one attended on me as midwife or physician at the time the child was born.

Minnie x Johnson

Witnesses To Mark:
  Alex Posey
  DC Skaggs

Subscribed and sworn to before me this 14 day of March, 1905.

Drennan C Skaggs
Notary Public.

BIRTH AFFIDAVIT.

DEPARTMENT OF THE INTERIOR.
COMMISSION TO THE FIVE CIVILIZED TRIBES.

IN RE APPLICATION FOR ENROLLMENT, as a citizen of the Creek Nation, of Carr Raymond Johnson, born on the 15 day of March, 1904

Name of Father:	"Norbe"	a citizen of the	Creek	Nation.
Name of Mother:	Minnie Johnson	a citizen of the	Shawnee	Nation.

Postoffice   Paden, I.T.

Applications for Enrollment of Creek Newborn
Act of 1905   Volume V

AFFIDAVIT OF MOTHER.

UNITED STATES OF AMERICA, Indian Territory, ⎫
 Western   DISTRICT.   ⎬

I, Minnie Johnson , on oath state that I am 31 years of age and a citizen by blood , of the Shawnee Nation; that I am the lawful wife of "Norbe" , who is a citizen, by blood of the Creek Nation; that a male child was born to me on 15" day of March , 1904 , that said child has been named Carr Raymond Johnson , and was living March 4, 1905, and is now living.

                                  her
                           Minnie x Johnson
                                mark

Witnesses To Mark:
{ J McDermott
  Billi Mahardy

Subscribed and sworn to before me this 13 day of October , 1905.
My Commission
Expires July 25 1907   J McDermott
                                Notary Public.

AFFIDAVIT OF ATTENDING PHYSICIAN OR MID-WIFE.

UNITED STATES OF AMERICA, Indian Territory, ⎫
 Western   DISTRICT.   ⎬

I, Sallie Ellie , a midwife , on oath state that I attended on Mrs. Minnie Johnson , not the wife of "Norbi" on the 15" day of March , 1904 : that there was born to her on said date a male child; that said child was living March 4, 1905, and is said to have been named Carr Raymond Johnson

                           her
                       Sallie x Ellis
Witnesses To Mark: mark
{ J McDermott
  Bille Mahardy

Subscribed and sworn to before me this 13 day of October , 1905.
My Commission
Expires July 25 1907   J McDermott
                                Notary Public.

Applications for Enrollment of Creek Newborn
Act of 1905 Volume V

BIRTH AFFIDAVIT.

DEPARTMENT OF THE INTERIOR.
COMMISSION TO THE FIVE CIVILIZED TRIBES.

IN RE APPLICATION FOR ENROLLMENT, as a citizen of the Creek Nation, of Carr Raymond Warrior, born on the 15" day of March, 1904

Name of Father: Sam Warrior   a citizen of the   Creek   Nation.
Name of Mother: Minnie Johnson   a citizen of the   Shawnee Nation.

Postoffice   Paden, Indian Territory

AFFIDAVIT OF MOTHER.

UNITED STATES OF AMERICA, Indian Territory,
  Western   DISTRICT.

I, Minnie Johnson, on oath state that I am about 30 years of age and a citizen by blood, of the Shawnee Nation; that I am not the lawful wife of Sam Warrior, who is a citizen, by blood of the Creek Nation; that a male child was born to me on 15" day of March, 1904, that said child has been named Carr Raymond Warrior, and ~~is now~~ was living. March 4, 1905 That no one attended on me as midwife or physician at the time the child was born.

                                her
                        Minnie x Johnson
Witnesses To Mark: mark
  { Alex Posey
  { DC Skaggs

Subscribed and sworn to before me this 14 day of March, 1905.

                        Drennan C Skaggs
                        Notary Public.

N.C. 352

DEPARTMENT OF THE INTERIOR,
COMMISSION TO THE FIVE CIVILIZED TRIBES.
Muskogee, Indian Territory, June 28, 1905

In the matter of the application for the enrollment of Bessie Wilson as a citizen of the Creek Nation.

Applications for Enrollment of Creek Newborn
Act of 1905   Volume V

      Clark Wilson, being duly sworn, testified as follows through Sam John--Sunarkey-- sworn Euchee interpreter.

Q What is your name? A Cahcohethlon.
Q Have you an English name? A Clark Wilson.
Q How old are you? A About twentyfive.
Q What is your postoffice address? A Paden.
Q Are you a citizen of the Creek Nation? A Yes.
Q You are a full blood, are you? A Yes.
Q Are you married now? A Yes.
Q What is the name of your wife? A Minnie Johnson.
Q Have you a child named Bessie Wilson? A Yes
Q Is that it there? A Yes, in my arms.
Q What is the name of the mother of that child? A Minnie Johnson.
Q When was Bessie born? A Two years ago December 10, 1904
Q That would make it three years old next December 10, is that right? A Yes.
Q That is your child is it? A Yes, I belong to that baby.

      Minnie Johnson, being duly sworn, testified as follows through Sam John--Sunarkey--sworn Shawnee interpreter.

Q What is your name? A Minnie Johnson.
Q How old are you? A I don't know, about thirty.
Q What is your postoffice address? A Paden.
Q Are you a citizen of the Creek Nation? A No, a Shawnee.
Q What is the name of your husband now at this time? A This man here.
Q How about Sam Warrior? A He went down to Shawnee City and married another woman.
Q Did you marry this man after that, Wilson here? A She married this fellow first and then when this fellow went off she married Sam Warrior after a little while, then Sam went off to Shawnee City and married another woman and then she came back to Wilson. This man Wilson didn't know anything about it.
Q Did he have a child by both this man and by Warrior? A Yes. Bessie by Wilson and the other by Warrior.
Q Both these men are citizens of the Creek Nation are they? A Yes

      Clark Wilson re-called.
Q What is the name of your father? A Artarkinnay.
Q Is he living? A He is dead.
Q What was your father English name? A Called him old man Wolf.

NOTE: Witness is identified as Cahcohethlon on Creek Indian card 2780 and his name is contained in a partial list of citizens by blood of the Creek Nation, approved by the Secretary of the Interior March 28, 1902, opposite aoll[sic] number 7919.

      I, Anna Garrigues, on oath state that the above and foregoing is a full and true transcript of my stenographic notes taken in said cause on said date.

Applications for Enrollment of Creek Newborn
Act of 1905 Volume V

Anna Garrigues

Subscribed and sworn to before me this 28th day of June, 1905.

Edw C Griesel
Notary Public.

BIRTH AFFIDAVIT.

DEPARTMENT OF THE INTERIOR.
COMMISSION TO THE FIVE CIVILIZED TRIBES.

IN RE APPLICATION FOR ENROLLMENT, as a citizen of the Creek Nation, of Bessie Wilson, born on the 10 day of December, 1902

Name of Father:	Clark Wilson	a citizen of the	Creek	Nation.
Name of Mother:	Minnie Johnson	a citizen of the	Shawnee	Nation.

Postoffice   Paden, Indian Territory

AFFIDAVIT OF MOTHER.

UNITED STATES OF AMERICA, Indian Territory, }
    Western   DISTRICT.

I, Minnie Johnson, on oath state that I am about 30 years of age and a citizen by blood, of the Shawnee Nation; that I ~~am~~ was formerly the lawful wife of Clark Wilson, who is a citizen, by blood of the Creek Nation; that a female child was born to me on 10 day of December, 1902, that said child has been named Bessie Wilson, and was living March 4, 1905.

                                              her
Witnesses To Mark: Minnie x Johnson
  { Alex Posey   mark
  { DC Skaggs

Subscribed and sworn to before me this 14 day of March, 1905.

Drennan C Skaggs
Notary Public.

Applications for Enrollment of Creek Newborn
Act of 1905   Volume V

AFFIDAVIT OF ATTENDING PHYSICIAN OR MID-WIFE.

UNITED STATES OF AMERICA, Indian Territory,
Western   DISTRICT.

I, Sally Ellis, a midwife, on oath state that I attended on Mrs. Minnie Johnson, formerly the lawful wife of Clark Wilson on the 10 day of December, 1902; that there was born to her on said date a female child; that said child was living March 4, 1905, and is said to have been named Bessie Wilson

          her
         Sally x Ellis
Witnesses To Mark: mark
 Alex Posey
 D C Skaggs
Subscribed and sworn to before me this 14 day of March, 1905.

         Drennan C Skaggs
         Notary Public.

BIRTH AFFIDAVIT.

DEPARTMENT OF THE INTERIOR.
COMMISSION TO THE FIVE CIVILIZED TRIBES.

IN RE APPLICATION FOR ENROLLMENT, as a citizen of the Creek Nation, of Bessie Wilson, born on the 10" day of Dec., 1902

Name of Father: Clark Wilson (Cah-co-ke-thlon) a citizen of the Creek Nation.
Name of Mother: Minnie Johnson a citizen of the Shawnee Nation.

      Postoffice Paden

AFFIDAVIT OF ~~MOTHER~~ Father

UNITED STATES OF AMERICA, Indian Territory,
Western   DISTRICT.

I, Clark Wilson, on oath state that I am about 25 years of age and a citizen by blood, of the Creek Nation; that I am the lawful ~~wife~~ husband of Minnie Johnson, who is a citizen, by blood of the Shawnee Nation; that a female child was born to me on 10 day of December, 1902, that said child has been named Bessie Wilson, and was living March 4, 1905.

        his
      Clark x Wilson
       mark

Applications for Enrollment of Creek Newborn
Act of 1905 Volume V

Witnesses To Mark:
{ H.G. Hains
  Anna Garrigues

    Subscribed and sworn to before me this 28" day of June, 1905.

                              Henry G. Hains
                                  Notary Public.

                                        NC 352.

                    Muskogee, Indian Territory, June 1, 1905.

Minnie Johnson,
    Paden, Indian Territory.

Dear Madam:

    In the matter of the application for the enrollment of your minor child, Bessie Wilson, you are advised that it is necessary for Clarke Wilson, the father of said child, to appear before the Commission at its office in Muskogee, Indian Territory, to give testimony under oath. For this purpose fifteen days will [sic] allowed.

                          Respectfully,

                                      Com. in Ch
                                      ~~Chairman~~.

Creek Newborn
352.

                    Muskogee, Indian Territory, August 2, 1905.

James F. Randlett, Col. U. S. A.
    United States Indian Agent,
        Anadarko, Oklahoma Territory.

Dear Sir:

    On March 14, 1905 an application was made to the Commission to the Five Civilized Tribes for the enrollment of Bessie Wilson, born December 10, 1902, as a citizen by blood of the Creek Nation. It is stated in said application that the father of said child is Clark Wilson, who is identified as Coh-co-ke-thlon, number 7910 upon the final roll is citizens by blood of the Creek Nation, and that the mother of said child is Minnie Johnson, a citizen by blood of the Shawnee tribe of Indians.

Applications for Enrollment of Creek Newborn
Act of 1905   Volume V

You are requested to inform this office as to whether the said Bessie Wilson has been enrolled by your agency as a citizen of the Shawnee tribe of Indians and whether she has received a share of the tribal property of that tribe.

Respectfully,

Commissioner.

DEPARTMENT OF THE INTERIOR.

INDIAN SCHOOL SERVICE.

U.S. Indian Agency,
Shawnee, Okla, Aug. 8, 1905.

Hon. Tams Bixby,
   Commissioner,
      Muskogee, Ind. Ter.

Dear Sir:

    This will acknowledge receipt of your letter of the 2nd instant to Col. Jas. F. Randlett at Anadarko, Oklahoma, in which you make inquiry relative to one Bessie Wilson daughter of Minnie Johnson, member of the Absentee Shawnee tribe of Indians of this agency, and Clark Wilson alias Cah-co-ke-thlon of your agency.

    Replying thereto I have to advise that said Bessie Wilson has never received any benefits whatsoever as an Absentee Shawnee Indian. She is enrolled with her mother at this agency in the same name "Bessie Wilson" but was never allotted here.

Very respectfully,

(Signed) Frank A. Thackery.

Supt. & Spcl. Disbg. Agent.

NC 352

Muskogee, Indian Territory, March 1, 1907.

Minnie Johnson,
   c/o Clark Wilson,
      Paden, Indian Territory.

Dear Madam:

Applications for Enrollment of Creek Newborn
Act of 1905   Volume V

You are hereby advised that on February 15, 1907, the Secretary of the Interior approved the enrollment of your minor child, Bessie Wilson, as a citizen by blood of the Creek Nation, and that the name of said child appears upon the roll of New Born citizens by blood of the Creek Nation, enrolled under the Act of Congress approved March 3rd, 1905, as number 1137.

The child is now entitled to allotment and application therefor should be made without delay at the Creek Land Office, Muskogee, Indian Territory.

Respectfully,

Commissioner.

AFFIDAVIT OF ATTENDING PHYSICIAN OR MID-WIFE.

UNITED STATES OF AMERICA, Indian Territory,
Western Judicial   DISTRICT.

acquaintance

I, John Lilly[sic] , a ~~(blank)~~ , on oath state that I ~~attended~~ on Mrs. Amanda J. Frank, wife of Tingo Frank on the 12 day of March , 1904 ; that there was born to her on said date a male child; that said child was living March 4, 1905, and is said to have been named William Frank

John Lilley

Witnesses To Mark:
{

Subscribed and sworn to before me this 13 day of July, 1905.

my Com. Exp. Aug 19-1908   Tupper Dunn
                                  Notary Public.

AFFIDAVIT OF ACQUAINTANCE.

UNITED STATES OF AMERICA, Indian Territory,
Western Judicial   DISTRICT.

I, Ella Davis , on oath state that I am 25 years of age, and a citizen by blood of the Creek Nation; that my postoffice address is Arbeka , Ind. Ter.; that I was personally acquainted with William Frank who ~~was a citizen~~ is citizen, by blood , of the Creek ~~Nation~~ Nation; and that said William Frank was living ~~died~~ on the 4 day of March , 1905. was borned[sic] 12 day of March, 1904

Ella Davis

Applications for Enrollment of Creek Newborn
Act of 1905   Volume V

Witnesses To Mark:

{

Subscribed and sworn to before me this 13 day of July, 1905.

my Com. Exp. Aug 19" 1908   Tupper Dunn
                                  Notary Public.

BIRTH AFFIDAVIT.

DEPARTMENT OF THE INTERIOR.
COMMISSION TO THE FIVE CIVILIZED TRIBES.

IN RE APPLICATION FOR ENROLLMENT, as a citizen of the Creek Nation, of William Frank, born on the 12 day of March, 1904

Name of Father: Tingo Frank   a citizen of the   Creek   Nation.
Name of Mother: Amanda J. Frank a citizen of the   Creek   Nation.

                    Postoffice   Arbeka, Ind. Ter.

AFFIDAVIT OF MOTHER.

UNITED STATES OF AMERICA, Indian Territory,
    Western   DISTRICT.

I, Amanda J. Frank, on oath state that I am 30 years of age and a citizen by blood, of the Creek Nation; that I am the lawful wife of Tingo Frank, who is a citizen, by blood of the Creek Nation; that a male child was born to me on the 12" day of March, 1904, that said child has been named William Frank, and was living March 4, 1905. That no one attended on me as physician or mid-wife at the time the child was born.

                                  Amanda J. Frank
Witnesses To Mark:

{

Subscribed and sworn to before me this 15 day of March, 1905.

                                  Drennan C Skaggs
                                  Notary Public.

Applications for Enrollment of Creek Newborn
Act of 1905   Volume V

NC-354

Muskogee, Indian Territory, May 29, 1905.

Louisa Fife,
    Dustin, Indian Territory.

Dear Madam:

    In the matter of the application for the enrollment of your minor child, James Fife, as a citizen of the Creek Nation, the Commission is unable to identify you under the name of Louisa Fife.

    You are requested to furnish the Commission with the name which you were enrolled, the names of your parents, the Creek Indian Town to which you belong, and, if possible, the roll number as it appears on your deeds to land in the Creek Nation.

    You are also requested to procure the affidavit of the midwife or physician in attendance at the birth of said child. For this purpose a blank form of birth affidavit is herewith enclosed you. In executing same, care should be taken to see that all blanks are properly filled, all names written in full, and in the event that the person signing the affidavit is unable to write, signature by mark must be attested by two witnesses. If said affidavit cannot be furnished, you are requested to procure the affidavits of two disinterested persons relating to the birth of said child.

                  Respectfully,

                                      Chairman.

1 B A

O. P. ROUGHTON, PRESIDENT   J. H. SWAFFORD, VICE-PRES. AND GEN. MANAGER
M. H. ROUGHTON, SECRETARY   C. M. SWAFFORD, TREASURER

Spokogee Mercantile Company.
(INCORPORATED)

Dustin, I. T., 6/14   1905.

Commission of the Five Civilized Tribes

My name on my allotment was Louisa Lowe My Father named was Con Nar Ky Lowe Mother Lena Lowe   Creek Town of Thlewarlee

                                    Respcfuly[sic]

Applications for Enrollment of Creek Newborn
Act of 1905   Volume V

Louisa Fife

BIRTH AFFIDAVIT.

DEPARTMENT OF THE INTERIOR.
COMMISSION TO THE FIVE CIVILIZED TRIBES.

IN RE APPLICATION FOR ENROLLMENT, as a citizen of the Creek Nation, of James Fife, born on the 23 day of March, 1904

Name of Father: Sundy Fife   a citizen of the   Creek   Nation.
Name of Mother: Louisa Fife   a citizen of the   Creek   Nation.

Postoffice   Dustin I.T.

AFFIDAVIT OF MOTHER.

UNITED STATES OF AMERICA, Indian Territory,
Western   DISTRICT.

I, Louisa Fife, on oath state that I am 30 years of age and a citizen by Birth, of the Creek Nation; that I am the lawful wife of Sundy Fife, who is a citizen, by Birth of the Creek Nation; that a male child was born to me on 23 day of March, 1904, that said child has been named James Fife, and was living March 4, 1905.

her
Louisa x Fife
mark

Witnesses To Mark:
Geo Canard
W.E. McQueen

Subscribed and sworn to before me this 14 day of June, 1905.

My Com Expires 1/31-1909   Dan Upton
Notary Public.

AFFIDAVIT OF ATTENDING PHYSICIAN OR MID-WIFE.

UNITED STATES OF AMERICA, Indian Territory,
Western   DISTRICT.

I, Sinda Law, a *(illegible)*, on oath state that I attended on Mrs. Louisa Fife, wife of Sinda[sic] Fife on the 23 day of March, 1904 : that there was born to her on said date a male child; that said child was living March 4, 1905, and is said to have been named James Fife

Cindy Lowe

Applications for Enrollment of Creek Newborn
Act of 1905 Volume V

Witnesses To Mark:

Subscribed and sworn to before me this 14 day of June, 1905.

My Com Expires 1/31-1909   Dan Upton
                                                    Notary Public.

BIRTH AFFIDAVIT.

DEPARTMENT OF THE INTERIOR.
COMMISSION TO THE FIVE CIVILIZED TRIBES.

IN RE APPLICATION FOR ENROLLMENT, as a citizen of the Creek Nation, of James Fife, born on the 23 day of March, 1904

Name of Father: Sandy Fife   a citizen of the   Creek   Nation.
Name of Mother: Louisa Fife   a citizen of the   Creek   Nation.

Postoffice   Dustin Ind. Ter.

AFFIDAVIT OF MOTHER.

UNITED STATES OF AMERICA, Indian Territory,
    Western   DISTRICT.

I, Louisa Fife, on oath state that I am about 30 years of age and a citizen by blood, of the Creek Nation; that I am the lawful wife of Sandy Fife, who is a citizen, by blood of the Creek Nation; that a male child was born to me on 23 day of March, 1904, that said child has been named James Fife, and was living March 4, 1905.

                                    her
                              Louisa x Fife
Witnesses To Mark: mark
  Alex Posey
  D C Skaggs

Subscribed and sworn to before me this 20 day of March, 1905.

                              Drennan C Skaggs
                                    Notary Public.

Applications for Enrollment of Creek Newborn
Act of 1905 Volume V

AFFIDAVIT OF ATTENDING PHYSICIAN OR MID-WIFE.

UNITED STATES OF AMERICA, Indian Territory,
(blank) DISTRICT.

I, Cindy Lowe, a (blank), on oath state that I attended on Mrs. Louisa Fife, wife of Sandy Fife on the 23 day of March, 1904 ; that there was born to her on said date a male child; that said child was living March 4, 1905, and is said to have been named James Fife

Cindy Lowe

Witnesses To Mark:

Subscribed and sworn to before me this 20 day of March, 1905.

Drennan C Skaggs
Notary Public.

AFFIDAVIT OF TWO WITNESSES.

We Wisey Soloman of Okemah, I.T. and Jackson Knight of Boley, I.T.

On oath state that we are well acquainted with Lucy Michiley (nee Hill) who is a Citizen of the Creek Nation and wife of Michiley, and know that to be a fact that there was born to her on or about Feb. 16, 1905 & Oct. 5, 1902 a both Male children child, that said children wasere living March 4, 19056, and wis[sic] said to have been named Ralph and Roy Mitchell.

her
Wisey x Soloman
mark

WITNESSES TO MARK:

his
Jackson x Knight
mark

John D. Richards

John H. Phillips

Subscribed and sworn to before me this 23rd day of July, 1906.

My Commission Expires   John H. Phillips
Sept. 6, 1906   Notary Public.

Applications for Enrollment of Creek Newborn
Act of 1905 Volume V

BIRTH AFFIDAVIT.

DEPARTMENT OF THE INTERIOR.
COMMISSION TO THE FIVE CIVILIZED TRIBES.

IN RE APPLICATION FOR ENROLLMENT, as a citizen of the Creek Nation, of Roy Mitchiley, born on the 5th day of October, 1902

Name of Father: Mitchiley	a citizen of the	Creek Nation.
Name of Mother: Lucy Hill Mitchiley	a citizen of the Creek	Nation.

Postoffice *(blank)*

AFFIDAVIT OF MOTHER.

UNITED STATES OF AMERICA, Indian Territory,
   Western Judicial   DISTRICT.

I, Lucy Mitchiley, on oath state that I am 35 years of age and a citizen by Blood, of the Creek Nation; that I am the lawful wife of Mitchiley, who is a citizen, by Blood of the Creek Nation; that a male child was born to me on 5th day of Oct., 1902, that said child has been named Roy Mitchiley, and was living March 4, 1905.

                                        her
                              Lucy x Mitchiley

Witnesses To Mark: mark
  { Dan M. Baker
   John H. Phillips

Subscribed and sworn to before me this 25th day of August, 1905.

My Commission Expires Sept. 6th 1906.   John H. Phillips
                                                  Notary Public.

AFFIDAVIT OF ATTENDING PHYSICIAN OR MID-WIFE.

UNITED STATES OF AMERICA, Indian Territory,
   Western Judicial   DISTRICT.

I, Mitchiley, a Husband, on oath state that I attended on Mrs. Lucy Mitchiley, my wife ~~of~~ *(blank)* on the 5th day of Oct, 1902; that there was born to her on said date a male child; that said child was living March 4, 1905, and is said to have been named Roy Mitchiley

                                    Mitchiley

Witnesses To Mark:
  {

Applications for Enrollment of Creek Newborn
Act of 1905   Volume V

Subscribed and sworn to before me this 25th day of August, 1905.

My Commission Expires Sept. 6th 1906.

John H. Phillips
Notary Public.

BIRTH AFFIDAVIT.

DEPARTMENT OF THE INTERIOR.
COMMISSION TO THE FIVE CIVILIZED TRIBES.

IN RE APPLICATION FOR ENROLLMENT, as a citizen of the Creek Nation, of Ralph Mitchiley, born on the 24th day of Feb., 1905

Name of Father: Mitchiley   a citizen of the   Creek   Nation.
Name of Mother: Lucy Hill nee Mitchiley   a citizen of the   Creek   Nation.

Postoffice   Okemah, I.T.

AFFIDAVIT OF MOTHER.

UNITED STATES OF AMERICA, Indian Territory,
Western Judicial   DISTRICT.

I, Lucy Mitchiley, on oath state that I am 35 years of age and a citizen by Blood, of the Creek Nation; that I am the lawful wife of Mitchiley, who is a citizen, by Blood of the Creek Nation; that a male child was born to me on 24th day of FebRuary[sic], 1905, that said child has been named Ralph Mitchiley, and was living March 4, 1905.

                                      her
                              Lucy x Mitchiley
Witnesses To Mark: mark
  Dan M. Baker
  Jno H. Phillips

Subscribed and sworn to before me this 25th day of August, 1905.

My Commission Expires Sept. 6th 1906.

John H. Phillips
Notary Public.

AFFIDAVIT OF ATTENDING PHYSICIAN OR MID-WIFE.

UNITED STATES OF AMERICA, Indian Territory,
Western Judicial   DISTRICT.

I, Mitchiley, a Husband, on oath state that I attended on Mrs. Lucy Mitchiley, my wife ~~of~~ *(blank)* on the 24th day of Feb., 1905 ; that there was born to

Applications for Enrollment of Creek Newborn
Act of 1905   Volume V

her on said date a male child; that said child was living March 4, 1905, and is said to have been named Ralph Mitchiley

Mitchiley

Witnesses To Mark:

{

    Subscribed and sworn to before me this 25th day of August, 1905.

My Commission Expires Sept. 6th 1906.   John H. Phillips
Notary Public.

N.C. 355.

Muskogee, Indian Territory, June 22, 1906.

Lucy Hill (Lucy Mitchiley),
    Okemah, Indian Territory.

Dear Madam:

    In the matter of the application for the enrollment of your minor children, Roy Mitchiley and Ralph Mitchiley, as citizens of the Creek Nation, you are advised that it is required that you furnish this office with the affidavits of yourself and the midwife in attendance at the birth of said children. For this purpose there are inclosed[sic] blank forms of birth affidavit. Each of said affidavits should show the name of the child, the names of its parents, the date of its birth and whether or not it was living March 4, 1906.

    This matter should receive your prompt attention.

Respectfully,

2 BA   Commissioner.

Applications for Enrollment of Creek Newborn
Act of 1905   Volume V

BIRTH AFFIDAVIT.

Department of the Interior,
COMMISSION TO THE FIVE CIVILIZED TRIBES.

IN RE Application for Enrollment, as a citizen of the Creek Nation, of Martha & Marry Mayes, born on the first day of January, 1903

Name of Father: Wyatt Mayes   a citizen of the Tennessee ~~Nation~~.
Name of Father: Martha Mayes   a citizen of the   Creek   Nation.

Post Office: Newby I T

AFFIDAVIT OF MOTHER.

UNITED STATES OF AMERICA,
    INDIAN TERRITORY,
    Western   District.

I, Martha Mayes, on oath state that I am 25 years of age and a citizen by birth, of the Creek Nation; that I am the lawful wife of Wyatt Mayes, who is a citizen, by marriage of the Creek Nation; that a w female children was born to me on first day of January, 1903, that said children has been named Martha & Marry Mayes, and is now living.

                                    Martha Mayes

WITNESSES TO MARK:
    Henry Mason
    Mattie Hartman

Subscribed and sworn to before me this 16 day of March, 1905.

                        L H Evert
                            Notary Public.
                        My commission expires May 31 1908

AFFIDAVIT OF ATTENDING PHYSICIAN OR MID-WIFE.

UNITED STATES OF AMERICA,
    INDIAN TERRITORY,
    Western   District.

I, Martha Mayes, a Midwife, on oath state that I attended on Mrs. Martha Mayes my daughter in law, wife of Wyatt Mayes on the first day of January, 1903; that there was born to her on said date a 2 female children; that said children is now living and is said to have been named Martha & Marry Mayes

Applications for Enrollment of Creek Newborn
Act of 1905   Volume V

WITNESSES TO MARK:
{ Henry Mason
{ Mattie Hartman

her
Martha x Mayes
mark

Subscribed and sworn to before me this 16 *day of* March, *1905*.

L H Evert
Notary Public.
My commission exp May 31 1908

BA NE 94.

DEPARTMENT OF THE INTERIOR,
COMMISSION TO THE FIVE CIVILIZED TRIBES.
MUSKOGEE, I.T. May 18, 1905.

In the matter of the application for the enrollment of John Whitlow as a citizen by blood of the Creek Nation.

William
~~John~~ Whitlow being duly sworn, testified as follows; through Official Interpreter, Jesse McDermott.

By the Commission.   William
Q What is your name? A ~~John~~ Whitlow.
Q What is your age? A About 28.
Q What is your post office address? A Dustin.
Q Are you a citizen of the Creek Nation? A I am a citizen of the Seminole Nation
Q Have you a child named John Whitlow? A Yes sir.
Q Is that child living? A Yes sir.
Q When was the last time you saw it? A Yesterday
Q What is the name of the mother of this child? A Simhoye.
Q Is she a citizen of the Creek Nation? A Yes sir.

Simhoye Whitlow is identified on Creek Indian Card, Field Number 2830.

Q Are you and she living together? A Yes sir.
Q If it should be found that this child has rights in both the Creek and Seminole Nation, in which nation do you now elect to have him enrolled and receive his allotment of land? A In the Creek Nation.
Q Do you know whether your wife wants him to be enrolled and take his allotment in the Creek Nation? A She is willing.

Applications for Enrollment of Creek Newborn
Act of 1905   Volume V

An affidavit executed by you and Simhoye Whitlow, the mother of said child, and Dinah Beaver, midwife, on the 22nd of April, 1903, heretofore filed in this case is made a part of the record herein.

Lona Merrick, being duly sworn, states that the above and foregoing is a true and correct transcript of her stenographic notes as taken in said cause on said date.

            Lona Merrick

Subscribed and sworn to before me this 18th day of May, 1905.

            Edw C Griesel
              Notary Public.

N.C.

        DEPARTMENT OF THE INTERIOR.
     COMMISSIONER TO THE FIVE CIVILIZED TRIBES.
        DUSTIN, I. T., DECEMBER 13, 1906.

In the matter of the application for the enrollment of John Whitlow as a citizen by blood of the Creek Nation.

WILLIAM WHITLOW, being first duly sworn by Jesse McDermott, a Notary Public, and examined through Alex Posey, Official Interpreter, testified as follows:

BY THE COMMISSIONER:

Q What is your name? A William Whitlow.
Q How old are you? A I do not know how old I am, but I am over 30.
Q What is your postoffice address? A Dustin.
Q Are you a citizen of the Creek Nation? A Yes sir I was a citizen of the Creek Nation and belonged to Thlewathe town by[sic] I am enrolled as a citizen of the Seminole Nation and have taken my allotment of land there.
Q Are you married? A Yes sir.
Q What is the name of your wife? A Semhoye.
Q Is your wife a citizen of the Creek Nation? A Yes sir.
Q To what Creek town does she belong? A Arbeka Tulledega.
Q Have you and your wife a minor child named John Whitlow? [sic]
Q Have you personally appeared before the Commissioner to the Five Civilized Tribes and made application for the enrollment of your minor child, you are advised that the Commission requires further evidence as to the birth of said child, of your child? A No sir, but we made affidavits relative to the birth of the child before a Notary at Dustin and transmitted them to the Commissioner at Muskogee. I made application for the child three years ago and the child is now ~~six years~~ five years old.

Applications for Enrollment of Creek Newborn
Act of 1905   Volume V

Q Do you know the date of the birth of John? A He was born on or about October 20, and was five years old last October.
Q Was the child born in 1901? A Yes sir, according to my best recollections that is the year in which it was born.
Q Is John now living? A ~~A~~ Yes sir. After I made application for the child I ~~w~~ received a letter from the Commission requesting a joint affidavit of two disinterested witnesses, but I Have[sic] not yet furnished the affidavits.
Q Have you and Semhoye any other children? A Yes sir, Edward, Edmond and Sissy, all of whom are enrolled.
Q How are you enrolled in the Seminole Nation? A Simply as Whitlow.
Q How is your wife enrolled? A Simply as Semhoye.

J. B. Myers, being first duly sworn, states, that as stenographer to the Commissioner to the Five Civilized Tribes, he recorded the testimony in the foregoing proceedings, and that the above is a true and correct transcript of his stenographic notes thereof.

JB Myers

Subscribed and sworn to before me,
this 13th day of December, 1906.

Alex Posey
JBM   Notary Public.

N.C. 357.   F.H.W.

DEPARTMENT OF THE INTERIOR,
COMMISSIONER TO THE FIVE CIVILIZED TRIBES.

In the matter of the application for the enrollment of John Whitlow as a citizen by blood of the Creek Nation.

DECISION.

The record in this case shows that on April 28, 1903, application was made, in affidavit form, for the enrollment of John Whitlow, as a citizen by blood of the Creek Nation. Further proceedings were had May 18, 1905, before the Commission to the Five Civilized Tribes, at Muskogee, Indian Territory, and on December 13, 1906, before a Creek enrollment field party, at Dustin, Indian Territory. A supplemental affidavit executed December 13, 1906, is attached to and made a part of the record herein.

The evidence shows that the said John Whitlow is the child of William Whitlow, a citizen of the Seminole Nation, and Simhoya whose name appears on a partial schedule of citizens by blood of the Creek Nation, approved by the Secretary of the Interior March 28, 1902, opposite roll No. 8014. It further appears that an election was made for the applicant to be enrolled as a citizen of the Creek Nation.

The evidence further shows that said John Whitlow was born October 20, 1901, and was still living December 13, 1906.

Applications for Enrollment of Creek Newborn
Act of 1905   Volume V

The Act of Congress approved March 3, 1905 (33 Stat., 1048), provides in part as follows:

"That the Commission to the Five Civilized Tribes is authorized for sixty days after the date of the approval of this Act to receive and consider applications for enrollments of children born subsequent to May twenty five, nineteen hundred and one, and prior to March fourth, nineteen hundred and five, and living on said latter date, to citizens of the Creek tribe of Indians whose enrollment has been approved by the Secretary of the Interior prior to the approval of this Act: and to enroll and make allotments to such children."

It is therefore, ordered and adjudged that the said John Whitlow is entitled to enrollment as a citizen by blood of the Creek Nation, in accordance with the provisions of the Act of Congress above quoted, and the application for his enrollment as such is accordingly granted.

Tams Bixby Commissioner.

Muskogee, Indian Territory.

January 15, 1907

NC 357.

Muskogee, Indian Territory, June 5, 1905.

Semhoye Whitlow,
  Dustin, Indian Territory.

Dear Madam:

In the matter of the application for the enrollment of your minor child, Sissie Whitlow, as a citizen of the Creek Nation, you are advised that the Commission requires the affidavit of the midwife or physician in attendance at the birth of said child, and if same cannot be procured the affidavits of two disinterested witnesses as to the date of its birth.

There are herewith enclosed two blank forms of birth affidavit, and in executing same care should be exercised to see that all blanks are properly filled, all names written in full and in the event that either of the persons signing the affidavits is unable to write, signatures by mark must be attested by two witnesses. Each affidavit must be executed before a Notary Public and the notarial seal and signature of the officer must be attached to each separate affidavit.

Respectfully,

2 BA.   Commissioner in Charge.

Applications for Enrollment of Creek Newborn
Act of 1905   Volume V

N.C. 357

Muskogee, Indian Territory, July 7, 1905.

William Whitlow,
    Dustin, Indian Territory.

Dear Sir:

    In the matter of the application for the enrollment of your minor child, Sissie Whitlow, as a citizen of the Creek Nation, you are advised that you will be allowed a reasonable time to appear at this office for the purpose of electing in which nation you desire to have said child enrolled and take her allotment of land.

    Respectfully,

Commissioner.

NC. 357.

Muskogee, Indian Territory, July 14, 1905.

Commissioner to the Five Civilized Tribes,
    Seminole Enrollment Division,
        Muskogee, Indian Territory.

Gentlemen:

    March 24, 1905, application was made to the Commission to the Five Civilized Tribes for the enrollment of Sissie Whitlow, born September 18, 1904, as a citizen by blood of the Creek Nation. It is stated in said application that the father of said child is William Whitlow, a citizen of the Seminole Nation, and that the mother is Simhoye, a citizen of the Creek Nation.

    You are requested to inform the Creek Enrollment Division as to whether application has been made for the enrollment of Sissie Whitlow, as a citizen of the Seminole Nation, and if so, what disposition has been made of the same.

    Respectfully,

Commissioner.

Applications for Enrollment of Creek Newborn
Act of 1905   Volume V

DEPARTMENT OF THE INTERIOR.
COMMISSION TO THE FIVE CIVILIZED TRIBES.

Muskogee, Indian Territory, July 18, 1905.

Chief Clerk,
    Creek Enrollment Division.

Dear Sirs:

    Receipt is acknowledged of your letter of July 14, 1905 stating that an application was made to the Commission to the Five Civilized Tribes for the enrollment of Sissie Whitlow, born September 18, 1904, child of William Whitlow, a citizen of the Seminole Nation, and Simhoye, a citizen of the Creek Nation, as a citizen by blood of the Creek Nation and requesting to be informed as to whether an application has been made for the enrollment of said child as a citizen of the Seminole Nation.

    In reply to your letter you are advised that it does not appear from an examination of the records of this office that any application was made to the Commission to the Five Civilized Tribes for the enrollment of said Sissie Whitlow as a citizen of the Seminole Nation.

    Respectfully,

Tams Bixby   Commissioner.

NC-357.

Muskogee, Indian Territory, August 2, 1905.

William Whitlow,
    Dustin, Indian Territory.

Dear Sir:

    In the matter of the application for the enrollment of your minor son John Whitlow, born August 20, 1901, as a citizen by blood of the Creek Nation you are advised that the affidavits as to the birth of said child, now on file with this office, show only that he was living March 4, 1905 on April 22, 1903.

    It is necessary, before his rights as such citizen can be finally determined, that affidavits be filed with this office showing whether or not he was living on March 4, 1905. For that purpose a blank for[sic] of proof of birth partially filled out is inclosed[sic] herewith and you are requested to have the same properly executed and return to this office in the inclosed[sic] envelope. In case any signature is by mark it must be attested by two disinterested witnesses. Be careful to see that the notary public, before whom the affidavits are sworn to, attaches his name and seal to each affidavit.

Applications for Enrollment of Creek Newborn
Act of 1905   Volume V

Respectfully,

CTD-10   Commissioner.
Env.

NC 357

Muskogee, Indian Territory, November 2, 1906.

Chief Clerk,
    Seminole Enrollment Division,
        General Office.

Dear Sir:

You are hereby advised that the name of Sissie Whitlow, born September 18, 1904, to William Whitlow, an alleged citizen of the Seminole Nation, and Simhoye Whitlow, a citizen b blood of the Creek Nation, is contained in a schedule of New Born citizens of the Creek Nation, approved by the Secretary of the Interior September 27, 1905, opposite Roll No. 374.

Respectfully,

Commissioner.

NC 357.

Muskogee, Indian Territory, March 1, 1907.

Simhoye Whitlow,
    C/o[sic] William Whitlow,
        Dustin, Indian Territory.

Dear Madam:

You are hereby advised that on February 15, 1907, the Secretary of the Interior approved the enrollment of your minor child, John Whitlow, as a citizen by blood of the Creek Nation, and that the name of said child appears upon the roll of New Born citizens by blood of the Creek Nation, enrolled under the Act of Congress approved March 3rd, 1905, as number 1138.

The child is now entitled to allotment, and application therefor should be made without delay at the Creek Land Office, Muskogee, Indian Territory.

Applications for Enrollment of Creek Newborn
Act of 1905   Volume V

                              Respectfully,

                                                    Commissioner.

Western District,
Indian Territory   SS

    We, the undersigned, on oath state that we are personally acquainted with Semhoye Whitlow wife of William Whitlow and that on or about the 20 day of October, 1904, a male child was born to them and has been named John Whitlow; that said child was living March 4, 1906, and is now living

    We further state that we have no interest in the above case.

                                                W E McQueen
                                                Charley Wesby

Witness to mark.
    Alex Posey
    JB Myers
    Alex Posey
    JB Myers

Subscribed and sworn to before
me this 13 day of Dec 1906.
                                      Alex Posey
                                        Notary Public.

BIRTH AFFIDAVIT.
                      DEPARTMENT OF THE INTERIOR.
             COMMISSION TO THE FIVE CIVILIZED TRIBES.

    IN RE APPLICATION FOR ENROLLMENT, as a citizen of the Creek Nation, of Sissie Whitlow, born on the 18th day of Sept, 1904

Name of Father: William Whitlow   a citizen of the Seminole Nation.
Name of Mother: Semhoye Whitlow   a citizen of the   Creek   Nation.

                            Postoffice   Dustin Ind. Ter.

Applications for Enrollment of Creek Newborn
Act of 1905   Volume V

AFFIDAVIT OF MOTHER.

UNITED STATES OF AMERICA, Indian Territory, ⎱
    Western   DISTRICT. ⎰

    I, Simhoye Whitlow , on oath state that I am 28 years of age and a citizen by Birth , of the Creek   Nation; that I am the lawful wife of William Whitlow , who is a citizen, by Birth of the Seminole   Nation; that a Female male child was born to me on 18th   day of September , 1904 , that said child has been named Sissie Whitlow , and was living March 4, 1905.

                                                        her
                                          Semhoye x Whitlow
Witnesses To Mark: mark
   ⎰ Joe Brown
   ⎱ E Carpenter

    Subscribed and sworn to before me this 3 day of July , 1905.

My Com Expires 1/31/1909   Dan Upton
                                            Notary Public.

                              Witness
             AFFIDAVIT OF ~~ATTENDING PHYSICIAN OR MID-WIFE~~.

UNITED STATES OF AMERICA, Indian Territory, ⎱
    Western   DISTRICT. ⎰

                                                  personally know
    I, George Kanard , a witness , on oath state that I ~~attended on~~ Mrs. Semhoye Whitlow , wife of William Whitlow on the 18th day of Sept , 1904 ; that there was born to her on said date a Female child; that said child was living March 4, 1905, and is said to have been named Sissie Whitlow

                                          Geo Kanard
Witnesses To Mark:
   ⎰
   ⎱

    Subscribed and sworn to before me this 3 day of July , 1905.

My Commission Expires 1/31/1909   Dan Upton
                                            Notary Public.

BIRTH AFFIDAVIT.
                            DEPARTMENT OF THE INTERIOR.
            COMMISSION TO THE FIVE CIVILIZED TRIBES.

    IN RE APPLICATION FOR ENROLLMENT, as a citizen of the Creek Nation, of Sissie Whitlow, born on the 18th day of Sept , 1904

Applications for Enrollment of Creek Newborn
Act of 1905   Volume V

Name of Father: William Whitlow   a citizen of the Seminole Nation.
Name of Mother: Semhoye Whitlow   a citizen of the Creek   Nation.

Postoffice   Dustin Ind. Ter.

AFFIDAVIT OF MOTHER.

UNITED STATES OF AMERICA, Indian Territory,
Western   DISTRICT.

I, Simhoye Whitlow, on oath state that I am 28 years of age and a citizen by Birth, of the Creek Nation; that I am the lawful wife of William Whitlow, who is a citizen, by Birth of the Seminole Nation; that a Female child was born to me on 18th day of September, 1904, that said child has been named Sissie Whitlow, and was living March 4, 1905.

                                      her
                            Semhoye x Whitlow
Witnesses To Mark: mark
  Joe Brown
  E Carpenter
Subscribed and sworn to before me this   3 day of July, 1905.

My Com Expires 1/31/1909   Dan Upton
                                      Notary Public.

Witness
AFFIDAVIT OF ~~ATTENDING PHYSICIAN OR MID-WIFE~~.

UNITED STATES OF AMERICA, Indian Territory,
Western   DISTRICT.

                                      personally know
I, W.E. McQueen, a Witness, on oath state that I ~~attended on~~ Mrs. Semhoye Whitlow, wife of William Whitlow on the 18th day of Sept, 1904 ; that there was born to her on said date a Female child; that said child was living March 4, 1905, and is said to have been named Sissie Whitlow

                                      W.E. McQueen
Witnesses To Mark:

Subscribed and sworn to before me this   3 day of July, 1905.

My Commission Expires 1/31/1909   Dan Upton
                                        Notary Public.

Applications for Enrollment of Creek Newborn
Act of 1905   Volume V

BIRTH AFFIDAVIT.

DEPARTMENT OF THE INTERIOR.
COMMISSION TO THE FIVE CIVILIZED TRIBES.

IN RE APPLICATION FOR ENROLLMENT, as a citizen of the Creek Nation, of John Whitlow, born on the 20th day of October, 1901

Name of Father:	William Whitlow	a citizen of the	Seminole	Nation.
Name of Mother:	Semhoye Whitlow	a citizen of the	Creek	Nation.

Postoffice   Spokogee

AFFIDAVIT OF MOTHER.

UNITED STATES OF AMERICA, Indian Territory,
Western   DISTRICT.

I, Semhoye Whitlow, on oath state that I am 28 years of age and a citizen by birth, of the Creek Nation; that I am the lawful wife of William Whitlow, who is a citizen, by birth of the Seminole Nation; that a male child was born to me on 20th day of October, 1901, that said child has been named John Whitlow, and is now living.

Witnesses To Mark:
{ W E McQueen
{ John Smith

her
Semhoye x Whitlow
mark

Subscribed and sworn to before me this 22^d day of April, 1903.

J.P. Boyle
Notary Public.

AFFIDAVIT OF ATTENDING PHYSICIAN OR MID-WIFE.

UNITED STATES OF AMERICA, Indian Territory,
Western   DISTRICT.

I, Dinah Beaver, a midwife, on oath state that I attended on Mrs. Semhoye Whitlow, wife of William Whitlow on the 20th day of October, 1901; that there was born to her on said date a male child; that said child is now living and is said to have been named John Whitlow.

Witnesses To Mark:
{ W.E. McQueen
{ John Smith

her
Dinah x Beaver
mark

Applications for Enrollment of Creek Newborn
Act of 1905   Volume V

Subscribed and sworn to before me this 22ᵈ day of April, 1903.

        J.P. Boyle
          Notary Public.

BIRTH AFFIDAVIT.

DEPARTMENT OF THE INTERIOR.
COMMISSION TO THE FIVE CIVILIZED TRIBES.

IN RE APPLICATION FOR ENROLLMENT, as a citizen of the Creek Nation, of Sissie Whitlow, born on the 18 day of September, 1904

Name of Father:	William Whitlow	a citizen of the	Seminole	Nation.
Name of Mother:	Semhoye Whitlow	a citizen of the	Creek	Nation.

      Postoffice Dustin Ind. Ter.

AFFIDAVIT OF MOTHER.

UNITED STATES OF AMERICA, Indian Territory,
 Western DISTRICT.

  I, Semhoye Whitlow, on oath state that I am about 28 years of age and a citizen by blood, of the Creek Nation; that I am the lawful wife of William Whitlow, who is a citizen, by blood of the Seminole Nation; that a female child was born to me on 18th day of September, 1904, that said child has been named Sissie Whitlow, and was living March 4, 1905.

          her
        Semhoye x Whitlow
Witnesses To Mark: mark
 { Alex Posey
 { D C Skaggs

Subscribed and sworn to before me this 21 day of March, 1905.

        Drennan C Skaggs
         Notary Public.

AFFIDAVIT OF ATTENDING PHYSICIAN OR MID-WIFE.

UNITED STATES OF AMERICA, Indian Territory,
 Western DISTRICT.

               my wife
  I, William Whitlow, a ~~(blank)~~, on oath state that I attended on ^ Mrs. Semhoye Whitlow, ~~wife of (blank)~~ on the 18 day of September, 1904; that there

Applications for Enrollment of Creek Newborn
Act of 1905   Volume V

was born to her on said date a female child; that said child was living March 4, 1905, and is said to have been named Sissie Whitlow

Witnesses To Mark:
{ Alex Posey
  D C Skaggs

his
William x Whitlow
mark

Subscribed and sworn to before me this 21 day of March , 1905.

Drennan C Skaggs
Notary Public.

COMMISSIONERS:
TAMS BIXBY,
THOMAS B. NEEDLES,
C.R. BRECKINBRIDGE.

WM. O. BEALL
Secretary

DEPARTMENT OF THE INTERIOR,
COMMISSIONER TO THE FIVE CIVILIZED TRIBES.

HGH
REFER IN REPLY TO THE FOLLOWING:

Cr NC-358

ADDRESS ONLY THE
COMMISSION TO THE FIVE CIVILIZED TRIBES.

Muskogee, Indian Territory, June 12, 1905.

Ellen Lewis,
    Checotah, Indian Territory.

Dear Madam:

    In the matter of the application for the enrollment of your minor children, Frank Turner and John David Lewis, as citizens of the Creek Nation, you are advised that the Commission cannot identify you on its rolls.

    You are requested to furnish the Commission with your maiden name, the names of your parents, the Creek Indian Town to which you claim to belong, your roll number as same appears on your deeds to land in the Creek Nation, and any other information which will help identify you as a citizen of said Nation.

Respectfully,

Tams Bixby Chairman.

Applications for Enrollment of Creek Newborn
Act of 1905 Volume V

copy

DEPARTMENT OF THE INTERIOR.
COMMISSION TO THE FIVE CIVILIZED TRIBES.

C 358.

Muskogee, Indian Territory, July 15, 1905.

J. B. Morrow,
    Checotah, Indian Territory.

Dear Sir:

    This office has been informed that you know the post office address of Ellen Lewis, the mother of Frank Turner and John David Lewis.

    You are requested to furnish this office with the post office address of said Ellen Lewis at an early date.

Respectfully,

(Signed) Tams Bixby,

Commissioner.

Checotah, I.T., July 17, 1905

Dear Sir:

    To the best of my knowledge Texanna, I.T. is the post office address of Ellen Lewis.

Respectfully,

Signed J.B. Morrow

HGH

DEPARTMENT OF THE INTERIOR.
COMMISSION TO THE FIVE CIVILIZED TRIBES.

NC. 358.

Muskogee, Indian Territory, July 15, 1905.

Ellen Lewis,
    Fame, Indian Territory.

Applications for Enrollment of Creek Newborn
Act of 1905   Volume V

Dear Madam:

In the matter of the application for the enrollment of your minor children, Frank Turner and John David Lewis, as citizens of the Creek Nation, you are advised that this office cannot identify you on its rolls of citizens of said Nation.

You are requested to state your maiden name, the names of your parents, the Creek Indian Town to which you claim to belong, and if possible, the numbers which appear on your deeds to land in the Creek Nation, and any other information which will help to identify you as a citizen of Creek Nation.

Respectfully,

Tams Bixby

Commissioner.

HGH

REFER IN REPLY TO THE FOLLOWING:

DEPARTMENT OF THE INTERIOR,
COMMISSIONER TO THE FIVE CIVILIZED TRIBES. N.C.358

Muskogee, Indian Territory, July 19, 1905.

Ellen Lewis,
    Texanna, Indian Territory.

Dear Madam:

In the matter of the application for the enrollment of your minor children, Frank Turner and John David Lewis, as citizens of the Creek Nation, you are advised that this office cannot, without further information, identify you on its rolls of said nation.

You are requested to state your maiden name, the names of your parents, the Creek Indian town to which you belong, and, if possible, the number on your deeds to land in the Creek Nation.

Respectfully,

Tams Bixby   Commissioner.

Applications for Enrollment of Creek Newborn
Act of 1905   Volume V

NC-358

Muskogee, Indian Territory, July 27, 1905.

Oskar Lewis,
    Checotah, Indian Territory.

Dear Sir:

    In the matter of the application for the enrollment of your minor children, Frank Turner and John David Lewis, as citizens of the Creek Nation, you are advised that this office is unable identify Ellen Lewis, the mother of said children, as a citizen of said Nation.

    You are requested to state her maiden name, the names of her parents, the Creek Indian Town to which she claims to belong, and, if possible, the roll number as same appears on her deeds to land in the Creek Nation, which will help identify her as a citizen thereof.

                          Respectfully,

                                             Commissioner.

DEPARTMENT OF THE INTERIOR,
COMMISSIONER TO THE FIVE CIVILIZED TRIBES.

REFER IN REPLY TO THE FOLLOWING:
C-375

Muskogee, Indian Territory, **October 3, 1905.**

Ellen Lewis,
    Texanna, Indian Territory.

Dear Madam:

    You are hereby advised that on **September 27, 1905**, the Secretary of the Interior approved the enrollment of your minor child, **Frank Turner Lewis**, as a citizen by blood of the **Creek** Nation, and that the name of said child appears upon the roll of new born citizens of the **Creek** Nation as Number **375**.

    The child is now entitled to an allotment, and application therefor should be made without delay at the Land Office for the Nation in which the prospective allotment is located.

    An entire allotment for said child must be selected at the time of the original application.

Applications for Enrollment of Creek Newborn
Act of 1905   Volume V

Respectively,

Tams Bixby

Commissioner.

DEPARTMENT OF THE INTERIOR,
COMMISSIONER TO THE FIVE CIVILIZED TRIBES.

REFER IN REPLY TO THE FOLLOWING:

C-376

Muskogee, Indian Territory, **October 3, 1905.**

Ellen Lewis,
  Texanna, Indian Territory.

Dear Madam:

You are hereby advised that on **September 27, 1905**, the Secretary of the Interior approved the enrollment of your minor child, **John Davis**[sic] **Lewis**, as a citizen by blood of the **Creek** Nation, and that the name of said child appears upon the roll of new born citizens of the **Creek** Nation as Number **376**.

The child is now entitled to an allotment, and application therefor should be made without delay at the Land Office for the Nation in which the prospective allotment is located.

An entire allotment for said child must be selected at the time of the original application.

Respectively,

Tams Bixby
Commissioner.

BIRTH AFFIDAVIT.

DEPARTMENT OF THE INTERIOR.
COMMISSION TO THE FIVE CIVILIZED TRIBES.

IN RE APPLICATION FOR ENROLLMENT, as a citizen of the Creek Nation, of Frank Turner Lewis, born on the 23^d day of June, 1901

Name of Father:	Oskar Lewis	a citizen of the United States	Nation.
Name of Mother:	Ellen Lewis	a citizen of the Creek	Nation.

Postoffice   Checotah, I.T.

Applications for Enrollment of Creek Newborn
Act of 1905   Volume V

AFFIDAVIT OF MOTHER.

UNITED STATES OF AMERICA, Indian Territory,
Western   DISTRICT.

I, Ellen Lewis, on oath state that I am 26 years of age and a citizen by Blood, of the Creek Nation; that I am the lawful wife of Oskar Lewis, who is a citizen, by *(blank)* of the United States Nation; that a male child was born to me on 23^d day of June, 1901, that said child has been named Frank Turner Lewis, and was living March 4, 1905.

           her
         Ellen x Lewis
Witnesses To Mark: mark
 { R.G. Dempsey *(Illegible)* I.T.
  A B Hill " "

Subscribed and sworn to before me this 18th day of March, 1905.

My Commission Expires July 1, 1906. J.B. Morrow
           Notary Public.

AFFIDAVIT OF ATTENDING PHYSICIAN OR MID-WIFE.

UNITED STATES OF AMERICA, Indian Territory,
Western   DISTRICT.

I, Lydia Wells, a Midwife, on oath state that I attended on Mrs. Ellen Lewis, wife of Oskar Lewis on the 23^d day of June, 1901 : that there was born to her on said date a male child; that said child was living March 4, 1905, and is said to have been named Frank Turner Lewis

         her
       Lydia x Wells
Witnesses To Mark: mark
 { R.G. Dempsey *(Illegible)* I.T.
  A B Hill " "

Subscribed and sworn to before me this 18th day of March, 1905.

My Commission Expires July 1, 1906. J.B. Morrow
           Notary Public.

BIRTH AFFIDAVIT.

DEPARTMENT OF THE INTERIOR.
COMMISSION TO THE FIVE CIVILIZED TRIBES.

IN RE APPLICATION FOR ENROLLMENT, as a citizen of the Creek Nation, of John David Lewis, born on the 18th day of March, 1904

Applications for Enrollment of Creek Newborn
Act of 1905   Volume V

Name of Father: Oskar Lewis   a citizen of the United States Nation.
Name of Mother: Ellen Lewis   a citizen of the   Creek   Nation.

Postoffice   Checotah, I.T.

AFFIDAVIT OF MOTHER.

UNITED STATES OF AMERICA, Indian Territory, ⎫
   Western   DISTRICT.   ⎭

I, Ellen Lewis , on oath state that I am 26 years of age and a citizen by Blood , of the Creek   Nation; that I am the lawful wife of   Oskar Lewis , who is a citizen, by *(blank)* of the United States Nation; that a male child was born to me on 18th day of March , 1904 , that said child has been named John David Lewis , and was living March 4, 1905.

                                                    her
                                            Ellen x Lewis
Witnesses To Mark: mark
  ⎧ R.G. Dempsey *(Illegible)* I.T.
  ⎩ A B Hill   "   "

Subscribed and sworn to before me this 18th day of March , 1905.

   My Commission Expires July 1, 1906.   J.B. Morrow
                                                    Notary Public.

AFFIDAVIT OF ATTENDING PHYSICIAN OR MID-WIFE.

UNITED STATES OF AMERICA, Indian Territory, ⎫
   Western   DISTRICT.   ⎭

I, Lydia Wells , a Midwife , on oath state that I attended on Mrs. Ellen Lewis , wife of Oskar Lewis on the 18th day of March , 1904 ; that there was born to her on said date a male child; that said child was living March 4, 1905, and is said to have been named John David Lewis

                                                    her
                                            Lydia x Wells
Witnesses To Mark: mark
  ⎧ R.G. Dempsey *(Illegible)* I.T.
  ⎩ A B Hill   "   "

Subscribed and sworn to before me this 18th day of March , 1905.

   My Commission Expires July 1, 1906.   J.B. Morrow
                                                    Notary Public.

Applications for Enrollment of Creek Newborn
Act of 1905   Volume V

N.C. 359.

DEPARTMENT OF THE INTERIOR,
COMMISSIONER TO THE FIVE CIVILIZED TRIBES,
Boley, Indian Territory, September 26, 1906.

In the matter of the application for the enrollment of Ida Wesley, deceased, as a citizen by blood of the Creek Nation.

EMMA JOHNSTON, being duly sworn, testified as follows:

BY COMMISSION:

Q What is your name? A Emma Johnston.
Q What is your age? A 26.
Q What is your postoffice address? A Boley.
Q Are you a Creek citizen? A No sir.
Q Do you know Thomas and Tochee Wesley? A Yes sir.
Q Do you [sic] a child of theirs named Ida? A Yes sir, I did.
Q Do you know when that child was born? A In February I was told.
Q Do you know that o be a fact? A No sir.
Q Just from hearsay? A Yes sir.
Q Is Ida living? A No sir.
Q Do you know when she died? A She died March the 8th last year.
Q In what year? A 1905.
Q How do you know that? A Cause I was there when they buried her.
Q Can you read and write? A Sure I can.
Q Are you positive that Ida died March 8th 1905? A Yes sir.
Q What time of the year was it? A It was early in the spring but still cold yet.
Q Is there anything that recalls your memory as to the exact date of the death of this child? A No, simply from recollection.
Q Are you interested in any way about the enrollment of this child? A None whatever.

HIRAM JOHNSTON, being duly sworn, testified as follows:

BY COMMISSIONER:

Q State your name, age and postoffice address? A Hiram Johnston; 28; Boley.
Q Are you a Creek citizen? A No sir.
Q Do you know Thomas and Tochee Wesley? A Yes sir
Q Do you know a child of theirs named Ida? A Yes sir.
Q Is Ida living? A No sir.
Q Do you know when she died? A She died in March last year but I couldn't tell you anything about the date.
Q Were you present when she died? A No sir.
Q Did you see her after she was dead? A Yes, I helped to dig the grave and let the coffin down that they buried her in.

Applications for Enrollment of Creek Newborn
Act of 1905 Volume V

Q Can you give me some idea about what day of the week it was that you helped to bury that child? A It was on Wednesday or Thursday.
Q Is there anything that helps you to remember that Ida died in March? A No sir, the only thing that I know is, that the child died in March.
Q Have you had a talk with Thomas about the enrollment of this child? A No sir, this is the first time that I've had a talk about this think. I am telling just what I know.

I, Jesse McDermott, on oath state that the above and foregoing is a full and true transcript of my notes as taken in said cause on said date.

Jesse McDermott

Subscribed and sworn to before me this 15th day of November, 1906.

Dan Upton
My Commission Expires   Notary Public.
Jan 31/09

[The above affidavit given again]

N.C. 359.

DEPARTMENT OF THE INTERIOR,
COMMISSIONER TO THE FIVE CIVILIZED TRIBES,
Okemah, Indian Territory, September 29, 1906.

In the matter of the application for the enrollment of Ida Wesley, deceased, as a citizen by blood of the Creek Nation.
THOMAS WESLEY, being duly sworn, testified as follows (through Jesse McDermott official interpreter):

BY COMMISSIONER:

Q What is your name? A Thomas Wesley
Q What is your age? A I am now 25.
Q What is your postoffice address? A Castle.

In your testimony on March 28, 1906, you stated that you had a record of the death of your child Ida, at home.

Q Have you that record with you? A Yes sir.

Applications for Enrollment of Creek Newborn
Act of 1905   Volume V

The witness presents a memorandum book and on page next to the last page of said book appears the following entry: "Ida Wesley died March 8th 1905. Born Feb'y 23rd 1904."

Q When did you make this record? A I am not sure whether I wrote that the same day that the child died, it may have been the next day.
Q How come you to write the date of the death first? A After I had written the date of her death then, that date of her birth came to my mind.

I, Jesse McDermott, on oath state that the above and foregoing is a full and true transcript of my notes as taken in said cause on said date.

                                        Jesse McDermott

Subscribed and sworn to before me this 15th day of November, 1906.

                                        Dan Upton
My Commission Expires 1/31-09   Notary Public.

N.C. 359.

DEPARTMENT OF THE INTERIOR.
COMMISSIONER TO THE FIVE CIVILIZED TRIBES.
Paden, I. T., May 28, 1906.

In the matter of the application for the enrollment of Ida Wesley as a citizen by blood of the Creek Nation.

THOMAS WESLEY, being duly sworn, testified as follows:

BY THE COMMISSIONER:
Q What is your name? Thomas Wesley.
Q How old are you? A Twenty-seven.
Q What is your post office address? A Castle.
Q Are you a citizen of the Creek Nation? A Yes, sir.
Q To what town do you belong? A Greenleaf.
Q Have you a child named Ida Wesley? A Yes, sir.
Q When was the child born? A February 23, 1904.
Q The child is dead is it? A Yes, sir.
Q When did it die? A March 8, 1905.
Q You made application for this child last year, did you not? A Yes, sir.
Q Have you a record showing the date of its birth and the date of its death? A Yes, sir. The record is at home.
Q How old was the child when it died? A A Year and a little over.

Applications for Enrollment of Creek Newborn
Act of 1905 Volume V

Q Where is the child buried? A About two miles south-east of Boley.
Q Is there a head-board on the grave? A No, sir. There is a grave house over the grave.
Q Is there any record on that grave-house? A No, sir.
Q Did you have a funeral when this child was buried? A No, sir. There was no one present except myself and wife and two white renters and a negro.
Q What are the names of the white people you mentioned? A Hiram Johnson[sic] and his wife, and a negro named Robwrt[sic] Jennings. Jennings is gone but Johnson still lives there.

Witness is advised that this office requires the affidavits of two disinterested witnesses who know the dates of the birth and death of Ida Wesley and the testimony of Hiram Johnson and his wife.

---oooOOOooo---

I, D. C. Skaggs, on oath state that the above and foregoing is a full and true transcript of my stenographic notes as taken in said cause on said date.

D. C. Skaggs

Subscribed and sworn to before me this 11th day of June, 1906.

Alex Posey
Notary Public.

AFFIDAVIT OF DISINTERESTED WITNESS.

UNITED STATES OF AMERICA,
Western DISTRICT,   SS
INDIAN TERRITORY.

We, the undersigned, on oath state that we are personally acquainted with Toche Wesley wife of Thomas Wesley ; that there was born to her a female child on or about the 23^d day of February 1904 ; that the said child has been named Ida Wesley and was living March 4, 1905.

Witnesses:

_____

_____

Eli McGirt

Cindy Herrod

Subscribed and sworn to before me this 29th day of Sept. 1906.

Applications for Enrollment of Creek Newborn
Act of 1905   Volume V

My Commission
Expires July 28" 1907

J McDermott
Notary Public.

DEPARTMENT OF THE INTERIOR.
COMMISSION TO THE FIVE CIVILIZED TRIBES.

In the matter of the death of Ida Wesley   a citizen of the Creek Nation, who formerly resided at or near Castle , Ind. Ter., and died on the 8 day of March , 1905.

AFFIDAVIT OF RELATIVE.

UNITED STATES OF AMERICA, Indian Territory,
Western   DISTRICT.

I, Toche Wesley , on oath state that I am 21 years of age and a citizen by blood , of the Creek Nation; that my postoffice address is Castle , Ind. Ter.; that I am mother of Ida Wesley who was a citizen, by blood , of the Creek Nation and that said Ida Wesley died on the 8 day of March , 1905.

Toche Wesley

Witnesses To Mark:

Subscribed and sworn to before me this 14" day of March, 1905.

Drennan C Skaggs
Notary Public.

AFFIDAVIT OF ACQUAINTANCE.

UNITED STATES OF AMERICA, Indian Territory,
Western   DISTRICT.

I, Wilson Knight , on oath state that I am 49 years of age, and a citizen by blood of the Creek Nation; that my postoffice address is Boley , Ind. Ter.; that I was personally acquainted with Ida Wesley who was a citizen, by blood , of the Creek Nation; and that said Ida Wesley died on the 8 day of March , 1905.

his
Wilson x Knight
mark

Witnesses To Mark:
Alex Posey
D C Skaggs

Applications for Enrollment of Creek Newborn
Act of 1905   Volume V

Subscribed and sworn to before me this 14" day of March, 1905.

Drennan C Skaggs
Notary Public.

BIRTH AFFIDAVIT.

DEPARTMENT OF THE INTERIOR.
COMMISSION TO THE FIVE CIVILIZED TRIBES.

IN RE APPLICATION FOR ENROLLMENT, as a citizen of the Creek Nation, of Ida Wesley, born on the 23 day of February, 1904

Name of Father: Thomas Wesley   a citizen of the   Creek   Nation.
Name of Mother: To-che Wesley (nee Knight)   a citizen of the   Creek   Nation.

Postoffice   Castle, Indian Territory

AFFIDAVIT OF MOTHER.

UNITED STATES OF AMERICA, Indian Territory,
Western   DISTRICT.

I, Toche Wesley   , on oath state that I am   21   years of age and a citizen by blood, of the Creek   Nation; that I am the lawful wife of Thomas Wesley , who is a citizen, by   blood of the Creek   Nation; that a female   child was born to me on 23 day of February , 1904 , that said child has been named Ida Wesley , and was living March 4, 1905. That no one attended on me as midwife or physician at the time the child was born

Toche Wesley

Witnesses To Mark:

Subscribed and sworn to before me this 14" day of march , 1905.

Drennan C Skaggs
Notary Public.

(The above Birth Affidavit given again.)

Applications for Enrollment of Creek Newborn
Act of 1905   Volume V

DEPARTMENT OF THE INTERIOR.
COMMISSION TO THE FIVE CIVILIZED TRIBES.

In the matter of the death of Ida Wesley a citizen of the Creek Nation, who formerly resided at or near Castle , Ind. Ter., and died on the 8 day of March , 1905.

AFFIDAVIT OF RELATIVE.

UNITED STATES OF AMERICA, Indian Territory,
Western DISTRICT.

I, Toche Wesley , on oath state that I am 21 years of age and a citizen by blood , of the Creek Nation; that my postoffice address is Castle , Ind. Ter.; that I am mother of Ida Wesley who was a citizen, by blood , of the Creek Nation and that said Ida Wesley died on the 8 day of March , 1905.

Toche Wesley

Witnesses To Mark:

Subscribed and sworn to before me this 14" day of March, 1905.

Drennan C Skaggs
Notary Public.

AFFIDAVIT OF ACQUAINTANCE.

UNITED STATES OF AMERICA, Indian Territory,
Western DISTRICT.

I, Wilson Knight , on oath state that I am 49 years of age, and a citizen by blood of the Creek Nation; that my postoffice address is Boley , Ind. Ter.; that I was personally acquainted with Ida Wesley who was a citizen, by blood , of the Creek Nation; and that said Ida Wesley died on the 8 day of March, 1905.

his
Wilson x Knight
mark

Witnesses To Mark:
  Alex Posey
  D C Skaggs

Applications for Enrollment of Creek Newborn
Act of 1905 Volume V

Subscribed and sworn to before me this 14" day of March, 1905.

Drennan C Skaggs
Notary Public.

Cr. NC 359.

Muskogee, Indian Territory, June 8, 1905.

Toche Wesley,
    Castle, Indian Territory.

Dear Madam:

    In the matter of the application for the enrollment of your minor child, Iva[sic] Wesley (deceased), as a citizen of the Creek Nation, you are advised that it will be necessary for you to appear before the Commission, at its office, in Muskogee, Indian Territory, at an early date, with two disinterested witnesses who know the dates of the birth and death of said child, for the purpose of being examined under oath.

Respectfully,

Chairman.

NC-359.

Muskogee, Indian Territory, August 2, 1905.

Toche Wesley,
    Castle, Indian Territory.

Dear Madam:

    In the matter of the application for the enrollment of your minor daughter Iva[sic] Wesley, deceased, as a citizen by blood of the Creek Nation, you are advised that it will be necessary for you to appear before this office in Muskogee, Indian Territory, with two disinterested witnesses who know the dates of the birth and death of said child in order that you and they may be examined under oath in regard thereto.

    You were requested to so appear on June 8, 1905 and to such request no response has been received. It is advisable that you make such appearance in the near future.

Respectfully,

Commissioner.

Applications for Enrollment of Creek Newborn
Act of 1905   Volume V

NC 359

Okemah, Indian Territory, October 1, 1906.

Commissioner to the Five Civilized Tribes,
   Muskogee, Indian Territory.

Dear Sir:

There are herewith enclosed the affidavits of two disinterested witnesses in the matter of the application for the enrollment of your minor child, you are advised that the Commission requires further evidence as to the birth of said child, of Ida Wesley, as a citizen by blood of the Creek Nation. Testimony relative to the death of said child has been secured in the case.

Respectfully,

NC 359. EK

Muskogee, Indian Territory, March 1, 1907.

Toche Wesley,
   C/o Thomas Wesley,
      Castle, Indian Territory.

Dear Madam:

You are hereby advised that on February 15, 1907, the Secretary of the Interior approved the enrollment of your deceased minor child, Ida Wesley, as a citizen by blood of the Creek Nation, and that the name of said child appears upon the roll of New Born citizens by blood of the Creek Nation, enrolled under the Act of Congress approved March 3rd, 1905, as number 1139.

The child is now entitled to allotment, and application therefor should be made without delay at the Creek Land Office, Muskogee, Indian Territory.

Respectfully,

Commissioner.

Applications for Enrollment of Creek Newborn
Act of 1905 Volume V

NC.360.

Muskogee, Indian Territory, July 14, 1905.

Commissioner to the Five Civilized Tribes,
    Cherokee Enrollment Division,
    Muskogee, Indian Territory.

Gentlemen:

    March 21, 1905, application was made to the Commission to the Five Civilized Tribes for the enrollment of Reid Lee Hood, born April 1, 1903, as a citizen by blood of the Creek Nation. It is stated in said application that the father of said child is Sterling P. Hood, a citizen of the Cherokee Nation, and that the mother is Sarah Malinda Hood, a citizen of the Creek Nation.

    You are requested to advise the Creek Enrollment Division as to whether application has been made for the enrollment of said Reid Lee Hood, as a citizen of the Cherokee Nation, and if so, what disposition has been made of the same.

Respectfully,

Commissioner.

REFER IN REPLY TO THE FOLLOWING:

**DEPARTMENT OF THE INTERIOR,
COMMISSIONER TO THE FIVE CIVILIZED TRIBES.**

Muskogee, Indian Territory, July 18, 1905.

Chief Clerk,
    Creek Enrollment Division,
    Muskogee, Indian Territory.

Dear Sir:

    Replying to your letter of July 14, 1905, (NC. 360) asking to be advised whether or not any application has ever been made for the enrollment, as a citizen of the Cherokee Nation, of Reid Lee Hood, a child of Sterling P. Hood, a citizen of the Cherokee Nation, and Sarah Malinda Hood, a citizen of the Creek Nation, you are advised that from an examination of the records of the Cherokee Enrollment Division it does not appear that any application has ever been made for the enrollment of said child as a citizen of that nation.

Respectfully,

GHL   Tams Bixby   Commissioner.

Applications for Enrollment of Creek Newborn
Act of 1905   Volume V

BIRTH AFFIDAVIT.

DEPARTMENT OF THE INTERIOR.
COMMISSION TO THE FIVE CIVILIZED TRIBES.

IN RE APPLICATION FOR ENROLLMENT, as a citizen of the Creek Nation, of Reid Lee Hood, born on the 1st day of April, 1903

Name of Father: Sterling P. Hood   a citizen of the Cherokee Nation.
Name of Mother: Sarah Malinda Hood a citizen of the Creek   Nation.

Postoffice   Checotah I.T.

AFFIDAVIT OF MOTHER.

UNITED STATES OF AMERICA, Indian Territory,
Western   DISTRICT.

I, Sarah Malinda Hood, on oath state that I am 38 years of age and a citizen by Blood, of the Creek Nation; that I am the lawful wife of Sterling P. Hood, who is a citizen, by Blood of the Cherokee Nation; that a male child was born to me on 1st day of April, 1903, that said child has been named Reid Lee Hood, and was living March 4, 1905.

              her
            Sarah Malinda x Hood
Witnesses To Mark: mark
 { Oskar Lewis Checotah IT.
 { J B Lucas   " "
 JB Morrow

Subscribed and sworn to before me this 18th day of March, 1905.

            JB Morrow
My Commission Expires July 1, 1906. Notary Public.

AFFIDAVIT OF ATTENDING PHYSICIAN OR MID-WIFE.

UNITED STATES OF AMERICA, Indian Territory,
Western   DISTRICT.

I, Lydia Wells, a Midwife, on oath state that I attended on Mrs. Sarah Malinda Hood, wife of Sterling P Hood on the 1st day of April, 1903 ; that there was born to her on said date a Male child; that said child was living March 4, 1905, and is said to have been named Reid Lee Hood

          her
       Lydia x Wells
         mark

Applications for Enrollment of Creek Newborn
Act of 1905 Volume V

Witnesses To Mark:
{ AO Smith   Checotah IT
{ Luke Harrison   "   "

Subscribed and sworn to before me this 18th day of March, 1905.

JB Morrow

My Commission Expires July 1, 1906.

Notary Public.

BIRTH AFFIDAVIT.

DEPARTMENT OF THE INTERIOR.
COMMISSION TO THE FIVE CIVILIZED TRIBES.

IN RE APPLICATION FOR ENROLLMENT, as a citizen of the Creek Nation, of Olive A. Wright, born on the 16th day of March, 1902

Name of Father: C.J. Wright   a citizen of the United States Nation.
Name of Mother: Jane P. Wright   a citizen of the   Creek   Nation.

Postoffice   Checotah I.T.

AFFIDAVIT OF MOTHER.

UNITED STATES OF AMERICA, Indian Territory, }
    Western   DISTRICT.   }

I, Jane P. Wright, on oath state that I am 28 years of age and a citizen by Blood, of the Creek Nation; that I am the lawful wife of C. J. Wright, who is a citizen, by *(blank)* of the United States Nation; that a Female child was born to me on 16th day of March, 1902, that said child has been named Olive A. Wright, and was living March 4, 1905.

Jane P. Wright

Witnesses To Mark:
{

Subscribed and sworn to before me this 18th day of March, 1905.

JB Morrow

My Commission Expires July 1, 1906.

Notary Public.

Applications for Enrollment of Creek Newborn
Act of 1905 Volume V

AFFIDAVIT OF ATTENDING PHYSICIAN OR MID-WIFE.

UNITED STATES OF AMERICA, Indian Territory,
Western   DISTRICT.

I, G.R. Rucker , a Physician , on oath state that I attended on Mrs. Jane P. Wright , wife of C. J. Wright on the 16th day of March , 1902 ; that there was born to her on said date a Female child; that said child was living March 4, 1905, and is said to have been named Olive A. Wright

G. R. Rucker, M.D.

Witnesses To Mark:

Subscribed and sworn to before me this 18th day of March , 1905.

JB Morrow
Notary Public.

My Commission Expires July 1, 1906.

Cr NC-362

Muskogee, Indian Territory, June 8, 1905.

Hainey Moore,
    slumker[sic], Indian Territory.

Dear Madam:

In the matter of the application for the enrollment of your minor child, John Moore, as a citizen of the Creek Nation, you are advised that the Commission requires the affidavits of two disinterested witnesses as to the date of its birth.

For this purpose, there are herewith enclosed two blank forms of birth affidavit. In having same executed, care should be taken to see that all blanks are properly filled, all names written in full, and in the event that the person signing the affidavit is unable to write, signature by mark must be attested by two witnesses.

Respectfully,

Chairman
~~Commissioner in Charge~~.

2 B A

Applications for Enrollment of Creek Newborn
Act of 1905 Volume V

NC-362.

Muskogee, Indian Territory, August 2, 1905.

Hensy Moore,
    c/o John Moore,
        Slumker, Indian Territory.

Dear Madam:

    In the matter of the application for the enrollment of your minor son John Moore, born March 24, 1903, as a citizen by blood of the Creek Nation, you are advised that this office requires the affidavits of two disinterested persons relative to the birth of said child.

    Said affidavits must set for th[sic] the date of the birth of said child, the names of his parents and whether or not he was living on March 4, 1905.

    Please give this matter your prompt attention.

        Respectfully,

            Commissioner.

BIRTH AFFIDAVIT.

DEPARTMENT OF THE INTERIOR.
COMMISSION TO THE FIVE CIVILIZED TRIBES.

    IN RE APPLICATION FOR ENROLLMENT, as a citizen of the Creek Nation, of John Moore, born on the 24 day of March, 1903

Name of Father:	John Moore	a citizen of the Mexico	~~Nation~~.
Name of Mother:	Haney Moore	a citizen of the Creek	Nation.

        Postoffice   Slumker, Ind. Ter.

AFFIDAVIT OF MOTHER.

UNITED STATES OF AMERICA, Indian Territory, }
    Western   DISTRICT.

    I, Haney Moore, on oath state that I am about 37 years of age and a citizen by blood, of the Creek Nation; that I am the lawful wife of John Moore, who is a citizen, ~~by~~ *(blank)* of ~~the~~ Mexico ~~Nation~~; that a male child was born to me on 24

Applications for Enrollment of Creek Newborn
Act of 1905   Volume V

day of March, 1903, that said child has been named John Moore, and was living March 4, 1905. That no one attended on me as midwife or physician at the birth of the children.

                                          her
                                  Haney x Moore

Witnesses To Mark: mark
   { Alex Posey
     DC Skaggs

Subscribed and sworn to before me this 20 day of March, 1905.

                                    Drennan C Skaggs
                                      Notary Public.

BIRTH AFFIDAVIT.

DEPARTMENT OF THE INTERIOR.
COMMISSION TO THE FIVE CIVILIZED TRIBES.

IN RE APPLICATION FOR ENROLLMENT, as a citizen of the Creek Nation, of John Moore, born about 24 day of March, 1903

Name of Father: John W. Moore   a citizen of the   Mexico   Nation.
Name of Mother: Hainey Moore   a citizen of the   Creek   Nation.
                               Postoffice   Trenton I.T.

                                  disinterested witness
                    AFFIDAVIT OF ~~MOTHER~~.

UNITED STATES OF AMERICA, Indian Territory, }
    Western   DISTRICT.

I, Jailler Proctor, on oath state that I am 40 years of age and a citizen by blood, of the Creek Nation; that I ~~am the lawful wife of~~ know Hainey Moore, who is a citizen, by blood of the Creek Nation; that a male child was born to ~~me~~ her on about 24 day of March, 1903, that said child has been named John Moore, and was living March 4, 1905.

                                      his
                                Jailler x Proctor
Witnesses To Mark: mark
   { Caesar Kelley
     J.A. Depue

Subscribed and sworn to before me this 11th day of August, 1905.

                                  T.T. Caves
My Commission expires Nov 28=1906   Notary Public.

Applications for Enrollment of Creek Newborn
Act of 1905   Volume V

AFFIDAVIT OF ATTENDING PHYSICIAN OR MID-WIFE.

UNITED STATES OF AMERICA, Indian Territory, ⎱
   Western   DISTRICT. ⎰

    I, Sukie Sieka , a ----- , on oath state that I ~~attended on Mrs~~. know Hainey Moore , wife of John W. Moore and that about 24 day of March , 1903 ; that there was born to her on said date a male child; that said child was living March 4, 1905, and is said to have been named John Moore

                                                  her
Witnesses To Mark: Sukie x Sieka
  ⎰ Caesar Kelley   mark
  ⎱ J.A. Depue

    Subscribed and sworn to before me this 11th day of August , 1905.

                                  T.T. Caves
My Commission expires   Notary Public.
        Nov 28-1906

                                                                      NC-363

DEPARTMENT OF THE INTERIOR,
COMMISSIONER TO THE FIVE CIVILIZED TRIBES.

        Muskogee, Indian Territory, July 28, 1905.

    In the matter of the application for the enrollment of Louisa Canard as a citizen by blood of the Creek Nation.

    Kizzie Canard, being duly sworn, testified as follows (through Jesse McDermott, Official Interpreter):

EXAMINATION BY THE COMMISSION:
Q What is your name? A Kizzie Canard
Q How does your name appear on the final roll? A Kizzie Yarhola.
Q What is your father's name? A Fushutche Yarhola.
Q What is your mother's name? A Mary Yarhola.
Q How old are you? A I am over 20.
Q What is your postoffice address? A Weleetka.
Q Have you a child named Louisa Canard? A Yes sir.
Q Is she living? A Yes sir.
Q When was she born? A September 20

Applications for Enrollment of Creek Newborn
Act of 1905   Volume V

Q What year? A I don't know the year, only I know the child was born September 20th.
Q How old will she be next September 20th? A She will be four years old.
Q Was born in 1901, then, was she? A I don't know.
Q You made out one affidavit before the Commission's field party and said the child was born in 1901; afterwards you went before a notary public and said the child was born in 1902--you think 1901 is correct, do you? A I am sure that the child will be four years old next September.
Q Before the Commission's notary public you stated that there was no midwife present at the birth of that child, and afterwards there was one sent in here--affidavit stating that Kate Barnett was the midwife. How do you explain that? A There was no one present when the child was born, only my husband, but I understood they required some one who had come there shortly after the birth of the child, so I gave the name Kate as midwife.
Q If she said 1902 she was mistaken because that would not make the child four years old? A I was mistaken.

Billy Canard, being duly sworn, testified as follows:

EXAMINATION BY THE COMMISSION:

Q What is your name? A Billy Canard.
Q How old are you? A About 40.
Q What is your postoffice? A Weleetka.
Q Are you a citizen of the Creek Nation? A Yes sir.
Q What is the name of your father? A Hallake Yarhola.
Q Have you a child named Louisa Canard? A Yes sir.
Q Do you know when she was born, the names of her parents and whether or not she was living March 4, 1905 born? A No, I don't know.
Q Is she living? A Yes sir.
Q About how old is she? A She is part three years old.
Q Was born in the fall? A Yes sir.
Q Will she be four years old this fall? A Yes sir.

Alex Lowe, being duly sworn, testified as follows:

EXAMINATION BY THE COMMISSION:
Q What is your name? A Alex Lowe.
Q How old are you? A I am 25.
Q What is your postoffice address? A Weleetka.
Q Are you a citizen of the Creek Nation? A Yes sir.
Q Do you know Billy and Kizzie Canard? A Yes sir.
Q Any kin to them? A Distant relation to him.
Q Do you know when Louisa was born? A No sir; I don't know when she was born, the names of her parents and whether or not she was living March 4, 1905 born.
Q Do you know about how old she is? A Yes sir.
Q How old? A She is past three, I know.
Q Is she living? A Yes sir.

Applications for Enrollment of Creek Newborn
Act of 1905 Volume V

Q Do you know anything about who the midwife was that was present when the child was born? A Yes sir. She told Patterson the notary public that nobody was present; but just as this woman states now, she thought she had to have somebody, and this woman came in shortly after the child was born. Didn't actually officiate as midwife. She was asked to help take care of the child and of the woman.

INDIAN TERRITORY, Western District.

I, J. Y. Miller, a stenographer to the Commissioner to the Five Civilized Tribes, do hereby certify that the above and foregoing is a true and complete translation of my notes as same appear in my stenographic report of this case.

JY Miller

Sworn to and subscribed before me
this the 2nd day of August,
1905.

Edw C Griesel
Notary Public.

BIRTH AFFIDAVIT.

DEPARTMENT OF THE INTERIOR.
COMMISSION TO THE FIVE CIVILIZED TRIBES.

IN RE APPLICATION FOR ENROLLMENT, as a citizen of the Creek Nation, of Millie Canard, born on the 2 day of February , 1904

Name of Father:	Billy Canard	a citizen of the	Creek	Nation.
Name of Mother:	Kizzie Canard	a citizen of the	Creek	Nation.

Postoffice   Weleetka, Ind. Ter.

AFFIDAVIT OF MOTHER.

UNITED STATES OF AMERICA, Indian Territory,
Western   DISTRICT.

I, Kizzie Canard , on oath state that I am about 25 years of age and a citizen by blood , of the Creek Nation; that I am the lawful wife of Billy Canard , who is a citizen, by blood of the Creek Nation; that a female child was born to me on 2 day of February , 1904 , that said child has been named Millie Canard , and was living March 4, 1905.

                                                      her
Witnesses To Mark: Kizzie x Canard
  { Alex Posey   mark
  { DC Skaggs

Applications for Enrollment of Creek Newborn
Act of 1905   Volume V

Subscribed and sworn to before me this 20 day of March , 1905.

                                      Drennan C Skaggs

                                            Notary Public.

BIRTH AFFIDAVIT.

DEPARTMENT OF THE INTERIOR.
COMMISSION TO THE FIVE CIVILIZED TRIBES.

IN RE APPLICATION FOR ENROLLMENT, as a citizen of the Muskogee (Creek) Nation, of Millie Canard, born on the 2nd day of Feb , 1904

Name of Father:	Billy Canard	a citizen of the	Creek	Nation.
Name of Mother:	Kizzie Canard	a citizen of the	Creek	Nation.

                              Postoffice   Weleetka, Ind. Ter.

AFFIDAVIT OF MOTHER.

UNITED STATES OF AMERICA, Indian Territory,
    Western   DISTRICT.

    I, Kizzie Canard , on oath state that I am 24 years of age and a citizen by Birth, of the Creek   Nation; that I am the lawful wife of Billy Canard , who is a citizen, by Birth   of the Muskogee (Creek) Nation; that a Female   child was born to me on 2nd day of February , 1904 , that said child has been named Millie Canard , and was living March 4, 1905.

                                          her
Witnesses To Mark: Kizzie x Canard
    { E.L. Blackman   mark
    { Alex Lowe

    Subscribed and sworn to before me this 17 day of June , 1905.

                                     John B. Patterson
MY COMMISSION EXPIRES FEBY. 29, 1906.   Notary Public.

AFFIDAVIT OF ATTENDING PHYSICIAN OR MID-WIFE.

UNITED STATES OF AMERICA, Indian Territory,
    Western   DISTRICT.

    I, Katie Barnett , a Midwife , on oath state that I attended on Mrs. Kizzie Canard , wife of Billy Canard on the 2nd day of Feb. , 1904 ; that there was born to

Applications for Enrollment of Creek Newborn
Act of 1905 Volume V

her on said date a Female child; that said child was living March 4, 1905, and is said to have been named Millie Canard

Katie Bannatt[sic]

Witnesses To Mark:
{

Subscribed and sworn to before me this 17 day of June, 1905.

John B. Patterson

MY COMMISSION EXPIRES FEBY. 29, 1906.   Notary Public.

BIRTH AFFIDAVIT.

DEPARTMENT OF THE INTERIOR.
COMMISSION TO THE FIVE CIVILIZED TRIBES.

IN RE APPLICATION FOR ENROLLMENT, as a citizen of the Creek Nation, of Louisa Canard, born on the 20 day of September, 1901

| Name of Father: | Billy Canard | a citizen of the | Creek | Nation. |
| Name of Mother: | Kizzie Canard | a citizen of the | Creek | Nation. |

Postoffice   Weleetka, Ind. Ter.

AFFIDAVIT OF MOTHER.

UNITED STATES OF AMERICA, Indian Territory, ⎫
    Western   DISTRICT.   ⎬

I, Kizzie Canard , on oath state that I am about 25 years of age and a citizen by blood, of the Creek   Nation; that I am the lawful wife of Billy Canard , who is a citizen, by blood of the Creek Nation; that a female child was born to me on 20 day of September , 1901 , that said child has been named Louisa Canard , and was living March 4, 1905.

                        her
                  Kizzie x Canard
Witnesses To Mark: mark
{ Alex Posey
  DC Skaggs

Subscribed and sworn to before me this 20 day of March, 1905.

Drennan C Skaggs
Notary Public.

Applications for Enrollment of Creek Newborn
Act of 1905   Volume V

N.C. 363.

Department of the Interior,
COMMISSION TO THE FIVE CIVILIZED TRIBES.

In re Application for Enrollment as a Citizen of the Creek Nation of Louisa Canard, born on the 20" day of September, 1901.
Name of Father: Billy Canard, a citizen of the Creek Nation.
Name of Mother: Kizzie Canard, a citizen of the Creek Nation.

Postoffice, Weleetka, Ind. Ter.

Affidavits of disinterested parties.

United States of America,   ) SS.
Western District of the Indian Territory.)

    I, Dick Barnett, on my oath state that I am a minister of the gospel; that I have known Billy Canard and his wife Kizzie Canard for the past 20 years or more; that I officiated as minister when they were married; that I remember the occasion of the birth of their child Louisa Canard on or about the 20 day of September, 1901, but of course do not remember the exact date of its birth; that I know the child was born about that time and that she was living on the 4" day of March, 1905, and is still living and that said child was named Louisa Canard; that I have no interest in this enrollment.

Ru[sic] Dick Barnett

Subscribed and sworn to before me this 15 day of January, 1906.

MY COMMISSION EXPIRES FEBY. 29, 1906.

John B. Patterson
Notary Public.

United States of America,   ) SS.
Western District of the Indian Territory.)

    I, Tucker Barnett, on my oath state that I have known both Billy Canard and his wife Kizzie Canard since their childhood; that I was personally well acquainted with them on or about the 20 day of September, 1901; that I know personally that on or about that date a female child was born to them; that said child was living on the 4" day of March, 1905 and that she was named Louisa Canard; that I am a citizen by birth of the Creek Nation, but that I have no interest in this case.

Tucker Barnett

Applications for Enrollment of Creek Newborn
Act of 1905   Volume V

Subscribed and sworn to before me this 15 day of January, 1906.

MY COMMISSION EXPIRES FEBY. 29, 1906.   John B. Patterson
                                                          Notary Public.

    I, J.B. Patterson, do hereby certify that I have known the family of Billy Canard and his wife Kizzie Canard for the past 3 years; that this little girl Louisa Canard has been living with them all this time; that they have treated her and claimed her as their daughter since I first knew them, about April, 1902, and that she is still living with them and is still regarded by all who know the family as their daughter.

MY COMMISSION EXPIRES FEBY. 29, 1906.   John B. Patterson

BIRTH AFFIDAVIT.

DEPARTMENT OF THE INTERIOR.
COMMISSION TO THE FIVE CIVILIZED TRIBES.

    IN RE APPLICATION FOR ENROLLMENT, as a citizen of the Muskogee (Creek) Nation, of Millie Canard, born on the 2nd day of Feb, 1904

Name of Father: Billy Canard   a citizen of the   Creek   Nation.
Name of Mother: Kizzie Canard   a citizen of the   Creek   Nation.

                  Postoffice   Weleetka, Ind. Ter.

AFFIDAVIT OF MOTHER.

UNITED STATES OF AMERICA, Indian Territory, }
   Western   DISTRICT.

    I, Kizzie Canard, on oath state that I am 24 years of age and a citizen by Birth, of the Creek Nation; that I am the lawful wife of Billy Canard, who is a citizen, by Birth of the Muskogee (Creek) Nation; that a Female child was born to me on 2nd day of February, 1904, that said child has been named Millie Canard, and was living March 4, 1905.

                                  her
                            Kizzie x Canard
Witnesses To Mark: mark
   { E.L. Blackman
     Alex Lowe

    Subscribed and sworn to before me this 17 day of June, 1905.

                            John B. Patterson
MY COMMISSION EXPIRES FEBY. 29, 1906.   Notary Public.

Applications for Enrollment of Creek Newborn
Act of 1905   Volume V

AFFIDAVIT OF ATTENDING PHYSICIAN OR MID-WIFE.

UNITED STATES OF AMERICA, Indian Territory,
  Western   DISTRICT.

I, Katie Barnett , a Midwife , on oath state that I attended on Mrs. Kizzie Canard , wife of Billy Canard on the 2nd day of Feb. , 1904 ; that there was born to her on said date a Female child; that said child was living March 4, 1905, and is said to have been named Millie Canard

             Katie Bannatt[sic]

Witnesses To Mark:
{

Subscribed and sworn to before me this 17 day of June , 1905.

           John B. Patterson
MY COMMISSION EXPIRES FEBY. 29, 1906.   Notary Public.

              Cr NC-363

      Muskogee, Indian Territory, June 8, 1905.

Kizzie Canard,
  Weleetka, Indian Territory.

Dear Madam:

  In the matter of the application for the enrollment of your minor child, Millie Canard, as a citizen of the Creek Nation, you are advised that the Commission requires the affidavit of the midwife or physician in attendance at the birth of said child.

  In the matter of the application for the enrollment of your minor child, Louisa Canard, as a citizen of the Creek Nation, you are advised that the Commission requires the affidavits of two disinterested persons as to the date of its birth.

  For the purpose herein stated, there are herewith enclosed three blank forms of birth affidavit. In having same executed, care should be taken to see that all blanks are properly filled, all names written in full, and in the event that the person signing an affidavit is unable to write, signatures by mark must be attested by two witnesses.

        Respectfully,
             Chairman
           ~~Commissioner in Charge~~.

3 B A

Applications for Enrollment of Creek Newborn
Act of 1905   Volume V

HGH

COMMISSIONERS:
TAMS BIXBY,
THOMAS B. NEEDLES,
C.R. BRECKINBRIDGE.

WM. O. BEALL
Secretary

**DEPARTMENT OF THE INTERIOR,
COMMISSIONER TO THE FIVE CIVILIZED TRIBES.**

REFER IN REPLY TO THE FOLLOWING:

NC 363.

ADDRESS ONLY THE
COMMISSION TO THE FIVE CIVILIZED TRIBES.

Muskogee, Indian Territory, June 30, 1905.

Kizzie Canard,
    Weleetka, Indian Territory.

Dear Madam:

    In the matter of the application for the enrollment of your minor children, Louisa and Millie Canard, you are advised that the Commission cannot identify you on its rolls.

    You are requested to furnish the Commission with your maiden name, the names of your parents, the Creek Indian Town to which you belong, and if possible, the numbers which appear on your deeds to land in the Creek Nation.

                  Respectfully,

                             Tams Bixby   Chairman.

Maiden Name - Kizzie Yahola
Parents Names - Mother - Mary Yahola
                    Father - Fushushte[sic] Yahola

Town - Alabama
Allotment - S E 4 - Sec 14 - Twp 17 - R 11.

NC. 363.

Muskogee, Indian Territory, July 18, 1905.

Kizzie Canard,
    Weleetka, Indian Territory.

Dear Madam:

    In the matter of the application for the enrollment of your minor child, Louisa Canard, as a citizen of the Creek Nation, you are advised that you will be allowed fifteen days from date hereof within which to appear before the Commissioner to the Five Civilized Tribes at Muskogee, Indian Territory, for the purpose of being examined under oath.

Applications for Enrollment of Creek Newborn
Act of 1905   Volume V

Respectfully,

Commissioner.

NC-363

Muskogee, Indian Territory, July 26, 1905.

Kizzie Canard,
    Weleetka, Indian Territory.

Dear Madam:

In the matter of the application for the enrollment of your minor child, Louisa Canard, as a citizen of the Creek Nation, you are advised that you will be allowed fifteen days from date hereof within which to appear before the Commissioner to the Five Civilized Tribes at Muskogee, Indian Territory, for the purpose of being examined under oath.

Respectfully,

Commissioner.

---

n[sic]   Cr NC-364

Muskogee, Indian Territory, June 8, 1905.

Melinda Benham,
    Carson, Indian Territory.

Dear Madam:

In the matter of the application for the enrollment of your minor child, James Albert Benham, as a citizen of the Creek Nation, you are advised that the Commission requires the affidavits of two disinterested witnesses as to the date of its birth.

For this purpose there are herewith enclosed two blank forms of birth affidavit. In having same executed, care should be taken to see that all blanks are properly filled, all names written in full, and in the event that the person signing the affidavit is unable to write, signature by mark must be attested by two witnesses.

Respectfully,

Chairman
~~Commissioner in Charge~~.

2 B A

Applications for Enrollment of Creek Newborn
Act of 1905 Volume V

BIRTH AFFIDAVIT.

DEPARTMENT OF THE INTERIOR.
COMMISSION TO THE FIVE CIVILIZED TRIBES.

IN RE APPLICATION FOR ENROLLMENT, as a citizen of the Creek Nation, of James Albert Benham , born on the 1 day of February , 1903

Name of Father:	Claude Benham	a citizen of the United States	Nation.
Name of Mother:	Melinda Benham	a citizen of the Creek	Nation.

Postoffice   Carson, Ind. Ter.

AFFIDAVIT OF MOTHER.

UNITED STATES OF AMERICA, Indian Territory,
Western   DISTRICT.

I, Melinda Benham , on oath state that I am about 23 years of age and a citizen by blood , of the Creek Nation; that I am the lawful wife of Claude Benham , who is a citizen, ~~by~~ *(blank)* of the United States Nation; that a male child was born to me on 1 day of February , 1903 , that said child has been named James Albert Benham , and was living March 4, 1905. That the woman (Mrs. Boshaw) who attended on me at the birth of the child is now out of the country and cannot appear to make affidavit.

Melinda Benham

Witnesses To Mark:
{

Subscribed and sworn to before me this 20 day of March , 1905.

Drennan C Skaggs
Notary Public.

BIRTH AFFIDAVIT.

DEPARTMENT OF THE INTERIOR.
COMMISSION TO THE FIVE CIVILIZED TRIBES.

IN RE APPLICATION FOR ENROLLMENT, as a citizen of the Creek Nation, of James Albert Benham , born on the 1st day of Feb , 1903

Name of Father:	C. A Benham	a citizen of the U. S	~~Nation~~.
Name of Mother:	Melinda Benham	a citizen of the Creek	Nation.

Postoffice   Carson, I. T.

Applications for Enrollment of Creek Newborn
Act of 1905 Volume V

AFFIDAVIT OF MOTHER.

UNITED STATES OF AMERICA, Indian Territory,
Western DISTRICT.

I, Malinda Benham, on oath state that I am 20 years of age and a citizen by Blood, of the Muscogee[sic] Nation; that I am the lawful wife of C A Benham, who is a citizen, by U.S. of the (blank) Nation; that a male child was born to me on 1st day of Feb, 1903, that said child has been named James Albert, and was living March 4, 1905.

                                  Melinda Benham

Witnesses To Mark:

Subscribed and sworn to before me this 2 day of Aug, 1905.

Com Ex Spt 4-06-   Barney C Robison
                                        Notary Public.

AFFIDAVIT OF ATTENDING PHYSICIAN OR MID-WIFE.

UNITED STATES OF AMERICA, Indian Territory,
Western DISTRICT.

I, Ida Robison, a midwife, on oath state that I attended on Mrs. Malinda Benham, wife of C A Benham on the 1st day of Feb, 1903; that there was born to her on said date a male child; that said child was living March 4, 1905, and is said to have been named James Albert

                                  Ida Robison

Witnesses To Mark:

Subscribed and sworn to before me this 2 day of Aug, 1905.

Com Ex Spt 4-06   Barney C Robison
                                        Notary Public.

BIRTH AFFIDAVIT.

DEPARTMENT OF THE INTERIOR.
COMMISSION TO THE FIVE CIVILIZED TRIBES.

IN RE APPLICATION FOR ENROLLMENT, as a citizen of the Creek Nation, of James Albert Benham, born on the 1st day of Feb, 1903

Applications for Enrollment of Creek Newborn
Act of 1905   Volume V

Name of Father: C. A Benham   a citizen of the   U. S   ~~Nation~~.
Name of Mother: Malinda[sic] Benham a citizen of the   Creek   Nation.

Postoffice   Carson, I. T.

AFFIDAVIT OF MOTHER.

UNITED STATES OF AMERICA, Indian Territory, ⎫
    Western   DISTRICT. ⎭

    I, Malinda Brown[sic]   , on oath state that I am 20 years of age and a citizen by Blood , of the Muscogee[sic] Creek Nation; that I am the lawful wife of C A Benham , who is a citizen, ~~by~~ white of the U. S. Nation; that a male   child was born to me on 1st   day of Feb , 1903 , that said child has been named James Albert Benham, and was living March 4, 1905.

                                    Melinda Benham

Witnesses To Mark:
  {

    Subscribed and sworn to before me this 19 day of July , 1905.

                                      Barney C Robison
                                            Notary Public.

AFFIDAVIT OF ATTENDING PHYSICIAN OR MID-WIFE.

UNITED STATES OF AMERICA, Indian Territory, ⎫
    (blank)   DISTRICT. ⎭

    I, Mrs Nancy S Bashaw , a mid-wife   , on oath state that I attended on Mrs. Malinda Benham , wife of C A Benham on the 1st day of Feb. , 1903 ; that there was born to her on said date a male   child; that said child was living March 4, 1905, and is said to have been named James Albert

                                + Nancy S. BaShaw
Witnesses To Mark:
  {

    Subscribed and sworn to before me this 27 day of July , 1905.

My Commission expires Feb. 2, 1906.   Geo. W. Moon
                                          Notary Public.

Applications for Enrollment of Creek Newborn
Act of 1905 Volume V

BIRTH AFFIDAVIT.

DEPARTMENT OF THE INTERIOR.
COMMISSION TO THE FIVE CIVILIZED TRIBES.

IN RE APPLICATION FOR ENROLLMENT, as a citizen of the Creek Nation, of Lucy Etta Benham, born on the 6 day of February, 1905

Name of Father: Claude Benham   a citizen of the United States Nation.
Name of Mother: Melinda Benham   a citizen of the   Creek   Nation.

Postoffice   Carson, Ind. Ter.

AFFIDAVIT OF MOTHER.

UNITED STATES OF AMERICA, Indian Territory,
Western   DISTRICT.

I, Melinda Benham, on oath state that I am about 23 years of age and a citizen by Bblood, of the Creek Nation; that I am the lawful wife of Claude Benham, who is a citizen, ~~by~~ *(blank)* of the United States Nation; that a female child was born to me on 6 day of February, 1905, that said child has been named Lucy Etta Benham, and was living March 4, 1905.

                                        Melinda Benham
Witnesses To Mark:
{

Subscribed and sworn to before me this 20 day of March, 1905.

                        Drennan C Skaggs
                            Notary Public.

AFFIDAVIT OF ATTENDING PHYSICIAN OR MID-WIFE.

UNITED STATES OF AMERICA, Indian Territory,
Western   DISTRICT.

I, Martha Scott ~~a~~   , on oath state that I attended on Mrs. Melinda Benham, wife of Claude Benham on the 6 day of February, 1905 : that there was born to her on said date a *(blank)* child; that said child was living March 4, 1905, and is said to have been named Lucy Etta Benham
                                        Martha Scott
Witnesses To Mark:
{

Applications for Enrollment of Creek Newborn
Act of 1905 Volume V

Subscribed and sworn to before me this 20 day of March, 1905.

> Drennan C Skaggs
> Notary Public.

BIRTH AFFIDAVIT.

Department of the Interior,
COMMISSION TO THE FIVE CIVILIZED TRIBES.

IN RE-Application for Enrollment, as a citizen of the Creek Nation, of Kattie Musquito, born on the 15 day of March, 1904

Name of Father:	Albert Musquito	a citizen of the	Creek	Nation.
	(nee Polly Bear)			
Name of Father:	Polly Mosquito[sic]	a citizen of the	Creek	Nation.

Post-office   Bristow Ind Tery

AFFIDAVIT OF MOTHER.

UNITED STATES OF AMERICA,
  INDIAN TERRITORY,
  Western   District.

I, Polly Mosquito, on oath state that I am 24 years of age and a citizen by Birth, of the Creek Nation; that I am the lawful wife of Albert Mosquito, who is a citizen, by Birth of the Creek Nation; that a Female child was born to me on 15 day of March, 1904, that said child has been named Kattie Mosquito, and is now living.

> Polly Mosquito

WITNESSES TO MARK:
{ A.C. Henkins

Subscribed and sworn to before me this 18 day of March, 1905.

> E W Sims
> Notary Public.

Applications for Enrollment of Creek Newborn
Act of 1905   Volume V

AFFIDAVIT OF ATTENDING PHYSICIAN OR MID-WIFE.

UNITED STATES OF AMERICA,
   INDIAN TERRITORY,
Western   District.

I, So. con-thla-ney Tiger , a Midwife , on oath state that I attended on Mrs. Polly Musquito , wife of Albert Mosquito on the 15 day of March , 1904 ; that there was born to her on said date a Female child; that said child is now living and is said to have been named Kattie Mosquito

                                                her
                       So.con-thla-ney Tiger x
WITNESSES TO MARK: mark
  A.C. Henkins
  M.D. Guilfoyle

Subscribed and sworn to before me this 18 day of March, 1905.

                E W Sims
                        Notary Public.

BIRTH AFFIDAVIT.

DEPARTMENT OF THE INTERIOR.
COMMISSION TO THE FIVE CIVILIZED TRIBES.

IN RE APPLICATION FOR ENROLLMENT, as a citizen of the CREEK Nation, of Myrtle Hewlett , born on the 17th day of February , 1904

Name of Father: Will Hewlett   ~~a citizen of the~~ white man   ~~Nation~~.
Name of Mother: Katie Cowans   a citizen of the   Creek   Nation.

                Postoffice   Tulsa I.T.

Child Brought in Mar 22-05 - Gr

AFFIDAVIT OF MOTHER.

UNITED STATES OF AMERICA, Indian Territory,
   WESTERN   DISTRICT.

I, Katie Cowans , on oath state that I am nineteen years of age and a citizen by birth , of the Creek Nation; that I am ~~the lawful wife of~~ unmarried . ~~who is a citizen, by (blank) of the (blank) Nation~~: that a female child was born to me on 17th day of February, 1904 , that said child has been named Myrtle Hewlett , and is now living.

                    Katie Cowans

Applications for Enrollment of Creek Newborn
Act of 1905   Volume V

Witnesses To Mark:
{

Subscribed and sworn to before me this 20th day of March, 1905.

Benjamin F. Rice, Jr.
Notary Public.

AFFIDAVIT OF ATTENDING PHYSICIAN OR MID-WIFE.

UNITED STATES OF AMERICA, Indian Territory, ⎫
   WESTERN   DISTRICT.   ⎬
                                ⎭

I, Nancy Sawyer , a midwife , on oath state that I attended on Mrs. Katie Cowans, ~~wife of~~ unmarried on the 17th day of February , 1904 ; that there was born to her on said date a female child; that said child is now living and is said to have been named Myrtle Hewlett

her
Nancy x Sawyer
mark

Witnesses To Mark:
{ B F Sawyer Tulsa I.T.
{ J H *(Illegible)*

Subscribed and sworn to before me this 20th day of March, 1905.

Benjamin F. Rice, Jr.
Notary Public.

Cr NC-367.

Muskogee, Indian Territory, June 10, 1905.

Patience F. Tarvin,
   Okomah[sic], Indian Territory.

Dear Madam:

In the matter of the application for the enrollment of your minor child, Marie Louisa Tarvin, as a citizen of the Creek Nation, you are advised that the Commission requires the affidavit of the midwife or physician in attendance at its birth.

For this purpose, there is herewith enclosed a blank form of birth affidavit. In having same executed, care should be taken to see that all blanks are properly filled, all names written in full and in the event that the person signing the affidavit is unable to

Applications for Enrollment of Creek Newborn
Act of 1905   Volume V

write, signatures by mark must be attested by two witnesses same care should be exercised to see that all blanks are properly filled, all names written in full and in the event that the person signing the affidavit is unable to write, signature by mark must be attested by two witnesses.

Respectfully,

Chairman.

1 B A

BIRTH AFFIDAVIT.

DEPARTMENT OF THE INTERIOR.
COMMISSION TO THE FIVE CIVILIZED TRIBES.

IN RE APPLICATION FOR ENROLLMENT, as a citizen of the Muskogee or Creek Nation, of Marie Louisa Tarvin, born on the 14 day of March, 1903

			or Creek
Name of Father:	Pharauh F. Tarvin	a citizen of the Muskogee	Nation.
Name of Mother:	Patience F. Tarvin	a citizen of the Non citizen	Nation.

Postoffice   Okemah, Ind. Ter.

AFFIDAVIT OF MOTHER.

UNITED STATES OF AMERICA, Indian Territory, }
   Western   DISTRICT.

I, Patience F. Tarvin , on oath state that I am 36 years of age and a citizen by Non citizen , of the Muskogee or Creek Nation; that I am the lawful wife of Pharauh F. Tarvin , who is a citizen, by Blood of the Muskogee or Creek Nation; that a female child was born to me on 14 day of March , 1903 , that said child has been named Marie Louisa Tarvin , and was living March 4, 1905.

Patience F. Tarvin

Witnesses To Mark:

Subscribed and sworn to before me this 17 day of July , 1905.

Geo. A. Harvison
Notary Public.

Applications for Enrollment of Creek Newborn
Act of 1905 Volume V

AFFIDAVIT OF ATTENDING PHYSICIAN OR MID-WIFE.

UNITED STATES OF AMERICA, Indian Territory, ⎫
    Western   DISTRICT.   ⎬

    I, Nicolasa Vivero , a *(blank)* , on oath state that I attended on Mrs. Patience F. Tarvin , wife of Pharauh F. Tarvin on the 14 day of March , 1903 ; that there was born to her on said date a female child; that said child was living March 4, 1905, and is said to have been named Marie Louisa Tarvin

                          (Her mark)   Nicolasa Vivero

Witnesses To Mark: x
⎧ M. C. Van Cott
⎩ Estoban Palacios

    Subscribed and sworn to before me this 7th day of July, 1905.

                                Philip C *(Illegible)*
                                ~~Notary Public~~.
                  CONSUL GENERAL OF THE UNITED STATES
                              Monterey Mexico.

BIRTH AFFIDAVIT.

DEPARTMENT OF THE INTERIOR.
COMMISSION TO THE FIVE CIVILIZED TRIBES.

    IN RE APPLICATION FOR ENROLLMENT, as a citizen of the CREEK Nation, of Marie Louisa , born on the 14th day of March , 1903

Name of Father: Pleasant[sic] F. Tarvin   a citizen of the   Creek   Nation.
Name of Mother: Patience F. Tarvin   a ~~citizen of the~~ Non-Citizen ~~Nation~~.

                          Postoffice   Okemah Creek Nation I.T.

AFFIDAVIT OF MOTHER.

UNITED STATES OF AMERICA, Indian Territory, ⎫
    WESTERN   DISTRICT.   ⎬

    I, Patience F. Tarvin , on oath state that I am 36 years of age and a ~~citizen by~~ non-citizen , of the Creek Nation; that I am the lawful wife of Pleasant[sic] F. Tarvin , who is a citizen, by blood of the Creek Nation; that a Female child was born to me on 14th day of March , 1903 , that said child has been named Marie Louisa , and is now living.

                                Patience F. Tarvin

Applications for Enrollment of Creek Newborn
Act of 1905   Volume V

My Commission Expires Aug 2-1906

Witnesses To Mark:

Subscribed and sworn to before me this 16 day of March, 1905.

Geo. A. Harvison
Notary Public.

United States of America
Western District, Indian Terr.

I, Pleasant F. Tarvin on oath state that I am the lawful husband of Patience F. Tarvin and there was born to her on 14$^{\underline{th}}$ day of March 1903 a female child and has been named Marie Louisa, and is now living, and I am the father of the child.

I am a citizen by Blood of the Muskogee Nation.

Pleasant F. Tarvin

Subscribed and sworn to before me this
23 day of March, 1905
Geo. A. Harvison

Department of the Interior,
COMMISSION TO THE FIVE CIVILIZED TRIBES.

IN RE Application for Enrollment, as a citizen of the Creek Nation, of James Pier Henry, born on the 28 day of October, 1904

Name of Father: James S Henry   a citizen of the   U. S.   ~~Nation~~.
Name of Father: Lucy Henry   a citizen of the   Creek   Nation.

Post Office: Dustin, I.T.

Applications for Enrollment of Creek Newborn
Act of 1905 Volume V

AFFIDAVIT OF MOTHER.

UNITED STATES OF AMERICA, ⎫
    INDIAN TERRITORY,   ⎬
  Western   District. ⎭

    I, Lucy Henry , on oath state that I am 26 years of age and a citizen by blood , of the Creek Nation; that I am the lawful wife of J.S. Henry , who is a citizen, by *(blank)* of the United States Nation; that a boy child was born to me on 28 day of October , 1904 , that said child has been named James Pier Henry , and is now living.

                          Lucy Henry

Subscribed and sworn to before me this 18th day of March, 1905.

                          E.E. Lewis
                              Notary Public.

AFFIDAVIT OF ATTENDING PHYSICIAN OR MID-WIFE.

UNITED STATES OF AMERICA, ⎫
    INDIAN TERRITORY,   ⎬
  Western   District. ⎭

    I, *(Illegible)* Robertson , a midwife , on oath state that I attended on Mrs. Lucy Henry , wife of J.S. Henry on the 28 day of October , 1904 ; that there was born to her on said date a boy child; that said child is now living and is said to have been named James Pier Henry   her
                                  (Illegible) x Robertson
Witness to mark   mark
  J.S. Henry
  E.E. Lewis

Subscribed and sworn to before me this 18th day of March, 1905.

                          E.E. Lewis
                              Notary Public.

Department of the Interior,
COMMISSION TO THE FIVE CIVILIZED TRIBES.

    IN RE Application for Enrollment, as a citizen of the Creek Nation, of Viola Velmer Henry , born on the 29 day of June , 1902

Applications for Enrollment of Creek Newborn
Act of 1905 Volume V

Name of Father: James S Henry   a citizen of the   U. S.   Nation.
Name of Father: Lucy Henry   a citizen of the   Creek   Nation.

Post Office: Dustin, I.T.

AFFIDAVIT OF MOTHER.

UNITED STATES OF AMERICA,
    INDIAN TERRITORY,
Western   District.

I, Lucy Henry, on oath state that I am 26 years of age and a citizen by blood, of the Creek Nation; that I am the lawful wife of J.S. Henry, who is a citizen, by ~~United States~~ of the United States Nation; that a girl child was born to me on 29 day of June, 1902, that said child has been named Viola Velmer Henry, and is now living.

Lucy Henry

Subscribed and sworn to before me this 18th day of March, 1905.

E.E. Lewis
Notary Public.

AFFIDAVIT OF ATTENDING PHYSICIAN OR MID-WIFE.

UNITED STATES OF AMERICA,
    INDIAN TERRITORY,
Western   District.

I, Lula Henry, a midwife, on oath state that I attended on Mrs. Lucy Henry, wife of J.S. Henry on the 29 day of June, 1902; that there was born to her on said date a girl child; that said child is now living and is said to have been named Viola Velmer Henry

Lula Henry

Subscribed and sworn to before me this 18th day of March, 1905.

E.E. Lewis
Notary Public.

Applications for Enrollment of Creek Newborn
Act of 1905   Volume V

B.A. 10.

DEPARTMENT OF THE INTERIOR,
COMMISSIONER TO THE FIVE CIVILIZED TRIBES.
Muskogee, Indian Territory, August 22, 1905.

In the matter of the application for the enrollment of Lueree Brown as a citizen by blood of the Creek Nation.

Jeff Brown, being duly sworn, testified as follows:

Q What is your name? A Jeff Brown.
Q What is your age? A 53
Q What is your post office? A Wewoka.
Q You have some new-born children here for whom you are making application? A Yes, sir
Q When was McKinley born? A To the best of my recollection 20th September 1902
Q Is McKinley living? A Yes, sir
Q When was Lueree born? A I think long in March or April 1903
Q Is she living? A No, sir dead
Q When did she die? A About a year ago
Q She dies during 1904? A Yes, sir
Q Who was the mother of all these children? A Julia Brown
Q Your wife Julia Brown is a citizen of the Creek Nation? A Yes
Q You are not a citizen of nay nation are you? A No, sir

Julia Brown the mother of these children is identified on Creek Indian care field No. 357 opposite roll No. 1180

I, Anna Garrigues, on oath state that the above and foregoing is a true and correct copy of my stenographic notes taken in said case on said date.

Anna Garrigues

Subscribed and sworn to before
me this 23 day of August 1905

Edw C Griesel
Notary Public.

N.C. 369.   F.H.W.

DEPARTMENT OF THE INTERIOR,
COMMISSIONER TO THE FIVE CIVILIZED TRIBES.

In the matter of the application for the enrollment of Lueree Brown, deceased, as a citizen by blood of the Creek Nation.

Applications for Enrollment of Creek Newborn
Act of 1905   Volume V

STATEMENT AND ORDER.

The record in this case shows that on August 22, 1905, Jeff Brown appeared before the Commissioner to the Five Civilized Tribes, at Muskogee, Indian Territory, and made application by oral testimony for the enrollment of his minor child, Lueree Brown, deceased, as a citizen by blood of the Creek Nation.

It appears from the evidence that said Lueree Brown was born some time in March or April, 1903, and <u>died during the year 1904</u>.

It is, therefore, adjudged that there is no authority of law for the enrollment of Lueree Brown, deceased, as a citizen by blood of the Creek Nation, and the application for her enrollment as such is hereby ordered dismissed.

Tams Bixby   Commissioner.

Muskogee, Indian Territory.
FEB 13 1907

BIRTH AFFIDAVIT.

DEPARTMENT OF THE INTERIOR.
COMMISSION TO THE FIVE CIVILIZED TRIBES.

IN RE APPLICATION FOR ENROLLMENT, as a citizen of the Creek Nation, of   Lueree Brown, born on the 24" day of February, 1903

Name of Father:	Jeff Brown	a citizen of the United States Nation.
Name of Mother:	Julia Brown	a citizen of the Creek Nation.

Postoffice   Wewoka, I.Ter.

AFFIDAVIT OF MOTHER.

UNITED STATES OF AMERICA, Indian Territory,
  Western   DISTRICT.

I, Julia Brown, on oath state that I am 30 years of age and a citizen by blood, of the Creek   Nation; that I am the lawful wife of   Jeff Brown, who is a citizen, by U.S. of the ----- ~~Nation~~; that a   female   child was born to me on   24th day of Feb, 1903, that said child has been named   lueree[sic] Brown, and is now living.

Julia Brown

Witnesses To Mark:
  Ellen Simon

Applications for Enrollment of Creek Newborn
Act of 1905 Volume V

Subscribed and sworn to before me this 28th day of March, 1903.

J.R. Dunzy
Notary Public.

AFFIDAVIT OF ATTENDING PHYSICIAN OR MID-WIFE.

UNITED STATES OF AMERICA, Indian Territory,
Western   DISTRICT.

I, Chaney Wallace, a midwife, on oath state that I attended on Mrs. Julia Brown, wife of Jeff Brown on the 24th day of Feb, 1903 ; that there was born to her on said date a female child; that said child is now living and is said to have been named lueree[sic] Brown

Chaney Wallas

Witnesses To Mark:
  Ellen Simon
  (No other name given)

Subscribed and sworn to before me this 28th day of March, 1903.

J.R. Dunzy
Notary Public.

NC 369 JLD

DEPARTMENT OF THE INTERIOR,
COMMISSIONER TO THE FIVE CIVILIZED TRIBES.

. . . .

In the matter of the application for the enrollment of Lueree Brown, deceased, as a citizen by blood of the Creek Nation.

. . . .

STATEMENT AND ORDER.

The record in this case shows that on March 31, 1903, application was made, in affidavit form, and that on August 22, 1905, supplemental testimony was introduced, for the enrollment of Lueree Brown, deceased, as a citizen by blood of the Creek Nation. Said affidavit is considered as an original application for the enrollment of said child under the provisions of the Act of Congress approved March 3, 1905.

It appears that the evidence filed in this matter that said Lueree Brown, deceased, was born February 24, 1903, and died in the year 1904..

The act of Congress approved March 3, 1905, (33 Stats., 1048), provides:

"That the Commission to the Five Civilized Tribes is authorized for sixty days after the date of the approval of this act to receive and consider applications for

Applications for Enrollment of Creek Newborn
Act of 1905 Volume V

enrollment, of children, born subsequent to May twenty-fifth, nineteen hundred and one, and prior to March fourth, nineteen hundred and five, and living on said latter date, to citizens of the Creek tribe of Indians whose enrollment has been approved by the Secretary of the Interior prior to the approval of this act; and to enroll and make allotments to such children."

It is, therefore, ordered that the application for the enrollment of Lueree Brown, deceases, as a citizen by blood of the Creek Nation, be, and the same is hereby dismissed.

                                      Tams Bixby Commissioner.

Muskogee, Indian Territory.
    JAN 4 – 1907

Western District)
Indian Territory) SS

    We, the undersigned, on oath state that we are personally acquainted with   Julia Brown   wife of   F.J. Brown   : that on or about the   20   day of Sept , 1901, a male child was born to them and has been named   McKinley Brown   ; and that said child was living March 4, 1905.

    We further state that we have no interest in the above case.

                                                      W M Townsend
                                                                 his
                                                   S.W. Wallace x
Witness to mark: mark

B. H. Mills

Jno E. Turner

Subscribed and sworn to before
me this 19 day of May 1906.   Nat Williams
                                                   Notary Public
My Com Exp. July 1-1906.

Applications for Enrollment of Creek Newborn
Act of 1905 Volume V

N.C. 369

Muskogee, Indian Territory, December 13, 1905.

Julia Brown,
    Care Jeff Brown,
        Wewoka, Indian Territory.

Dear Madam:

    In the matter of the application for the enrollment of your minor child, McKinley Brown, born September 20, 1901, as a citizen by blood of the Creek Nation, it will be necessary for you to file with this office your affidavit and the affidavit of the midwife in attendance at the birth of said child showing whether or not said McKinley Brown was living on March 4, 1905. For this purpose there is herewith enclosed blank form of birth affidavit which you are requested to have executed before a notary public and return to this office in the enclosed envelope.

                Respectfully,

                                      Commissioner.

BA
Env.

NC-369

Muskogee, Indian Territory, December 21, 1905.

Julia Brown,
    Care of Jeff Brown,
        Wewoka, Indian Territory.

Dear Madam:

    In the matter of the application for the enrollment of your minor child, McKinley Brown, born September 20, 1901, as a citizen by blood of the Creek Nation, you are notified that the affidavit of the physician in attendance on you at the birth of said child is defective, inasmuch as it does not state the date of the birth of said child.

    From the fact that the date "September 20, 1901" has been erased from said affidavit, it appears that Virgil Berry, M.D., the affiant, either did not know the date of the birth of said child or he did not believe that said September 20, 1901, was the correct date of its birth. If said Virgil Berry, M.D. does not know the exact date of the birth of said child, you are requested to secure his affidavit as to whether or not said McKinley Brown was born subsequent to May 25, 1901, and prior to March 4, 1905. In the event that such affidavit cannot be obtained from said Virgil Berry, M.D., it will be necessary for you to furnish this Office with the affidavits of two disinterested persons relative to

Applications for Enrollment of Creek Newborn
Act of 1905   Volume V

the birth of said child. Said affidavit must set forth said child's name, the names of its parents, the date of its birth and whether or not it was living March 4, 1905. A blank for this purpose is herewith enclosed.

                                Respectfully,

                                            Commissioner.

Dis

                                                               HGH

REFER IN REPLY TO THE FOLLOWING:

DEPARTMENT OF THE INTERIOR,
COMMISSIONER TO THE FIVE CIVILIZED TRIBES.

                        Muskogee, Indian Territory, October 23, 1906.

Julia Brown,
    Wewoka, Indian Territory.

Dear Madam:

    You are hereby advised that the name of your minor child, McKinley Brown, is contained in the partial list of citizens by blood of the Creek Nation, approved by the Secretary of the Interior the Interior October 15, 1906, and that a selection of land in the Creek Nation may now be made for said child at the Creek Land Office in Muskogee, Indian Territory.

    This matter should receive your prompt attention.

                          Respectfully,

                                Tams Bixby
                                      Commissioner.

NC-369.   JWH

                      Muskogee, Indian Territory, February 14, 1907.

Julia Brown,
    c/o Jeff Brown,
        Wewoka, Indian Territory.

Dear Madam:--

    There is enclosed herewith copy of statement and order of the Commissioner to the Five Civilized Tribes, dated February 13, 1907, dismissing the application made by

Applications for Enrollment of Creek Newborn
Act of 1905   Volume V

you for the enrollment of your deceased minor child, Lueree Brown, as a citizen by blood of the Creek Nation.

Respectfully,

Registered

JWH 14-2   Commissioner.

BIRTH AFFIDAVIT.

DEPARTMENT OF THE INTERIOR.
COMMISSION TO THE FIVE CIVILIZED TRIBES.

IN RE APPLICATION FOR ENROLLMENT, as a citizen of the Creek Nation, of McKinley Brown , born on the 20" day of Sept. , 1901

Name of Father:	Jeff Brown	a citizen of the	U.S.	Nation.
	(Illegible) Town			
Name of Mother:	Julia Brown	a citizen of the	Creek	Nation.
Parents:	Caesar Simon			
	Charity "	Postoffice ~~Wew~~	Mautee I.T.	

AFFIDAVIT OF MOTHER.

UNITED STATES OF AMERICA, Indian Territory, ⎤
      Western   DISTRICT.   ⎦

I, Julia Brown , on oath state that I am 35 years of age and a citizen by blood , of the Creek Nation; that I am the lawful wife of Jeff Brown , who is a citizen, by ----- of the U.S. Nation; that a male child was born to me on 20" day of Sept. , 1901 , that said child has been named McKinley Brown , and was living March 4, 1905.

Julia Brown

Witnesses To Mark:
{

Subscribed and sworn to before me this 14" day of December , 1905.

Henry G. Hains
Notary Public.

Applications for Enrollment of Creek Newborn
Act of 1905   Volume V

BIRTH AFFIDAVIT.

DEPARTMENT OF THE INTERIOR.
COMMISSION TO THE FIVE CIVILIZED TRIBES.

IN RE APPLICATION FOR ENROLLMENT, as a citizen of the Muskogee (Creek) Nation, of McKinley Brown, born on the 20th day of Sept., 1901

Name of Father: Jeff Brown   a citizen of the   U.S. Nation.

Name of Mother: Julia Brown   a citizen of the Muskogee (Creek) Nation.

Postoffice   Mautee I.T.

AFFIDAVIT OF MOTHER.

UNITED STATES OF AMERICA, Indian Territory,
    DISTRICT.

I, _____, on oath state that I am ____ years of age and a citizen by ____ of the ____ Nation; that I am the lawful wife of ____, who is a citizen, by ____ of the ____ Nation; that a ____ child was born to me on ____ day of ____, 1 ____, that said child has been named ____ and was living March 4, 1905.

Witnesses To Mark:

Subscribed and sworn to before me this ____ day of ____, 1905.

                Notary Public.

AFFIDAVIT OF ATTENDING PHYSICIAN OR MID-WIFE.

UNITED STATES OF AMERICA, Indian Territory,
   (blank)   DISTRICT.

                                  know

I, Virgil Berry M.D. , a Physician , on oath state that I ~~attended~~ on Mrs. Julia Brown , wife of Jeff Brown on the 20 day of Sept. , 1901 ; that there was born to her on ~~said~~ a date a male child; that said child was living March 4, 1905, and is said to have been named McKinley Brown and that I performed a surgical operation on said child during the month of Nov. 1905.

                Virgil Berry

Applications for Enrollment of Creek Newborn
Act of 1905 Volume V

Witnesses To Mark:
{ Walker Jackson
{ F W Shaber

    Subscribed and sworn to before me this 15" day of Dec, 1905.

                              BB Chitwood
                                  Notary Public.

BIRTH AFFIDAVIT.

                  DEPARTMENT OF THE INTERIOR.
       COMMISSION TO THE FIVE CIVILIZED TRIBES.

    IN RE APPLICATION FOR ENROLLMENT, as a citizen of the Creek Nation, of McKinley Brown, born on the 20 day of Sept, 1901

| Name of Father: | Jeff Brown | a citizen of the | U.S. | Nation. |
| Name of Mother: | Julia Brown | a citizen of the | Creek | Nation. |

                Postoffice   Wewoka, I.T.

             AFFIDAVIT OF ~~MOTHER~~. Father

UNITED STATES OF AMERICA, Indian Territory, }
    Western   DISTRICT. }

    I, Jeff Brown, on oath state that I am 53 years of age and a citizen by -----, of the U.S. ~~Nation~~; that I am the lawful ~~wife~~ Husband of Julia Brown, who is a citizen, by blood of the Creek Nation; that a male child was born to me on 20 day of Sept, 1901, that said child has been named McKinley Brown, and is now living.

                                  Jeff Brown
Witnesses To Mark:
{
{

    Subscribed and sworn to before me this 22 day of Aug, 1905.

                                Edw C Griesel
                                  Notary Public.

Applications for Enrollment of Creek Newborn
Act of 1905 Volume V

BIRTH AFFIDAVIT.

Department of the Interior,
COMMISSION TO THE FIVE CIVILIZED TRIBES.

IN RE Application for Enrollment, as a citizen of the Creek Nation, of McKinley Brown, born on the 20" day of Sept., 1901

Name of Father: Jeff Brown   a citizen of the United States Nation.
Name of Father: Julia Brown   a citizen of the Creek Nation.

Post Office: Wewoka, I.T.

AFFIDAVIT OF MOTHER.

UNITED STATES OF AMERICA,
   INDIAN TERRITORY,
Western   District.

I, Julia Brown, on oath state that I am 30 years of age and a citizen by blood, of the Creek Nation; that I am the lawful wife of Jeff Brown, who is a citizen, by U.S. of the United States Am ~~Nation~~; that a male child was born to me on 20 day of Sept, 1901, that said child has been named McKinley Brown, and is now living.

                        Julia Brown

WITNESSES TO MARK:
   (No other name given)
   Chaney Wallas

Subscribed and sworn to before me this 28 day of March, 1903.

                        J.R. Dunzy
                           Notary Public.

AFFIDAVIT OF ATTENDING PHYSICIAN OR MID-WIFE.

UNITED STATES OF AMERICA,
   INDIAN TERRITORY,
Western   District.

I, Ellen Simon, a midwife, on oath state that I attended on Mrs. Julia Brown, wife of Jeff Brown on the 20th day of Sept, 1901; that there was born to her on said date a male child; that said child is now living and is said to have been named McKinley Brown

                        Ellen Simon

Applications for Enrollment of Creek Newborn
Act of 1905   Volume V

WITNESSES TO MARK:

{ Chaney Wallas

Subscribed and sworn to before me this 28 day of March, 1905.

J.R. Dunzy
Notary Public.

BIRTH AFFIDAVIT.

DEPARTMENT OF THE INTERIOR.
COMMISSION TO THE FIVE CIVILIZED TRIBES.

IN RE APPLICATION FOR ENROLLMENT, as a citizen of the Creek Nation, of Ruby Mildred Childers, born on the 23" day of April, 1902

Name of Father:	Daniel Childers	a citizen of the	Creek	Nation.
Name of Mother:	Mildred Childers	a citizen of the	Creek	Nation.

Postoffice   Broken Arrow, Ind. Ter.

AFFIDAVIT OF MOTHER.

UNITED STATES OF AMERICA, Indian Territory, }
  Western   DISTRICT.

I, Mildred Childers , on oath state that I am 30 years of age and a citizen by Blood , of the Creek Nation; that I am the lawful wife of Daniel Childers , who is a citizen, by Blood of the Creek Nation; that a Female child was born to me on 23" day of April , 1902 , that said child has been named Ruby Mildred Childers , and is now living.

Mildred Childers

Witnesses To Mark:

{

Subscribed and sworn to before me this 17" day of March , 1905.

Z.I.J. Holt
My Commission expires May 9" 1907   Notary Public.

Applications for Enrollment of Creek Newborn
Act of 1905   Volume V

AFFIDAVIT OF ATTENDING PHYSICIAN OR MID-WIFE.

UNITED STATES OF AMERICA, Indian Territory,
    Western   DISTRICT.

I, Mrs Mal Hundley , a Mid-wife , on oath state that I attended on Mrs. Mildred Childers , wife of Daniel Childers on the 23" day of April , 1902 : that there was born to her on said date a Female child; that said child is now living and is said to have been named Ruby Mildred Childers

                                    her
                            Mrs Mal x Hundley

Witnesses To Mark: mark
   F S Hurd
   Inez Craig

Subscribed and sworn to before me this 17" day of March , 1905.

                            Z.I.J. Holt
My Commission expires May 9" 1907   Notary Public.

BIRTH AFFIDAVIT.

DEPARTMENT OF THE INTERIOR.
COMMISSION TO THE FIVE CIVILIZED TRIBES.

IN RE APPLICATION FOR ENROLLMENT, as a citizen of the Muskogee or Creek Nation, of George Cameron Foster , born on the 17 day of Sept. , 1901

Name of Father: William C. Foster   a citizen of the Muskogee   Nation.
Name of Mother: Jennie May Foster   a citizen of the non citizen Nation.

                      Postoffice   Fentress I.T.

AFFIDAVIT OF MOTHER.

UNITED STATES OF AMERICA, Indian Territory,
    Western   DISTRICT.

I, Jennie May Foster , on oath state that I am 23 years of age and a citizen by non citizen , of the Muskogee Nation; that I am the lawful wife of William C. Foster , who is a citizen, by Blood of the Muskogee Nation; that a Male child was born to me on 17 day of Sept , 1901 , that said child has been named George Cameron Foster , and was living March 4, 1905.

                                  her
                        Jennifer x May Foster
                            mark

Applications for Enrollment of Creek Newborn
Act of 1905   Volume V

Witnesses To Mark:
{ Hazel *(Illegible)*
{ J.B. Stamper

Subscribed and sworn to before me this 14 day of March, 1905.

J.B. Stamper
Notary Public.

AFFIDAVIT OF ATTENDING PHYSICIAN OR MID-WIFE.

UNITED STATES OF AMERICA, Indian Territory, }
   Western   DISTRICT.

I, J.H. Hudson, a *(blank)*, on oath state that I attended on Mrs. Jennie May Foster, wife of William C. Foster on the 17 day of Sept., 1901; that there was born to her on said date a male child; that said child was living March 4, 1905, and is said to have been named George Cameron Foster

J H Hudson M.D.

Witnesses To Mark:
{ Scott Ralsten
{ J.B. Stamper

Subscribed and sworn to before me this 14 day of March, 1905.

J.B. Stamper
Notary Public.

BIRTH AFFIDAVIT.

DEPARTMENT OF THE INTERIOR.
COMMISSION TO THE FIVE CIVILIZED TRIBES.

IN RE APPLICATION FOR ENROLLMENT, as a citizen of the Creek Nation, of George Cameron Foster, born on the 17th day of September, 1901

Name of Father: William C. Foster   a citizen of the Muskogee Nation.
Name of Mother: Jennie May Foster   a citizen of the United States Nation.

Postoffice   Fentress I.T.

Applications for Enrollment of Creek Newborn
Act of 1905   Volume V

AFFIDAVIT OF MOTHER.

UNITED STATES OF AMERICA, Indian Territory,
Western   DISTRICT.

I, William C. Foster, on oath state that I am 24 years of age and a citizen by blood, of the Creek Nation; that I am the lawful ~~wife~~ husband of Jennie May Foster, who is a citizen, by *(blank)* of the United States ~~Nation~~; that a male child was born to ~~me~~ us on 17th day of September, 1901, that said child has been named George Cameron Foster, and was living March 4, 1905.

William C. Foster

Witnesses To Mark:
  { Tupper Dunn
  { *(Name Illegible)*

Subscribed and sworn to before me this 24 day of August, 1905.

Creed T. Huddleston
Notary Public.

My Com expires March 12-1905[sic]

CERTIFICATE OF RECORD.

𝔘nited 𝔖tates of 𝔄merica,
Indian Territory,   ss.
Northern District.

I, **CHARLES A. DAVIDSON**, Clerk of the United States Court in the Northern District, Indian Territory, do hereby certify that the instrument hereto attached was filed for record in my office the 21" day of Jan 1901 at M., and duly recorded in Book K, Marriage Record, Page 258

WITNESS my hand and seal of said Court at Muscogee, in said Territory, this 6" day of May A. D. 190 1

Chas. A. Davidson   Clerk.
                  By   Deputy.

Applications for Enrollment of Creek Newborn
Act of 1905   Volume V

MARRIAGE LICENSE

🙞🙞🙞

United States of America,
   Indian Territory,   } ss.   No. **1590**
   Northern District.

To Any Person Authorized by Law to Solemnize Marriage---Greeting.

You are Hereby Commanded to Solemnize the Rite and publish the Banns of Matrimony between Mr.   Wm C. Foster   of   Fentress , in the Indian Territory, aged   20   years and Miss Jennie Cane   of   Fentress   in the Indian Territory aged   18   years according to law, and do you officially sign and return this License to the parties therein named.

WITNESS my hand and official seal at Muscogee Indian Territory this   19th   day of   December   A.D. 190 0

                          Chas. A. Davidson
                               Clerk of the U.S. Court

By   Saml E. Hannigan   Deputy

CERTIFICATE OF MARRIAGE.

🙞🙞

United States of America,
   Indian Territory,   } ss.
   Northern District.

I,   W.G. Merritt   , a Minister of the Gospel, DO HEREBY CERTIFY that on the   23rd day of   December   A. D. 1900, I did duly and according to law as commanded in the foregoing License, solemnize the Rite and publish the Banns of Matrimony between the parties therein named.

WITNESS my hand this   23rd day of   December   A. D. 1900

My credentials are recorded in the office of the Clerk of the United States Court, Indian Territory, Northern District, Book   , Page   .
Clerks Office
  at Muscogee   W.G. Merritt
                                                  A Minister of the Gospel

Applications for Enrollment of Creek Newborn
Act of 1905   Volume V

Note—This License and Certificate of Marriage must be returned to the Office of the Clerk of the United States Court in the Northern District, Indian Territory, from whence it was issued, within sixty days from the date thereof, or the party to whom the license was issued will be liable in the amount of the One Hundred Dollars ($100.00)

NC-371.

Muskogee, Indian Territory, August 2, 1905.

William C. Foster,
    Fentress, Indian Territory.

Dear Sir:

    In the matter of the application for the enrollment of your son George Cameron Foster, born September 17, 1901, as a citizen by blood of the Creek Nation, you are advised that it will be necessary before the rights of said child as such citizen can be finally determined, for you to file with this office either the original or a certified copy of the marriage license and certificate between you and Jennie May Foster, the noncitizen mother of said child.

    You are also requested to furnish this office with your affidavit as to the birth of said child and a blank for that purpose is inclosed[sic] herewith.

                Respectfully,

                              Commissioner.

CTD-11
Env.

Muskogee, Indian Territory, November 13, 1905.

W. C. Foster,
    Fentress, Indian Territory.

Dear Sir:

    Receipt is hereby acknowledged of your letter of November 7, 1905, in which you ask why you have not been notified in the matter of the application for the enrollment of your minor child, name not given.

    In reply to your letter you are advised that the matter of the application for the enrollment of George Cameron Foster, who is presumed to be the child referred to, is pending. It does not appear at this time that any further evidence is necessary. When final action is had in the matter you will be duly advised.

Applications for Enrollment of Creek Newborn
Act of 1905 Volume V

Respectfully,

Commissioner.

NC-372.

Muskogee, Indian Territory, August 2, 1905.

Eller Looney,
    Dustin, Indian Territory.

Dear Madam:

    In the matter of the application for the enrollment of your child Forest Leonard Looney, as a citizen by blood of the Creek Nation, you are advised that it will be necessary for you to furnish this office with corrected affidavits as to the birth of said child, his name having been omitted in the affidavits heretofore filed.

    There is, therefore, inclosed[sic] herewith a blank for proof of birth which has been partially filled out and you are requested to appear before a notary public with Dr. J. W. Robertson, who attended you at the birth of said child, and there have the affidavits properly executed. Be careful to see that the notary public before whom the same are sworn to attaches his name and seal to each affidavit.

Respectfully,

Commissioner.

CTD-12
Env.

BIRTH AFFIDAVIT.

DEPARTMENT OF THE INTERIOR.
COMMISSION TO THE FIVE CIVILIZED TRIBES.

    IN RE APPLICATION FOR ENROLLMENT, as a citizen of the Creek Nation, of Forest Leonard Looney , born on the 26th day of December, 1901

Name of Father:	N. W. Looney	a citizen of the United States Nation.
Name of Mother:	Eller Looney (nee Smith)	a citizen of the Creek Nation.

Postoffice   Dustin, I.T.

Applications for Enrollment of Creek Newborn
Act of 1905   Volume V

AFFIDAVIT OF MOTHER.

UNITED STATES OF AMERICA, Indian Territory, }
Western   DISTRICT.

I, Eller Looney, on oath state that I am 20 years of age and a citizen by blood, of the Creek Nation; that I am the lawful wife of N. W. Looney, who is a citizen, by *(blank)* of the United States ~~Nation~~; that a male child was born to me on 26th day of December, 1901, that said child has been named Forest Leonard Looney, and was living March 4, 1905.

                                                Eller Looney
Witnesses To Mark:
{
    Subscribed and sworn to before me this 8th day of August, 1905.

                                                E.E. Lewis
                                                Notary Public.
MY COMMISSION EXPIRES MAY 20, 1907

AFFIDAVIT OF ATTENDING PHYSICIAN OR MID-WIFE.

UNITED STATES OF AMERICA, Indian Territory, }
Western   DISTRICT.

I, J. W. Robertson, a physician, on oath state that I attended on Mrs. Eller Looney, wife of N. W. Looney on the 26th day of December, 1901 : that there was born to her on said date a male child; that said child was living March 4, 1905, and is said to have been named Forest Leonard Looney

                                                Dr. J.W. Robertson
Witnesses To Mark:
{
    Subscribed and sworn to before me this 8th day of August, 1905.

                                                E.E. Lewis
                                                Notary Public.
MY COMMISSION EXPIRES MAY 20, 1907

BIRTH AFFIDAVIT.

DEPARTMENT OF THE INTERIOR.
COMMISSION TO THE FIVE CIVILIZED TRIBES.

IN RE APPLICATION FOR ENROLLMENT, as a citizen of the Creek Nation, of Forest Leonard Looney, born on the 26th day of December, 1901

Applications for Enrollment of Creek Newborn
Act of 1905   Volume V

Name of Father: Newton Looney   a citizen of the United States Nation.
Name of Mother: Ella Looney (nee Smith)   a citizen of the Creek   Nation.

Postoffice   Dustin, Ind. Ter.

AFFIDAVIT OF MOTHER.

UNITED STATES OF AMERICA, Indian Territory, ⎱
    Western   DISTRICT.   ⎰

I, Ella Looney , on oath state that I am 20 years of age and a citizen by blood, of the Creek Nation; that I am the lawful wife of Newton Looney , who is a citizen, ~~by~~ *(blank)* of the United States Nation; that a male child was born to me on 26 day of December , 1901 , that said child has been named Forest Leonard Looney , and was living March 4, 1905. . That the physician (Dr. Robinson[sic]) who attended for me at the birth of the child has left the country.

Eller Looney

Witnesses To Mark:
{

Subscribed and sworn to before me this 20 day of March , 1905.

Drennan C Skaggs
Notary Public.

BIRTH AFFIDAVIT.

DEPARTMENT OF THE INTERIOR.
COMMISSION TO THE FIVE CIVILIZED TRIBES.

IN RE APPLICATION FOR ENROLLMENT, as a citizen of the Creek Nation, of Forest Leonard Looney , born on the 26 day of Dec, 1901

Name of Father: N. W. Looney   a citizen of the United States Nation.
Name of Mother: Ella Looney   a citizen of the   Creek   Nation.

Postoffice   Dustin, Ind. Ter.

AFFIDAVIT OF MOTHER.

UNITED STATES OF AMERICA, Indian Territory, ⎱
    Western   DISTRICT.   ⎰

I, Ella Looney , on oath state that I am 20 years of age and a citizen by Birth, of the Creek Nation; that I am the lawful wife of N. W. Looney , who is a citizen, by birth of the United States ~~Nation~~; that a male child was born to me on 26 day of

Applications for Enrollment of Creek Newborn
Act of 1905   Volume V

December, 1901, that said child has been named Forest Leonard Looney, and was living March 4, 1905.

                                          Eller Looney

Witnesses To Mark:
{

Subscribed and sworn to before me this 4th day of April, 1905.

                                     E.E. Lewis

Com Exp 5/20-07   Notary Public.

AFFIDAVIT OF ATTENDING PHYSICIAN OR MID-WIFE.

UNITED STATES OF AMERICA, Indian Territory, }
    Western   DISTRICT.

I, J. W. Robertson, a Physician, on oath state that I attended on Mrs. Ella Looney, wife of N. W. Looney on the 26 day of December, 1901; that there was born to her on said date a female[sic] child; that said child was living March 4, 1905, and is said to have been named *(blank)*

                                    J.W. Robertson M.D.

Witnesses To Mark:
{

Subscribed and sworn to before me this 4 day of April, 1905.

                                   E.E. Lewis

Com Exp 5/20-07   Notary Public.

BIRTH AFFIDAVIT.
DEPARTMENT OF THE INTERIOR.
COMMISSION TO THE FIVE CIVILIZED TRIBES.

IN RE APPLICATION FOR ENROLLMENT, as a citizen of the Creek Nation, of Leaster Knight, born on the 22 day of January, 1904

Name of Father:	Ramsey Knight	a citizen of the	Creek	Nation.
Name of Mother:	Amy Knight	a citizen of the	Creek	Nation.

                            Postoffice   Morse, I.T.

Applications for Enrollment of Creek Newborn
Act of 1905 Volume V

AFFIDAVIT OF MOTHER.

UNITED STATES OF AMERICA, Indian Territory, ⎫
    Western Judicial   DISTRICT. ⎬

    I, Amy Knight , on oath state that I am 29 years of age and a citizen by Blood , of the Muskokee[sic] or Creek Nation; that I am the lawful wife of Ramsey Knight , who is a citizen, by Blood of the Creek Nation; that a Female child was born to me on 22nd day of January , 1904 , that said child has been named Leaster Knight , and was living March 4, 1905.

                                                      her
Witnesses To Mark: Amy x Knight
  { Jno. Phillips   mark
  { J.F. Ryan

    Subscribed and sworn to before me this 18th day of March , 1905.

                                     John H. Phillips
My Commission Expires Sept 6th 1906.   Notary Public.

AFFIDAVIT OF ATTENDING PHYSICIAN OR MID-WIFE.

UNITED STATES OF AMERICA, Indian Territory, ⎫
    Western   DISTRICT. ⎬

    I, Upsie Fixico , a Mid-Wife , on oath state that I attended on Mrs. Amy Knight , wife of Ramsey Knight on the 22th[sic] day of January , 1904 ; that there was born to her on said date a Female child; that said child was living March 4, 1905, and is said to have been named Leaster Knight

                                                   her
Witnesses To Mark: Upsie x Fixico
  { Jno. Phillips   mark
  { J.F. Ryan

    Subscribed and sworn to before me this 18th day of March , 1905.

                                     John H. Phillips
My Commission Expires Sept 6th 1906.   Notary Public.

Applications for Enrollment of Creek Newborn
Act of 1905 Volume V

Cr NC-374

Muskogee, Indian Territory, June 12, 1905.

Jumbo Tiger,
    Bristow, Indian Territory.

Dear Sir:

    In the matter of the application for the enrollment of your minor child, Ada Tiger, as a citizen of the Creek Nation, you are advised that the Commission cannot identify the mother of said child on its citizenship rolls.

    You are requested to furnish the Commission with the maiden name of said mother, the names of her parents, the Creek Indian Town to which she claims to belong, and any other information which will help identify her as a citizen of the Creek Nation.

Respectfully,

Chairman.

DEPARTMENT OF THE INTERIOR,
COMMISSIONER TO THE FIVE CIVILIZED TRIBES.

REFER IN REPLY TO THE FOLLOWING:
C-390

Muskogee, Indian Territory, **October 4, 1905.**

Jumbo Tiger,
    Bristow, Indian Territory.

Dear Sir:

    You are hereby advised that on **September 4, 1905**, the Secretary of the Interior approved the enrollment of your minor child, **Ada Tiger**, as a citizen by blood of the **Creek** Nation, and that the name of said child appears upon the roll of new born citizens of the **Creek** Nation as Number **390**.

    The child is now entitled to an allotment, and application therefor should be made without delay at the Land Office for the Nation in which the prospective allotment is located.

    An entire allotment for said child must be selected at the time of the original application.

Applications for Enrollment of Creek Newborn
Act of 1905   Volume V

Respectively,

Tams Bixby
Commissioner.

BIRTH AFFIDAVIT.

DEPARTMENT OF THE INTERIOR.
COMMISSION TO THE FIVE CIVILIZED TRIBES.

IN RE APPLICATION FOR ENROLLMENT, as a citizen of the Creek Nation, of Ada Tiger, born on the 1st day of July, 1903

Name of Father:	Jumbo Tiger	a citizen of the Creek	Nation.
Name of Mother:	So.con.thla.ney Tiger	a citizen of the Creek	Nation.

Postoffice   Bristow, Ind. Tery

AFFIDAVIT OF MOTHER.

UNITED STATES OF AMERICA, Indian Territory,
Western   DISTRICT.

I, So.con.thla.ney Tiger, on oath state that I am 29 years of age and a citizen by Birth, of the Creek Nation; that I am the lawful wife of Jumbo Tiger, who is a citizen, by Birth of the Creek Nation; that a Female child was born to me on 1st day of July, 1903, that said child has been named Ada Tiger, and is now living.

                                                       her
Witnesses To Mark: So Com thla ney x Tiger
   Albert Skeeter   mark
   W.J. Ladd

Subscribed and sworn to before me this 18 day of March, 1905.

E.W. Simms
Notary Public.

AFFIDAVIT OF ATTENDING PHYSICIAN OR MID-WIFE.

UNITED STATES OF AMERICA, Indian Territory,
Western   DISTRICT.

I, Ah.ha.co.nan.ney Goodman, a Midwife, on oath state that I attended on Mrs. So.con.thla.ney Tiger, wife of Jumbo Tiger on the 1st day of July, 1903; that

Applications for Enrollment of Creek Newborn
Act of 1905   Volume V

there was born to her on said date a   Female   child; that said child is now living and is said to have been named   Ada Tiger   her

Ah-ha co.nan.ney x goodman[sic]
mark

Witnesses To Mark:
{ Albert Skeeter
  W.J. Ladd

Subscribed and sworn to before me this 18   day of March, 1905.

E.W. Simms
Notary Public.

BIRTH AFFIDAVIT.

DEPARTMENT OF THE INTERIOR.
COMMISSION TO THE FIVE CIVILIZED TRIBES.

IN RE APPLICATION FOR ENROLLMENT, as a citizen of the Creek Nation, of   Arney Hill, born on the 27 day of December, 1902

Name of Father: Elmer Hill   a citizen of the   Creek   Nation.
Name of Mother: Lottie Buck(nee) Hill   a citizen of the   Creek   Nation.

Postoffice   Okemah Ind. Ter.

AFFIDAVIT OF MOTHER.

UNITED STATES OF AMERICA, Indian Territory,
   Western   DISTRICT.

I, Lottie Buck(nee) Hill, on oath state that I am   24   years of age and a citizen by blood, of the   Creek   Nation; that I am the lawful wife of   Elmer Hill, who is a citizen, by blood of the   Creek   Nation; that a   female   child was born to me on   27   day of December, 1902, that said child has been named   Arney Hill, and was living March 4, 1905.
her
Lottie x Buck(nee) Hill
mark

Witnesses To Mark:
{ Elmer Hill
  Tupper Dunn

Applications for Enrollment of Creek Newborn
Act of 1905 Volume V

Subscribed and sworn to before me this 16 day of march, 1905.

Tupper Dunn
Notary Public.

My Com. Exp. Aug 19-1905

AFFIDAVIT OF ATTENDING PHYSICIAN OR MID-WIFE.

UNITED STATES OF AMERICA, Indian Territory,
Western   DISTRICT.

I, Mar wak kikee Yarhola , a midwife , on oath state that I attended on Mrs. Lottie Buck (nee) Hill , wife of Elmer Hill on the 27 day of December , 1902 ; that there was born to her on said date a female child; that said child was living March 4, 1905, and is said to have been named Arney Hill

her
Mar wak kikee x Yarhola
mark

Witnesses To Mark:
  Elmer Hill
  Tupper Dunn

Subscribed and sworn to before me this 16 day of March, 1905.

Tupper Dunn
Notary Public.

My Com. Exp. Aug 19-1905

N. C. 376.

DEPARTMENT OF THE INTERIOR,
COMMISSIONER TO THE FIVE CIVILIZED TRIBES.
Muskogee, Indian Territory, August 9, 1905.

In the matter of the application for the enrollment of Katie Fox as a citizen by blood of the Creek Nation.

Luke Fox, being duly sworn, testified as follows through Willie Fox sworn as an interpreter in this case.

Q What is your name? A Luke Fox.
Q What is your age? A 30
Q Are you the father of Katie Fox? A Yes, sir
Q Who is the mother of that child? A Maggie Fox.
Q Is she living? A No, she is dead.

Applications for Enrollment of Creek Newborn
Act of 1905   Volume V

Q Is Katie Fox living? A She is living.
Q When was Katie Fox born? A 1904 the 4th of July.
Q Who was present when said child was born? A Sukie Fox.
Q Who else? A And me.
Q There is an affidavit on file here sworn to by Sukie Fox in which she states that this child was born on the 4th of March 1903, is that a mistake? A Yes, a mistake.
Q As a matter of fact the child was born July 4, 1903? A Yes, sir

Willie Fox, being duly sworn, testified as follows.
Q What is your name? Willie Fox.
Q What is your age? A About 33
Q What relation are you to the man who just testified? A He is my brother.
Q Do you know a child of his named Katie Fox? A Yes, sir.
Q Who was the mother of that child? A Maggie Fox.
Q Is she living? A No, she is dead.
Q Do you know when this child was born? A Yes, 1903 July 4th.
W Is this child still living? A Yes, sir.
Q When did you see her last? A This morning.
Q Were you present when this child was born? A I was about a quarter of a mile away.

Luke Fox recalled.

Q What is the correct name of this child, Kate or Katie? A Katie.

Anna Garrigues on oath states that the above and foregoing is a true and correct copy of her stenographic notes taken in said cause on said date.

Anna Garrigues

Subscribed and sworn to before
me this 9th day of August 1905.
J McDermott
Notary Public.

BIRTH AFFIDAVIT.

DEPARTMENT OF THE INTERIOR.
COMMISSION TO THE FIVE CIVILIZED TRIBES.

IN RE APPLICATION FOR ENROLLMENT, as a citizen of the Creek - - - - - - - - Nation, of Katy Fox, - - - - - - - - - - - - - -, born on the 4th, day of July, 1903

Name of Father: Luke Fox. - - - - - - - - - - - a citizen of the   Creek. - - - Nation.
Name of Mother: Maggie Fox. - - - - - - - - - a citizen of the   Creek. - - - Nation.

Applications for Enrollment of Creek Newborn
Act of 1905   Volume V

Postoffice Bixby. Indian Territory. - - - - - -

AFFIDAVIT.

Western District,   SS
Indian Territory,
U. S. A.

    Personally appeared before me a Notary Public in and for the above district. Willie Fox and Luke Fox to me well known to be the identical persons to this affidavit and after being by me duly sworn according to law deposes and says, That The Mother of the applicant attached herewith Maggi Fox, was the natural Mother of the child Katy Fox and that the said mother died on the thirtyeth[sic] day of October, 1903.

                              Willie Fox
                              Luke Fox

Subscribed and sworn to before me this 18th day of March, 1905.

    My Commission expires Feb. 21, 1907.   R.Bantor
                                                Notary Public.

AFFIDAVIT OF ATTENDING PHYSICIAN OR MID-WIFE.

UNITED STATES OF AMERICA, Indian Territory,
    Western - - - - -   DISTRICT.

    I, Sukey Fox, - - --- - - - - - - - - - - - , a acting Midwife , on oath state that I attended on Mrs. Maggie Fox, - - - - - - - - , wife of Luke Fox. - - - - - - - - - on the 4th day of March, - - - - - , 1903 ; that there was born to her on said date a female child; that said child was living March 4, 1905, and is said to have been named Katy Fox. - - - -

                              Sukey Fox
Witnesses To Mark:

    Subscribed and sworn to before me this 18th, day of March, - - - - - 1905.

    My Commission expires Feb. 21, 1907.   R.Bantor
                                                  Notary Public.

Applications for Enrollment of Creek Newborn
Act of 1905 Volume V

BIRTH AFFIDAVIT.

DEPARTMENT OF THE INTERIOR.
COMMISSION TO THE FIVE CIVILIZED TRIBES.

IN RE APPLICATION FOR ENROLLMENT, as a citizen of the Creek Nation, of Katie Fox, born on the 4 day of July, 1903

Name of Father: Luke Fox   a citizen of the   Creek   Nation.
Euchee
Name of Mother: Maggie Fox   a citizen of the   Creek   Nation.
Euchee

Postoffice   Bixby

AFFIDAVIT OF ~~MOTHER~~. Father
Child Present

UNITED STATES OF AMERICA, Indian Territory,
Western   DISTRICT.

I, Luke Fox, on oath state that I am 30 years of age and a citizen by blood, of the Creek Nation; that I am the lawful ~~wife~~ Husband of Maggie Fox, who is a citizen, by blood of the Creek Nation; that a female child was born to me on 4 day of July, 1903, that said child has been named Katie Fox, and was living March 4, 1905.

Luke Fox

Witnesses To Mark:

Subscribed and sworn to before me this 25 day of April, 1905.

(Seal)   Edw C Griesel
Notary Public.

BIRTH AFFIDAVIT.

DEPARTMENT OF THE INTERIOR.
COMMISSION TO THE FIVE CIVILIZED TRIBES.

IN RE APPLICATION FOR ENROLLMENT, as a citizen of the Creek Nation, of Katie Fox, born on the 4 day of July, 1903

Name of Father: Luke Fox   a citizen of the   Creek   Nation.
(Euchee)
Name of Mother: Maggie Fox (deceased)   a citizen of the   Creek   Nation.
(Euchee)

Applications for Enrollment of Creek Newborn
Act of 1905 Volume V

Postoffice Bixby

Grand
AFFIDAVIT OF ^ **MOTHER.**   Child Present

UNITED STATES OF AMERICA, Indian Territory, ⎱
  Western   DISTRICT.   ⎰

I, Ta sa la Fox , on oath state that I am 60 years of age and a citizen by blood , of the Creek Nation; that I am the lawful ~~wife~~ mother of[sic] of Luke Fox , who is a citizen, by blood of the Creek Nation; that a female child was born to ~~me~~ Maggie Fox, wife of Luke Fox on 4 day of July , 1903 , that said child has been named Katie Fox , and was living March 4, 1905.

                                           her
                          Ta sa la x Fox
Witnesses To Mark: mark
 ⎰ David Shelby
 ⎱ Jesse McDermott

Subscribed and sworn to before me this 25 day of April , 1905.

                      Edw C Griesel
                            Notary Public.

BIRTH AFFIDAVIT.

DEPARTMENT OF THE INTERIOR.
COMMISSION TO THE FIVE CIVILIZED TRIBES.

IN RE APPLICATION FOR ENROLLMENT, as a citizen of the Creek Nation, of Kate Fox , born on the 4th day of July , 1903

Name of Father: Luke Fox   a citizen of the   Creek   Nation.
Name of Mother: Maggie Fox   a citizen of the   Creek   Nation.

Postoffice   Bixby, I.T.

AFFIDAVIT OF ~~MOTHER~~.   Father (mother died Oct 30-1903)

UNITED STATES OF AMERICA, Indian Territory, ⎱
  Western   DISTRICT.   ⎰

I, Luke Fox , on oath state that I am 30 years of age and a citizen by blood , of the Creek Nation; that I ~~am~~ was the lawful ~~wife~~ husband of Maggie Fox (deceased), who ~~is~~ was a citizen, by blood of the Creek Nation[sic] Nation; that a female child was

159

Applications for Enrollment of Creek Newborn
Act of 1905   Volume V

born to my wife on 4th day of July, 1903, that said child has been named Kate Fox, and was living March 4, 1905.

           Birth   Luke Fox
Witnesses To ~~Mark~~:
  { Willie Fox
    Sukey Fox

Subscribed and sworn to before me this 19th day of June, 1905.

                            J.F. Pauth
                                Notary Public.
                        My Commission Expires July 2nd, 1908.

AFFIDAVIT OF ATTENDING PHYSICIAN OR MID-WIFE.

UNITED STATES OF AMERICA, Indian Territory, ⎫
    Western   DISTRICT. ⎭

    I, Luke Fox, father & acting as midwife, on oath state that I attended on ~~Mrs.~~ my wife, Maggie Fox, deceased, ~~wife of~~ *(blank)* on the 4th day of July, 1903: that there was born to her on said date a female child; that said child was living March 4, 1905, and is said to have been named Kate Fox

           Birth   Luke Fox
Witnesses To ~~Mark~~:
  { Willie Fox
    Sukey Fox

Subscribed and sworn to before me this 19th day of June, 1905.

                            J.F. Pauth
                                Notary Public.
                        My Commission Expires July 2nd, 1908.

                                    Cr NC-376

                Muskogee, Indian Territory, June 12, 1905.

Maggie Fox,
    Bixby, Indian Territory.

Dear Madam:

Applications for Enrollment of Creek Newborn
Act of 1905 Volume V

In the matter of the application for the enrollment of your minor child, Katie Fox, as a citizen of the Creek Nation, you are advised that the Commission requires the affidavits of two disinterested witnesses relative to its birth.

For this purpose, there are herewith enclosed two blank forms of birth affidavit. In having same executed, care should be taken to see that all blanks are properly filled, all names written in full, and in the event that the person signing the affidavit is unable to write, signature by mark must be attested by two witnesses.

Respectfully,

Chairman.

2 B A

NC-376.

Muskogee, Indian Territory, August 2, 1905.

Maggie Fox,
    c/o Luke Fox,
        Bixby, Indian Territory.

Dear Madam:

In the matter of the application for the enrollment of your daughter Katie Fox, as a citizen by blood of the Creek Nation, it will be necessary for you to file with this office the affidavits of two disinterested persons relative to the birth of said child.

Said affidavits should set forth the date of her birth, the names of her parents and whether or not she was living on March 4, 1905.

Respectfully,

Commissioner.

Applications for Enrollment of Creek Newborn
Act of 1905   Volume V

N.C. 377

DEPARTMENT OF THE INTERIOR.
COMMISSIONER TO THE FIVE CIVILIZED TRIBES.
Muskogee, Indian Territory, January 16, 1906.

In the matter of the application for the enrollment of Hettie Brown as a citizen by blood of the Creek Nation.

John Chupco being duly sworn testified as follows through Alex Posey Official interpreter.

Q What is your name? A John Chupco.
Q What is your age? A About 39
Q What is your post office address? A Weleetka
Q Do you know a child named Hettie Brown? A Hettie is the child of my sister.
Q Is Hettie living? A Yes, sir
Q What is the name of the mother of Hettie? A Betsey
Q We have been unable to identify her under the name given in an affidavit, Monahee, do you know any other name she is known by? A Her proper name is Betsey Heneha but when she went before the Commission at Dustin she gave the name Betsey Monahee.
Q What was the name of Betsey's father? A Eblow Heneha
Q What was the name of her mother? A Jennie Sarls.
Q Is Betsey living? A She died last August.
Q What is the name of the father of Hettie Brown? A Joe Brown
Q Do you know what his father's name was? A Alex
Q What was the name of his mother? A Annie
Q To what Creek Indian town does Joe belong? A Ochiye
Q To what town did Betsey belong? A Hutchchuppa.

The mother of said child is identified as Betsey Heneha on Creek Indian card No. 1412, opposite roll No. 4493.

The father is identified as Josiah Brown on card 2612 opposite roll No. 7680.

Q Is Joe Brown ever known as Josiah? A I never heard him called Josiah, always heard him called Joe Brown.
Q Were Joe and Betsey married? A No, sir.
Q What is the name of Joe's wife? A Lizzie
Q Has he a child by her? A Yes, sir
Q What is its name? A They have a child but I do not know its name.
Q Abut how old is Hettie now? A About three years.

I, Anna Garrigues, on oath state that the above and foregoing is a true and correct transcript of my stenographic notes taken in said cause on said date.

Anna Garrigues

Applications for Enrollment of Creek Newborn
Act of 1905   Volume V

Subscribed and sworn to before me
this 17 day of January 1906.

J McDermott
Notary Public.

DEPARTMENT OF THE INTERIOR,
COMMISSIONER TO THE FIVE CIVILIZED TRIBES,
NEAR DUSTIN, INDIAN TERRITORY,
DECEMBER 7, 1906.

In the matter of the application for the enrollment of an unnamed minor child of Joe Brown and Betsy Barnett as a citizen by blood of the Creek Nation:

SUNTHLOPPA, being first duly sworn by and examined through Alex Posey, a Notary Public, and Official Interpreter, testified as follows:

BY THE COMMISSIONER:

Q What is your name? A Sunthloppa.
Q How old are you? A I do not know how old I am, but I became a mother three after the Civili[sic] War.
Q What is your postoffice address? A Dustin.
Q Are you a citizen of the Creek Nation? A Yes sir. My town is Hutchachuppa.
Q Have you the custody of an illigitimate[sic] child of Joe Brown and Betsy Barnett? A Yes sir.
Q What is the child's name? A Hettie Brown.
Q Has Betsy Brown, the child's mother, any other name? A Yes sir, she is known as Betsy Manawee and Betsy Hen, and she is probably enrolled under the latter name.
Q Do you know if application had already been made for the enrollment of this child? A Yes sir, the mother made application for the child's enrollment at Dustin in 1905.
Q Do you know what name she gave the child when she made application for its enrollment? A As Hettie Brown.
Q Joe Brown is not married to Betsy Barnett, is he? A No sir, they were never married.
Q Are either of the parties now living? A Joe is living. Betsy is now dead.
Q To what Creek town do the parents of this child belong? A Joe belongs to Okchiye and Betsy belonged to Hutchachuppa.
Q Is Hettie living? A Yes sir, here she is setting on the wagon tongue.
Q What relation is this child to you? A She is my grandchild.

- - - -

Statement by the witness.

Its[sic] my desire to have an arbitrary allotment set aside for this child by the Commissioner. I would like to have 80 acres set aside to her lying adjacent to and

Applications for Enrollment of Creek Newborn
Act of 1905   Volume V

between my allotment and the allotment of Betsy Barnett, or Hen, if the same is unallotted.

Q Has not selection of land been made to this child already? A No sir.
Q Under what name are you enrolled? A As Jennie Sarls.

Witness presents deed showing description of land allotted to her which is as follows:

East half of the northwestquarter[sic].
Northwest quarter of the northeast quarter.
Southwest quarter of the northeast quarter.
of Sec. 22. T. 20 N/? R. 12 E.

Q Where does the 80 acres which you desire to have allotted to your grandchild, lie with reference to your allotment? A On the east.

- - - - - -

J.B. Myers, being first duly sworn, states, that as stenographer to the Commissioner to the Five Civilized Tribes, he recorded the testimony in the foregoing proceedings, and that the above is a true and correct transcript of his stenographic notes thereof.

J.M. Myers

Subscribed and sworn to before me,
this 18 day of Dec . 1906.

Alex Posey
Notary Public.

BIRTH AFFIDAVIT.

DEPARTMENT OF THE INTERIOR.
COMMISSION TO THE FIVE CIVILIZED TRIBES.

IN RE APPLICATION FOR ENROLLMENT, as a citizen of the Creek Nation, of Hettie Brown, born on or about the 12 day of May , 1902

Name of Father: Joe Brown   a citizen of the   Creek   Nation.
Name of Mother: Betsey Madawee   a citizen of the   Creek   Nation.

Postoffice   Henryetta. Ind. Ter.

Applications for Enrollment of Creek Newborn
Act of 1905 Volume V

AFFIDAVIT OF MOTHER.

UNITED STATES OF AMERICA, Indian Territory,
Western DISTRICT.

I, Betsey Manawee, on oath state that I am about 25 years of age and a citizen by blood, of the Creek Nation; that I am not the lawful wife of Joe Brown, who is a citizen, by blood of the Creek Nation; that a female child was born to me on or about the 12 day of May, 1902, that said child has been named Hettie Brown, and was living March 4, 1905.

Witnesses To Mark:
{ Alex Posey
{ D C Skaggs

Betsey x Manawee
mark

Subscribed and sworn to before me this 21 day of March, 1905.

Drennan C Skaggs
Notary Public.

AFFIDAVIT OF ATTENDING PHYSICIAN OR MID-WIFE.

UNITED STATES OF AMERICA, Indian Territory,
Western DISTRICT.

I, Nancy Brown, a midwife, on oath state that I attended on Mrs. Betsey Manawee, ~~wife of~~ *(blank)* on or about the 12 day of May, 1902; that there was born to her on said date a *(blank)* child; that said child was living March 4, 1905, and is said to have been named Hettie Brown

Witnesses To Mark:
{ Alex Posey
{ D C Skaggs

Nancy x Brown
mark

Subscribed and sworn to before me this 21 day of March, 1905.

Drennan C Skaggs
Notary Public.

Applications for Enrollment of Creek Newborn
Act of 1905 Volume V

377
NC-~~327~~

Muskogee, Indian Territory, May 29, 1905.

Betsy Manawee,
    Henryetta, Indian Territory.

Dear Madam:

    In the matter of the application for the enrollment of your minor child, Hettie Brown, as a citizen of the Creek Nation, the Commission is unable to identify you under the name of Betsy Manawee on its rolls.

    You are requested to furnish the Commission with the name which you were enrolled, the names of your parents, the Creek Indian Town to which you belong, and, if possible, the roll number as it appears on your deeds to land in the Creek Nation.

                    Respectfully,

                              Chairman.

HGH

REFER IN REPLY TO THE FOLLOWING:
NC-377

DEPARTMENT OF THE INTERIOR,
COMMISSIONER TO THE FIVE CIVILIZED TRIBES.

Muskogee, Indian Territory, July 27, 1905.

Betsy Brown,
    Henryetta, Indian Territory.

Dear Madam:

    In the matter of the application for the enrollment of your minor child, Hettie Brown, as a citizen of the Creek Nation, you are advised that this office is unable to identify you as a citizen of the Creek Nation.

    You are requested to state your maiden name, the name of your parents, the Creek Indian Town to which you claim to belong, and, if possible, the roll number as same appears on your deeds to land in the Creek Nation, which will help to identify you as a citizen thereof.

                    Respectfully,

                    Tams Bixby   Commissioner.

Applications for Enrollment of Creek Newborn
Act of 1905 Volume V

NC-377

Muskogee, Indian Territory, July 27, 1905.

Joe Brown,
    Henryetta, Indian Territory.

Dear Sir:

    In the matter of the application for the enrollment of your minor child, Hettie Brown, as a citizen of the Creek Nation, you are advised that this office is unable to identify you as a citizen of the Creek Nation.

    You are requested to state the names of your parents, the Creek Indian Town to which you claim to belong, and, if possible, the roll number as same appears on your deeds to land in the Creek Nation, which will help identify you as a citizen thereof.

    Respectfully,

    Commissioner.

HGH

REFER IN REPLY TO THE FOLLOWING:

**DEPARTMENT OF THE INTERIOR,
COMMISSIONER TO THE FIVE CIVILIZED TRIBES.**

Muskogee, Indian Territory, October 23, 1906.

Joe Brown,
    Henryetta, Indian Territory.

Dear Sir:

    You are hereby advised that the name of your minor child, Hettie Brown, is contained in the partial list of citizens by blood of the Creek Nation, approved by the Secretary of the Interior October 15, 1906, and that a selection of land in the Creek Nation May now be made for said child at the Creek Land Office in Muskogee, Indian Territory.

    This matter should receive your prompt attention.

    Respectfully,

    Tams Bixby Commissioner.

Applications for Enrollment of Creek Newborn
Act of 1905   Volume V

NC-378.

(Address and Date blocked on letter.)

George Simmons,
    Slumker, Indian Territory.

Dear Sir:

    On March 22, 1905, you and your wife Martha Simmons appeared before the Commission to the Five Civilized Tribes and made application for the enrollment of your son William Simmons, born August 23, 1903, as a citizen by blood of the Creek Nation and at that time submitted your affidavits only as to the birth of said child.
    You are advised that it will be necessary, before the rights of said child can be finally determined, for you to file with this office the affidavit of the attending physician or midwife at the birth of said child or, in case there was no physician or midwife in attendance when said child was born, it will be necessary for you to file with this office the affidavits of two disinterested persons who are acquainted with the said William Simmons, know when he was born and whether or not he was living March 4, 1905.

    You should give this matter your immediate attention.

                    Respectfully,
B C
Env.   Commissioner.

(The above letter was given again but Address and Date were included.)

                                Muskogee, Indian Territory, August, 2, 1905.

BIRTH AFFIDAVIT.
DEPARTMENT OF THE INTERIOR.
COMMISSION TO THE FIVE CIVILIZED TRIBES.

    IN RE APPLICATION FOR ENROLLMENT, as a citizen of the Creek Nation, of William Simmons , born on the 23 day of August , 1903

Name of Father:	George Simmons	a citizen of the	Creek	Nation.
Name of Mother:	Martha Simmons	a citizen of the	Creek	Nation.

                        Postoffice   Slumker, Ind. Ter.

Applications for Enrollment of Creek Newborn
Act of 1905 Volume V

AFFIDAVIT OF MOTHER.

UNITED STATES OF AMERICA, Indian Territory, }
Western DISTRICT.

I, Martha Simmons , on oath state that I am about 24 years of age and a citizen by blood , of the Creek Nation; that I am the lawful wife of George Simmons , who is a citizen, by blood of the Creek Nation; that a male child was born to me on 23 day of August , 1903 , that said child has been named William Simmons , and was living March 4, 1905.

                                                              her
                                      Martha x Simmons

Witnesses To Mark: mark
{ Alex Posey
{ D C Skaggs

Subscribed and sworn to before me this 22 day of March , 1905.

                                          Drennan C Skaggs
                                          Notary Public.

AFFIDAVIT OF ATTENDING PHYSICIAN OR MID-WIFE.

UNITED STATES OF AMERICA, Indian Territory, }
Western DISTRICT.

                                                             my wife
I, George Simmons , ~~a (blank)~~ , on oath state that I attended on ^ Mrs. Martha Simmons , ~~wife of (blank)~~ on the 23 day of August , 1903 ; that there was born to her on said date a male child; that said child was living March 4, 1905, and is said to have been named William Simmons

                                          George Simmons

Witnesses To Mark:
{

Subscribed and sworn to before me this 22 day of March , 1905.

                                          Drennan C Skaggs
                                          Notary Public.

Applications for Enrollment of Creek Newborn
Act of 1905   Volume V

BIRTH AFFIDAVIT.

DEPARTMENT OF THE INTERIOR.
COMMISSION TO THE FIVE CIVILIZED TRIBES.

IN RE APPLICATION FOR ENROLLMENT, as a citizen of the Creek Nation, of William Simmons, born on the 23rd day of August, 1903

Name of Father:	George Simmons	a citizen of the	Creek	Nation.
Name of Mother:	Martha Simmons	a citizen of the	Creek	Nation.
	(Late Slumpker)			
		Postoffice	Trenton, I.T.	

AFFIDAVIT OF MOTHER.

UNITED STATES OF AMERICA, Indian Territory,
Western DISTRICT.

I, Martha Simmons, on oath state that I am about 24 years of age and a citizen by blood, of the Creek Nation; that I am the lawful wife of George Simmons, who is a citizen, by blood of the Creek Nation; that a male child was born to me on 23rd day of August, 1903, that said child has been named William Simmons, and was living March 4, 1905.

              her
           Martha x Simmons
Witnesses To Mark: mark
 Toney E. Proctor
 Willie Catch

Subscribed and sworn to before me this 7th day of Sept, 1905.

         (Illegible) Proctor
My Com Exp 5/30-07   Notary Public.

AFFIDAVIT OF ATTENDING PHYSICIAN OR MID-WIFE.

UNITED STATES OF AMERICA, Indian Territory,
Western DISTRICT.

I, Schoka Proctor, a midwife, on oath state that I attended on Mrs. Martha Simmons, wife of George Simmons on the 23rd day of August, 1903 ; that there was born to her on said date a Male child; that said child was living March 4, 1905, and is said to have been named William Simmons

            her
          Schoka x Proctor
Witnesses To Mark: mark
 Toney E Proctor
 Willie Catch

Applications for Enrollment of Creek Newborn
Act of 1905   Volume V

Subscribed and sworn to before me this 7th day of Sept , 1905.

My Com Exp 5/30-07

(Illegible) Proctor
Notary Public.

NC-379.

Muskogee, Indian Territory, August 2, 1905.

Rachel Smith,
 c/o J. W. Smith
  Summitt, Indian Territory.

Dear Madam:

  In the matter of the application for the enrollment of your daughter Gladdis G. Smith as a citizen by blood of the Creek Nation, it will be necessary for you to file with this office the certificate of the attending physician as to the birth of said child. Said certificate to show the date of the birth of said child and also whether or not she was living on March 4, 1905. A blank for that purpose which has been partially filled out is inclosed[sic] herewith and you are requested to have same properly executed and return to this office.

  The certificate of the attending physician which is now on file does not set forth the date of the birth of your said daughter nor does it show whether or not she was living on March 4, 1905.

         Respectfully,

CTD-13.
Env.

                      Commissioner.

Office of
DR. A. J. SNELSON
Physician and Surgeon

        OKTAHA, IND. TER. March 21st 1905

  This to certify that I, A.J. Snelson, a regular practicing physician was called to see and did wait on, in confinement, Rachel A Smith, wife of J.M. Smith and the dame date there was born to her a female child that has now been named Gladdis Gertrude Smith.

            A J Snelson M.D.

Applications for Enrollment of Creek Newborn
Act of 1905   Volume V

Subscribed and sworn to before me this March 21st 1905.

       R.M. Darling
       Notary Public.

BIRTH AFFIDAVIT.

DEPARTMENT OF THE INTERIOR.
COMMISSION TO THE FIVE CIVILIZED TRIBES.

(Child Present)

 IN RE APPLICATION FOR ENROLLMENT, as a citizen of the CREEK Nation, of Gladdis G Smith , born on the 7" day of Jany , 1905

Name of Father:	J M Smith	a citizen of the non citizen	Nation.
Name of Mother:	Rachel Smith	a citizen of the Creek	Nation.

    Postoffice Summitt, I.T.

AFFIDAVIT OF MOTHER.

UNITED STATES OF AMERICA, Indian Territory, }
 WESTERN DISTRICT. }

 I, Rachel Smith , on oath state that I am 21 years of age and a citizen by blood, of the Creek Nation; that I am the lawful wife of J.M. Smith , who is not a citizen, by *(blank)* of the Creek Nation; that a female child was born to me on 7" day of Jany , 1905 , that said child has been named Gladdis G. Smith , and is now living.

       Rachel Smith

Witnesses To Mark:
{

 Subscribed and sworn to before me this 24" day of Mar. , 1905.

       Edw C Griesel
       Notary Public.

BIRTH AFFIDAVIT.

DEPARTMENT OF THE INTERIOR.
COMMISSION TO THE FIVE CIVILIZED TRIBES.

 IN RE APPLICATION FOR ENROLLMENT, as a citizen of the Creek Nation, of Gladdis Gertrude Smith , born on the 7th day of January , 1905

Applications for Enrollment of Creek Newborn
Act of 1905 Volume V

Name of Father: J M Smith   a citizen of the United States Nation.
Name of Mother: Rachel Smith   a citizen of the   Creek   Nation.

Postoffice   Summitt, I.T.

AFFIDAVIT OF MOTHER.

UNITED STATES OF AMERICA, Indian Territory, }
   Western   DISTRICT.

I, ..., on oath state that I am ...... years of age and a citizen by ...., of the .... Nation; that I am the lawful wife of ...., who is a citizen, by .... of the .... Nation; that a .... child was born to me on ...... day of ...., 1......, that said child has been named ...., and was living March 4, 1905.

Witnesses To Mark:
{ ....
  .... }

....

Subscribed and sworn to before me this ...... day of ...., 1905.

....
Notary Public.

AFFIDAVIT OF ATTENDING PHYSICIAN OR MID-WIFE.

UNITED STATES OF AMERICA, Indian Territory, }
   Western   DISTRICT.

I, A.J. Snelson , a physician , on oath state that I attended on Mrs. Rachel Smith , wife of J.M. Smith on the 7th day of January , 1905 ; that there was born to her on said date a female child; that said child is now living and is said to have been named Gladdis Gertrude Smith

Andrew J. Snelson M.D.

Witnesses To Mark:
{ J.T. White
  J.E. Berryhill

Subscribed and sworn to before me this 12 day of Aug, 1905.

R.M. Darling
Notary Public.

Applications for Enrollment of Creek Newborn
Act of 1905 Volume V

----- OFFICE OF -----
DR. M. F. WILLIAMS.

MUSKOGEE, IND. TER., MAR 25 1905 190

To all whom it May concern: This is to certify that I did on the 14<u>th</u> day of January 1897, solemnize the rite of matrimony between John M. Davis and Mrs. Martha Ponoski.

                                              M.F. Williams
                                              Minister of the Gospel
                                              Book A. page 4
                                              U.S. Court records

                                                                   NC? 380.

                          Muskogee, Indian Territory, July 14, 1905.

Commissioner to the Five Civilized Tribes,
        Cherokee Enrollment Division,
                Muskogee, Indian Territory.
Gentlemen:

      March 22, 1905, application was made to the Commission to the Five Civilized Tribes for the enrollment of Annie Davis, born November 26, 1901, as a citizen by blood of the Creek Nation. It is stated in said application that the father of said child is John Davis, deceased, a citizen of the Creek nation, and that the mother is Martha Napier, a citizen of the Seminole Nation.

      You are requested to inform the Creek Enrollment Division as to whether application has been made for the enrollment of said Annie Davis, as a citizen of the Cherokee Nation, and if so, what disposition has been made of the same.

                                     Respectfully,

                                                Commissioner.

Applications for Enrollment of Creek Newborn
Act of 1905   Volume V

REFER IN REPLY TO THE FOLLOWING:

DEPARTMENT OF THE INTERIOR,
COMMISSIONER TO THE FIVE CIVILIZED TRIBES.

Muskogee, Indian Territory, July 18, 1905.

Chief Clerk,
    Creek Enrollment Division,
        Muskogee, Indian Territory.

Dear Sir:

    Replying to your letter of July 15, 1905, (NC. 380) asking to be advised whether or not any application has ever been made for the enrollment as a citizen of the Cherokee Nation of Annie Davis, a child of John Davis, deceased, a citizen of the Creek Nation, and Martha Napier, a citizen of the Seminole Nation, you are advised that from an examination of the records of the Cherokee Enrollment Division it does not appear that any application has ever been made for the enrollment of said child as a citizen of that nation.

                      Respectfully,

                      Tams Bixby
GHL   Commissioner.

NC-380

                Muskogee, Indian Territory, July 20, 1905.

Martha Napier,
    Tullahassee[sic], Indian Territory.
Dear Madam:

    In the matter of the application for the enrollment of your minor child, Annie Davis, as a citizen of the Creek Nation, you are advised that this office requires proof of your marriage to John Davis (deceased), the father of said minor child.

    You are requested to forward to this office at an early date a certified copy of your marriage license and certificate or other satisfactory proof of your marriage to said John Davis.

                      Respectfully,

                      Commissioner.

Applications for Enrollment of Creek Newborn
Act of 1905   Volume V

NC 380

Muskogee, Indian Territory, November 12, 1906.

Chief Clerk,
   Cherokee Enrollment Division,
      General Office.

Dear Sir:

You are hereby advised that the name of Annie Davis, born November 25, 1901, to John Davis, deceased, a citizen by blood of the Creek Nation, and Martha Napier, an alleged citizen of the Cherokee Nation, is contained in a schedule of New Born citizens of the Creek Nation, approved by the Secretary of the Interior September 27, 1905, opposite Roll No. 394.

                 Respectfully,

                        Commissioner.

BIRTH AFFIDAVIT.

DEPARTMENT OF THE INTERIOR.
COMMISSION TO THE FIVE CIVILIZED TRIBES.

IN RE APPLICATION FOR ENROLLMENT, as a citizen of the CREEK Nation, of Annie Davis, born on the 25 day of Nov., 1901.

Name of Father: John Davis (dcd)   a citizen of the   Creek   Nation.
Name of Mother: Martha Napier   a citizen of the   Cherokee   Nation.

                Postoffice   Tallahasee

(child present)

AFFIDAVIT OF MOTHER.

UNITED STATES OF AMERICA, Indian Territory,
   WESTERN   DISTRICT.

I, Martha Napier, on oath state that I am 39 years of age and a citizen by blood, of the Cherokee Nation; that I ~~am~~ was the lawful wife of John Davis (dc'd), who is a citizen, by blood of the Creek Nation; that a female child was born to me on 25 day of Nov., 1901, that said child has been named Annie Davis, and is now living.

                 Her
           Martha x Napier
               mark

Witnesses To Mark:
   Irwin Donovan
   EC Griesel

Applications for Enrollment of Creek Newborn
Act of 1905   Volume V

Subscribed and sworn to before me 22 day of March, 1905.

Edw C Griesel
Notary Public.

AFFIDAVIT OF ATTENDING PHYSICIAN OR MID-WIFE.

UNITED STATES OF AMERICA, Indian Territory,
WESTERN DISTRICT.

I, Susan D. McIntosh, a midwife, on oath state that I attended on Mrs. Martha Davis, wife of John Davis on the 25 day of Nov., 1901; that there was born to her on said date a female child; that said child is now living and is said to have been named Annie Davis

Her
Susan x D. McIntosh
mark

Witnesses To Mark:
{ Irwin Donovan
{ EC Griesel

Subscribed and sworn to before me 22 day of March, 1905.

Edw C Griesel
Notary Public.

BA-891-B

DEPARTMENT OF THE INTERIOR,
COMMISSION TO THE FIVE CIVILIZED TRIBES.

Muskogee, Indian Territory, March 22, 1905.

In the matter of the application for the enrollment of John Powell as a Creek.

Charles Powell, being duly sworn, testified as follows:

EXAMINATION BY THE COMMISSION:
Q What is your name? A Charles Powell.
Q What is your postoffice? A Henryetta.
Q How old are you? A I am 27 years old.
Q You have a new-born for whom you are applying? A Yes sir.
Q What is his name? A John Powell.
Q When was John born? A November 30, 1904.

Applications for Enrollment of Creek Newborn
Act of 1905   Volume V

Q You are presenting an affidavit which you had made out before Notary Public J. O. Hamilton, at Henryetta, in which it is stated that John was born the 30th of November, 1905; that is a mistake, is it not? A Yes sir.
Q You told him in 1904? A Yes sir.
Q The mother of this child is Martha Powell, nee Perryman? A Yes sir.
Q You are a Seminole? A Yes sir.
Q What Nation does she belong to? A Tulsa Canadian.
Q She is a citizen of the Creek Nation? A Yes sir.
Q She has her land? A Yes sir.
Q If it is found that John Powell has rights in both the Creek and Seminole Nations, do you wish to have him get an allotment in the Creek Nation? A In the Creek Nation.

)
INDIAN TERRITORY.)   I. J. Y. Miller, a stenographer to the Commission
Western District.   )   to the Five Civilized Tribes, do hereby certify
)   that the above and foregoing is a true and complete translation of my notes as same appear in my stenographic report of this case.

                                         J.Y. Miller

Sworn to and subscribed before me
this the 26 day of April, 1905.
                                Zera E. Parrish
   My comm. expires April 11, 1909.   Notary Public.

BIRTH AFFIDAVIT.
DEPARTMENT OF THE INTERIOR.
COMMISSION TO THE FIVE CIVILIZED TRIBES.

IN RE APPLICATION FOR ENROLLMENT, as a citizen of the Creek Nation, of John Powell, born on the 30th day of November, 1904

Name of Father:	Charles Powell	a citizen of the	Seminole	Nation.
		nee Perryman		
Name of Mother:	Martha Powell	a citizen of the	Creek	Nation.

                           Postoffice   Henryetta, I.T.

Applications for Enrollment of Creek Newborn
Act of 1905 Volume V

AFFIDAVIT OF MOTHER.

UNITED STATES OF AMERICA, Indian Territory,
Western DISTRICT.

    I, Martha Powell, on oath state that I am Twenty years of age and a citizen by Birth, of the Creek Nation; that I am the lawful wife of Charles Powell, who is a citizen, by Marriage of the Creek Nation; that a male child was born to me on 30th day of November, 1904, that said child has been named John Powell, and was living March 4, 1905.

                                                         her
                                          Martha x Powell
Witnesses To Mark: mark
   { John Bastable
   { J S Orr

    Subscribed and sworn to before me this 21st day of July, 1905.

                                          James O. Hamilton
                                                Notary Public.

AFFIDAVIT OF ATTENDING PHYSICIAN OR MID-WIFE.

UNITED STATES OF AMERICA, Indian Territory,
Western DISTRICT.

    I, Silla Perryman, a mid-wife, on oath state that I attended on Mrs. Martha Powell, wife of Charles Powell on the 30th day of November, 1904; that there was born to her on said date a male child; that said child was living March 4, 1905, and is said to have been named John Powell

                                            her
                                      Silla x Perryman
Witnesses To Mark: mark
   { John Bastable
   { J S Orr

    Subscribed and sworn to before me this 21st day of July, 1905.

                                          James O. Hamilton
                                              Notary Public.

Applications for Enrollment of Creek Newborn
Act of 1905   Volume V

BIRTH AFFIDAVIT.

DEPARTMENT OF THE INTERIOR.
COMMISSION TO THE FIVE CIVILIZED TRIBES.

IN RE APPLICATION FOR ENROLLMENT, as a citizen of the Creek Nation, of John Powell, born on the 30th day of Nov., 1905

Name of Father: Charles Powell   a citizen of the   Seminole   Nation.
Name of Mother: Martha Powell   a citizen of the   Creek   Nation.
                  nee Perryman
                       Postoffice   Henryetta, I.T.

AFFIDAVIT OF MOTHER.

UNITED STATES OF AMERICA, Indian Territory,
      Western   DISTRICT.

I, Martha Powell, on oath state that I am Twenty years of age and a citizen by Birth, of the Creek Nation; that I am the lawful wife of Charles Powell, who is a citizen, by Marriage of the Creek Nation; that a male child was born to me on 30th day of November, 1905, that said child has been named John Powell, and was living March 4, 1905.

                                          her
                              Martha x Powell
Witnesses To Mark: mark
  { John Bastable
  { John Freeman

Subscribed and sworn to before me this 20" day of March, 1905.

                              J. O. Hamilton
                                   Notary Public.
My Commission Expires January 18-1908

AFFIDAVIT OF ATTENDING PHYSICIAN OR MID-WIFE.

UNITED STATES OF AMERICA, Indian Territory,
      Western   DISTRICT.

I, Silla Perryman, a mid-wife, on oath state that I attended on Mrs. Martha Powell, wife of Charles Powell on the 30th day of November, 1905 : that there was born to her on said date a male child; that said child was living March 4, 1905, and is said to have been named John Powell

                                          her
                              Silla x Perryman
                                         mark

Applications for Enrollment of Creek Newborn
Act of 1905   Volume V

Witnesses To Mark:
{ John Bastable
{ J S Orr

Subscribed and sworn to before me this 20" day of March, 1905.

My Commission Expires January 18-1908

J. O. Hamilton
Notary Public.

NC. 381.

Muskogee, Indian Territory, July 14, 1905.

Martha Powell,
Henryetta, Indian Territory.

Dear Madam:

There are on file at this office affidavits executed by you and Silla Perryman, a midwife, in which it is stated that your minor child John Powell was born November 30, 1905.

For the correction of this error in the date, you are requested to have the enclosed affidavit executed before an officer authorized to administer oaths, and return same to this office in the enclosed envelope.

Respectfully,

LM-381.

Commissioner.

DEPARTMENT OF THE INTERIOR.
COMMISSION TO THE FIVE CIVILIZED TRIBES.

Muskogee, Indian Territory, July 18, 1905.

Chief Clerk,
Creek Enrollment Division.

Dear Sir:

Receipt is acknowledged of your letter of July 14, 1905 (NC-381) stating that an application was made to the Commission to the Five Civilized Tribes for the enrollment of John Powell, born November 30, 1904, child of Charles powell[sic], a citizen of the Seminole Nation, and Martha Powell, nee Perryman, a citizen of the Creek

Applications for Enrollment of Creek Newborn
Act of 1905   Volume V

Nation and requesting to be advised as to whether application has been made for the enrollment of said John Powell as a citizen of the Seminole Nation.

In reply to your letter you are advised that it does not appear from an examination of the records of this office that any application was made to the Commission to the Five Civilized Tribes for the enrollment of said John Powell as a citizen of the Seminole Nation.

Respectfully,

Tams Bixby   Commissioner.

NC 381

Muskogee, Indian Territory, November 12, 1906.

Chief Clerk,
    Seminole Enrollment Division,
        General Office.

Dear Sir:

    You are hereby advised that the name of John Powell, born November 30, 1904, to Charles Powell, an alleged citizen of the Seminole Nation, and Martha Powell, a citizen by blood of the Creek Nation, is contained in a schedule of New Born citizens of the Creek nation, approved by the Secretary of the Interior September 27, 1905, opposite roll No. 395.

Respectfully,

Commissioner.

NC 382.

Muskogee, Indian Territory, June 3, 1905.

Polly Stephenson,
    Weeletka[sic], Indian Territory.

Dear Madam:

    In the matter of the application for the enrollment of your minor child, Siney Stephenson, you are advised that the Commission requires the affidavits of two disinterested witnesses as to the birth of said child.

Applications for Enrollment of Creek Newborn
Act of 1905   Volume V

There are herewith enclosed two blank forms of birth affidavit, and in executing same care should be exercised to see that all blanks are properly filled, all names written in full, and in the event that either of the persons signing the affidavit is unable to write, signatures by mark must be attested by two witnesses. Each affidavit must be executed before a Notary Public and the notarial seal and signature of the officer must be attached to each separate affidavit.

Respectfully,

Commissioner in Charge.

2 BA

NC 382.

Muskogee, Indian Territory, June 22, 1905.

Polly Stephenson,
    Weleetka, Indian Territory.

Dear Madam:

In the matter of the application for the enrollment of your minor child, Siney Stephenson, as a citizen of the Creek Nation, you are advised that the affidavits on file with the Commission are conflicting.

You are advised that you will be allowed ten days from date within which to appear before the Commission at its office in Muskogee, Indian Territory, with the midwife who was in attendance at the birth of said child, for the purpose of being examined under oath.

Respectfully,

Chairman.

NC. 382.

DEPARTMENT OF THE INTERIOR,
COMMISSIONER TO THE FIVE CIVILIZED TRIBES.
Muskogee, I.T., July 8, 1905.

In the matter of the application for the enrollment of Siney Stephenson as a citizen by blood of the Creek Nation.

Polly Stephenson being duly sworn, testified as follows, through Official Interpreter, Jesse McDermott.

Applications for Enrollment of Creek Newborn
Act of 1905   Volume V

Examination by the Commissioner:
Q What is your name? A Polly Stephenson.
Q What is your ~~name~~ age? A 22.
Q What is your post office address? [sic] Weleetka.
Q In the affidavits you made out before Alex Posey, you state that you did not have a midwife and in your later affidavit sent in to this office it appears that Elizabeth Barnett seems to have acted as a midwife, how can you account for that? A At the time I made out the first affidavit Elizabeth Barnett was not with us at the time of the birth of the child, but she was there soon after the birth of the child and attended the mother and child. We did not have her affidavit because we thought it would do just as well without her affidavit. We received a letter from the Commission saying that witnesses were necessary and we went [sic] got her to sign the affidavit as midwife.

----------oOo----------

A.P. Stephenson, being duly sworn, testified as follows:

Q What is your name? A A.P. Stephenson.
Q How old are you? A 50 years old.
Q What is your post office address? A Weleetka.
Q You are not a citizen of any of the Five Civilized Tribes? A No sir.
Q Mr. Stephenson, how do you explain that your wife made an affidavit stating that there was no midwife present and then sometime later we got an affidavit signed by Elizabeth Barnett as midwife, who attended on your wife? A Well there was no midwife present.
Q There was no midwife when the child was actually born? ~~A~~ How then can Elizabeth Barnett sign an affidavit as midwife? A We afterwards sent for her right away and she got there the same day the child was born.
Q So she help waited on the mother after the child was born? A Yes sir.
Q She she[sic] helped to take [sic] of the mother and child? A Yes sir.
Q But she was not present when the child was born? A No sir.
Q So that when your wife made out the affidavit that there was no midwife, she meant that there was nobody there to help deliver the child? A A[sic] Yes sir. We got a letter from the Commission saying that they wanted some disinterested witnesses.

Elizabeth Barnett, being duly sworn testified as follows:

[sic] What is your name? A Elizabeth Barnett.
Q Yow old are you? A I don't know. Old people never have the age down. (Witness appears to be about 65).
Q What is your post office address? A Weleetka.
Q Are you a citizen of the Creek Nation? A Yes sir.
Q Do you know A.P. and Polly Stephenson? A Yes sir.
Q Do you know a child of theirs named Siney? A Yes sir.
Q Is that it there? A Yes sir. (Pointing to child).
Q Were you the midwife when that child was born? You were not there when the child was actually born. You were there to assist the mother after the child was delivered?
A Yes sir. I wasn't there when the child was born but I got there after. They sent for me.

Applications for Enrollment of Creek Newborn
Act of 1905 Volume V

Q So then when you made out an affidavit you didn't mean that you were the midwife, but was there to take care of the mother and child? A Yes sir. I helped to take care of the mother and child, but I wasn't there when the child was born.
Q You got there after the child was born but waited on the mother after the birth of her child? A Yes sir.

Lona Merrick, being duly sworn, states that the above and foregoing is a true and correct transcript of her stenographic notes as taken in said case on said date.

Lona Merrick

Subscribed and sworn to before me this 11th day of July, 1905.

Edw C Griesel
Notary Public.

BIRTH AFFIDAVIT.

DEPARTMENT OF THE INTERIOR.
COMMISSION TO THE FIVE CIVILIZED TRIBES.

IN RE APPLICATION FOR ENROLLMENT, as a citizen of the Creek Nation, of Siney Stephenson, born on the 20 day of July, 1902

Name of Father:	A.P. Stephenson	a citizen of the United States Nation.
Name of Mother:	Polly Stephenson	a citizen of the Creek Nation.

Postoffice   Weleetka, Ind. Ter.

AFFIDAVIT OF MOTHER.

UNITED STATES OF AMERICA, Indian Territory,
    Western   DISTRICT.

I, Polly Stephenson , on oath state that I am about 22 years of age and a citizen by blood , of the Creek Nation; that I am the lawful wife of A.P. Stephenson , who is a citizen, ~~by~~ *(blank)* of the United States Nation; that a female child was born to me on 20 day of July , 1902 , that said child has been named Siney Stephenson , and was living March 4, 1905. That no one attended on me as midwife or physician in attendance at the birth of said child physician at the birth of the child.

her
Polly x Stephenson
mark

Witnesses To Mark:
{ Alex Posey
{ DC Skaggs

Applications for Enrollment of Creek Newborn
Act of 1905   Volume V

Subscribed and sworn to before me this 20 day of March, 1905.

           Drennan C Skaggs
           Notary Public.

Department of the Interior,

Commission to the Five Civilized Tribes.

-----oOo-----

In re Application for Enrollment, as a Citizen of the Muskogee or Creek Nation of Siney Stephenson, born on the 20 day of July, 1902

Name of Father   A.P. Stephenson   a citizen of   U.S.   Nation. Name of Mother   Polly Stephenson   a citizen of the Creek Nation.

         Post Office, Weleetka, Indian Territory.

-----oOo-----

Affidavit of Disinterested Witness.

United States of America,   )
Western District of the Indian Territory) ss.
)

  I   John Webb   on oath state that I was present at the home of A.P. Stephenson and his wife Polly Stephenson, on the 20 day of   July   , 1902, that there was born to the said Polly Stephenson, wife of the said A.P. Stephenson on that date a female child; that said child was afterwards named   Siney Stephenson   and was living on the 4" day of March, 1905.

  I further state on oath that I have no interest in the above matter of the enrollment of Siney Stephenson as a citizen of the Creek Nation, and that the facts set forth in this, my affidavit, are true and correct and are within my own personal knowledge and observation.

           John Webb

Subscribed and sworn to before me this 3^d day of July, 1905.

MY COMMISSION EXPIRES FEBY. 29, 1906.   John B Patterson
                Notary Public.

Applications for Enrollment of Creek Newborn
Act of 1905   Volume V

BIRTH AFFIDAVIT.

DEPARTMENT OF THE INTERIOR.
COMMISSION TO THE FIVE CIVILIZED TRIBES.

IN RE APPLICATION FOR ENROLLMENT, as a citizen of the Muskogee (Creek) Nation, of Siney Stephenson, born on the 20 day of July, 1903

Name of Father: A.P. Stephenson   a citizen of the   U.S.   Nation.
Name of Mother: Polly Stephenson   a citizen of the   Creek   Nation.

Postoffice   Weleetka, Ind. Ter.

AFFIDAVIT OF MOTHER.

UNITED STATES OF AMERICA, Indian Territory,
Western   DISTRICT.

I, Polly Stephenson , on oath state that I am about 26 (?) years of age and a citizen by Birth , of the Muskogee (Creek, Ind. Ter.) Nation; that I am the lawful wife of A.P. Stephenson , who is a citizen, by Birth of the United States Nation; that a Female   child was born to me on 20"   day of July , 1902 , that said child has been named Siney Stephenson , and was living March 4, 1905.

               her
             Polly x Stephenson
Witnesses To Mark: mark
 { Austin Barnett
  (Name Illegible)

Subscribed and sworn to before me this 13" day of June, 1905.

MY COMMISSION EXPIRES FEBY. 29, 1906. John B Patterson
               Notary Public.

AFFIDAVIT OF ATTENDING PHYSICIAN OR MID-WIFE.

UNITED STATES OF AMERICA, Indian Territory,
Western   DISTRICT.

I, Elizabeth Barnett , a Midwife , on oath state that I attended on Mrs. Polly Stephenson , wife of A.P. Stephenson on the 20th day of July , 1902 ; that there was born to her on said date a Female child; that said child was living March 4, 1905, and is said to have been named Siney Stephenson   her
             Elizabeth x Barnett
              mark

Applications for Enrollment of Creek Newborn
Act of 1905   Volume V

Witnesses To Mark:
- Austin Barnett
- *(Name Illegible)*

Subscribed and sworn to before me this 13" day of June, 1905.

MY COMMISSION EXPIRES FEBY. 29, 1906.   John B Patterson
                                          Notary Public.

BIRTH AFFIDAVIT.

DEPARTMENT OF THE INTERIOR.
COMMISSION TO THE FIVE CIVILIZED TRIBES.

IN RE APPLICATION FOR ENROLLMENT, as a citizen of the Creek Nation, of Rufus Lucus, born on the 10 day of September, 1901

Name of Father: Thomas Lucus   a citizen of the United States Nation.
Name of Mother: Mary Lucus   a citizen of the Creek Nation.

Postoffice   Wetumka, Ind. Ter.

AFFIDAVIT OF MOTHER.

UNITED STATES OF AMERICA, Indian Territory,
     Western   DISTRICT.

I, Mary Lucus, on oath state that I am about 25 years of age and a citizen by blood, of the Creek Nation; that I am the lawful wife of Thomas Lucus, who is a citizen, ~~by~~ *(blank)* of the United States Nation; that a male child was born to me on 10 day of September, 1901, that said child has been named Rufus Lucus, and was living March 4, 1905.

                                          Mary Lucus

Witnesses To Mark:

Subscribed and sworn to before me this 22 day of March, 1905.

                                          Drennan C Skaggs
                                          Notary Public.

Applications for Enrollment of Creek Newborn
Act of 1905   Volume V

AFFIDAVIT OF ATTENDING PHYSICIAN OR MID-WIFE.

UNITED STATES OF AMERICA, Indian Territory, }
    Western   DISTRICT.

I, Martha Lucus , a midwife , on oath state that I attended on Mrs. Mary Lucus, wife of Thomas Lucus on the 10 day of September , 1901 ; that there was born to her on said date a male child; that said child was living March 4, 1905, and is said to have been named   Rufus Lucus

                                        her
                               Martha x Lucus
Witnesses To Mark: mark
  { Alex Posey
    DC Skaggs

Subscribed and sworn to before me this 22 day of March, 1905.

                                     Drennan C Skaggs
                                          Notary Public.

BIRTH AFFIDAVIT.

DEPARTMENT OF THE INTERIOR.
COMMISSION TO THE FIVE CIVILIZED TRIBES.

IN RE APPLICATION FOR ENROLLMENT, as a citizen of the Creek Nation, of   Josephine Lucus, born on the 29 day of November, 1904

Name of Father: Thomas Lucus   a citizen of the United States Nation.
Name of Mother: Mary Lucus   a citizen of the   Creek   Nation.

                              Postoffice   Wetumka, Ind. Ter.

AFFIDAVIT OF MOTHER.

UNITED STATES OF AMERICA, Indian Territory, }
    Western   DISTRICT.

I, Mary Lucus , on oath state that I am   about 25   years of age and a citizen by blood , of the   Creek   Nation; that I am the lawful wife of   Thomas Lucus   , who is a citizen, ~~by~~ *(blank)* of the United States   Nation; that a female   child was born to me on 29   day of November , 1904 , that said child has been named Josephine Lucus , and was living March 4, 1905.

                                      Mary Lucus
Witnesses To Mark:
  {

Applications for Enrollment of Creek Newborn
Act of 1905 Volume V

Subscribed and sworn to before me this 22 day of March, 1905.

                                        Drennan C Skaggs
                                        Notary Public.

AFFIDAVIT OF ATTENDING PHYSICIAN OR MID-WIFE.

UNITED STATES OF AMERICA, Indian Territory,
    Western   DISTRICT.

    I, Martha Lucus, a midwife, on oath state that I attended on Mrs. Mary Lucus, wife of Thomas Lucus on the 29 day of November, 1904; that there was born to her on said date a female child; that said child was living March 4, 1905, and is said to have been named Josephine Lucus

                                her
                         Martha x Lucus
Witnesses To Mark: mark
   { Alex Posey
      DC Skaggs

Subscribed and sworn to before me this 22 day of March, 1905.

                                        Drennan C Skaggs
                                        Notary Public.

BIRTH AFFIDAVIT.
DEPARTMENT OF THE INTERIOR.
COMMISSION TO THE FIVE CIVILIZED TRIBES.

    IN RE APPLICATION FOR ENROLLMENT, as a citizen of the Creek Nation, of Frank Lucus, born on the 1 day of March, 1903

Name of Father: Thomas Lucus   a citizen of the United States Nation.
Name of Mother: Mary Lucus   a citizen of the   Creek Nation.

                        Postoffice   Wetumka, Ind. Ter.

AFFIDAVIT OF MOTHER.

UNITED STATES OF AMERICA, Indian Territory,
    Western   DISTRICT.

    I, Mary Lucus, on oath state that I am about 25 years of age and a citizen by blood, of the Creek Nation; that I am the lawful wife of Thomas Lucus, who is a citizen, ~~by~~ *(blank)* of the United States Nation; that a male child was born to me on

Applications for Enrollment of Creek Newborn
Act of 1905   Volume V

1 day of March, 1903, that said child has been named Frank Lucus, and was living March 4, 1905.

Mary Lucus

Witnesses To Mark:
{

Subscribed and sworn to before me this 22 day of March, 1905.

Drennan C Skaggs
Notary Public.

AFFIDAVIT OF ATTENDING PHYSICIAN OR MID-WIFE.

UNITED STATES OF AMERICA, Indian Territory,
   Western   DISTRICT.

I, Martha Lucus, a midwife, on oath state that I attended on Mrs. Mary Lucus, wife of Thomas Lucus on the 1 day of March, 1903; that there was born to her on said date a male child; that said child was living March 4, 1905, and is said to have been named Frank Lucus

her
Martha x Lucus
mark

Witnesses To Mark:
{ Alex Posey
  DC Skaggs

Subscribed and sworn to before me this 22 day of March, 1905.

Drennan C Skaggs
Notary Public.

Department of the Interior,
COMMISSION TO THE FIVE CIVILIZED TRIBES.

IN RE Application for Enrollment, as a citizen of the Creek Nation, of Rufus James Lucus, born on the 10th day of September, 1901

		non
Name of Father:	Thos. Lucus	a ^ citizen ~~of the (blank) Nation~~.
Name of Father:	Mary A. Lucus	a citizen of the Creek Nation.

Post Office   Wetumka, Ind. Ter.

Applications for Enrollment of Creek Newborn
Act of 1905 Volume V

AFFIDAVIT OF MOTHER.

UNITED STATES OF AMERICA, INDIAN TERRITORY,
Western District.

I, Mary A. Lucus, on oath state that I am 21 years of age and a citizen by blood, of the Creek Nation; that I am the lawful wife of Thomas Lucus, who is a non citizen, ~~by (blank)~~ of the *(blank)* Nation; that a male child was born to me on 10th day of September, 1901, that said child has been named Rufus James Lucus, and is now living.

Mary Lucus

Subscribed and sworn to before me this 15th day of November, 1901.

A. V. Skelton
Notary Public.

My Commission Expires 4-16-1905

AFFIDAVIT OF ATTENDING PHYSICIAN OR MID-WIFE.

UNITED STATES OF AMERICA, INDIAN TERRITORY,
Western District.

I, Martha Lucus, a midwife, on oath state that I attended on Mrs. Mary A. Lucus, wife of Thomas Lucus on the 10th day of September, 1901; that there was born to her on said date a male child; that said child is now living and is said to have been named Rufus James Lucus

Martha Lucus

Subscribed and sworn to before me this 15th day of November, 1901.

A. V. Skelton
Notary Public.

My Commission Expires 4-16-1905

BIRTH AFFIDAVIT.

Department of the Interior,
COMMISSION TO THE FIVE CIVILIZED TRIBES.

IN RE Application for Enrollment, as a citizen of the Muskogee Nation, of Jenetta Knight. born on the 27 day of February, 1902

Applications for Enrollment of Creek Newborn
Act of 1905   Volume V

Name of Father: London Knight   a citizen of the Muskogee Nation.
Name of Father: Susan Knight   a citizen of the Muskogee Nation.

Post-office   Morse, I.T.

AFFIDAVIT OF MOTHER.

UNITED STATES OF AMERICA,
   INDIAN TERRITORY,
Western   District.

I, Susan Knight, on oath state that I am 30 years of age and a citizen by Blood, of the Muskogee Nation; that I am the lawful wife of London Knight, who is a citizen, by Blood of the Muskogee Nation; that a female child was born to me on 27 day of February, 1902, that said child has been named Jenetta Knight, and is now living.

                                  Susan Knight

WITNESSES TO MARK:
{

Subscribed and sworn to before me this 18 day of March, 1905.

                                  Geo. A. Harvison
                                  Notary Public.

AFFIDAVIT OF ATTENDING PHYSICIAN OR MID-WIFE.

UNITED STATES OF AMERICA,
   INDIAN TERRITORY,
Western   District.

I, Mahalla[sic] Johnson, a Midwife, on oath state that I attended on Mrs. Susan Knight, wife of London Knight on the 27 day of February, 1902; that there was born to her on said date a female child; that said child is now living and is said to have been named Jenetta Knight

                                  Mahala Johnson

WITNESSES TO MARK:
{

Subscribed and sworn to before me this 18 day of March, 1905.

                                  Geo. A. Harvison
                                  Notary Public.

My Commission Expires Aug 2-1906

Applications for Enrollment of Creek Newborn
Act of 1905   Volume V

BA-85-B.

Muskogee, Indian Territory, April 22, 1905.

James Porter.
Okfuskee, Indian Territory.

Dear Sir:

    The Commission is in receipt of your letter of April 14, 1905, in which you state that you filled out before a Notary Public at Okemah, Indian Territory, an affidavit relative to the birth of your child, Benjamin Porter. You ask to be informed if said affidavit has been received by the Commission.

    In reply you are advised that said affidavit has been received and filed with the Commission, and when action is had in the matter you will be duly notified.

Respectfully,

Chairman.

COPY----NC-386.

Okmulgee, Ind. Ter. November 10, 1906

Hon. Tams Bixby, Commissioner.
Muskogee, Ind. Ter.

Dear Sir:-

    I have your letter of the 3rd. instant in which you state that in relation to the enrollment of my minor child, Andrew Fife, you had written me in care of Sam Fife, that proof of my marriage to Sam Fife is necessary, and also an explanation of a discrepancy in the date of the child's birth is necessary.

    I beg to advise that I am enclosing herewith a certified copy of marriage license which you will kindly return to me when you are through with it.

    As to the discrepancy in date of birth beg to advise that the child was born on the 7th. day of September, 1905. This discrepancy must have be[sic] due to the fact that Sam Fife made an application to have the child enrolled and gave a different date, but the date given by me in my application is the correct date.

Yours very truly,

Sarah Fife.

1 enclosure.

Applications for Enrollment of Creek Newborn
Act of 1905 Volume V

MARRIAGE LICENSE

UNITED STATES OF AMERICA,)
)
Indian Territory,)
)
Western District.)

No. 370.

TO ANY PERSON AUTHORIZED BY LAW TO SOLEMNIZE MARRIAGE---GREETING:

YOU ARE HEREBY COMMANDED to solemnize the Rite and Publish the banns of Matrimony between Mr. Sam Fife of Okmulgee, in the Indian Territory, aged 23 years, and Miss Sarah Gray, of Okmulgee, in the Indian Territory, aged 22 years, according to law, and do you officially sign and return this license to the parties therein named.

WITNESS my hand and official seal at Okmulgee, Indian Territory, this 6" day of Aug., A. D. 1904.

By J. L. Peacock, Deputy.

R.P. Harrison,
Clerk of the U.S. Court.

CERTIFICATE OF MARRIAGE.

United States of America,)
Indian Territory,) SS.
Western District.)

I, M. L. Checote, a Minister of the Gospel, DO HEREBY CERTIFY, that on the 10th. day of August, A.D. 1904, did duly and according to law as commanded in the foregoing License, solemnize the Rite and Publish the Banns of Matrimony between the parties therein named.
WITNESS my hand this 10th. day of August, A. D. 1904.
My credentials are recorded in the office of the Clerk of the United States Court, Indian Territory, Western District, Book C, Page 41.

M. L. Checote
A Minister of the Gospel.

CERTIFICATE OF RECORD.

United States of America,)
INDIAN TERRITORY.) SS.
Western District.)

I, Robert P. Harrison, Clerk of the United States Court in the Western District, Indian Territory, do hereby certify that the instrument hereto attached was filed for record

Applications for Enrollment of Creek Newborn
Act of 1905   Volume V

in my office the 10 day of Sept. 1904, at ___M. and duly recorded in Book A, Marriage Record, Page 3.

    WITNESS my hand and seal of said Court at Muskogee, in said territory this 10 day of Sept. A.D. 1904.

                          Signed--R. P. Harrison. Clerk.

By John Harlan, Deputy.

I, Julia C. Laval on my oath state that the above and foregoing is a true and correct copy of the Marriage License issued to Sam Fife and Sarah Gray.

                          Julia C. Laval

Subscribed and sworn to before
me this 14 day of November, 1906.

                          Edward Merrick
                          Notary Public.

BIRTH AFFIDAVIT.

Department of the Interior,
COMMISSION TO THE FIVE CIVILIZED TRIBES.

    IN RE Application for Enrollment, as a citizen of the Muskogee or Creek Nation, of Benjamin Porter , born on the 31 day of March , 1903

Name of Father:	James E. Porter	a citizen of the Muskogee Nation.
Name of Father:	Nancy Porter	a citizen of the Muskogee Nation.

                      Post-office   Okfuskee Ind. Ter.

AFFIDAVIT OF MOTHER.

UNITED STATES OF AMERICA, ⎫
   INDIAN TERRITORY,   ⎬
    Western   District.   ⎭

    I, Nancy Porter   , on oath state that I am 30 years of age and a citizen by Blood , of the Muskogee   Nation; that I am the lawful wife of James E. Porter , who is a citizen, by Blood of the Muskogee Nation; that a Male   child was born to me on 31 day of March , 1903 , that said child has been named Benjamin Porter, and is now living.

                        Nancy Porter

WITNESSES TO MARK:

Applications for Enrollment of Creek Newborn
Act of 1905 Volume V

Subscribed and sworn to before me this 18 day of March, 1905.

          Geo. A. Harvison
          Notary Public.

AFFIDAVIT OF ATTENDING PHYSICIAN OR MID-WIFE.

UNITED STATES OF AMERICA,
 INDIAN TERRITORY,
 Western   District.

  I, Louisa Scott , a Midwife , on oath state that I attended on Mrs. ✚ Nancy Porter , wife of James E. Porter on the 31 day of March , 1903 ; that there was born to her on said date a male child; that said child is now living and is said to have been named Benjamin Porter

            her
          Louisa x Scott
            mark

WITNESSES TO MARK:
 Lelah Beaver
 London Knight

Subscribed and sworn to before me this 18 day of March, 1905.

          Geo. A. Harvison
          Notary Public.
My Commission Expires Aug 2-1906

NC-387.

        Muskogee, Indian Territory, August 2, 1905.

Eller Looney,
 Dustin, Indian Territory.

Dear madam[sic]:

  In the matter of the application for the enrollment of your daughter Della May Looney, as a citizen by blood of the Creek Nation, it appears from your affidavit that said child was born December 2, 1903, while from the affidavit of J. W. Robertson, the attending physician at the birth of said child, it appears that she was born on April 2, 1903.

  For the purpose of correcting this descrepancy[sic] there is inclosed[sic] herewith a blank for proof of birth partially filled out which you are requested to have executed and return to this office with as little delay as possible. Be careful to see that the notary

Applications for Enrollment of Creek Newborn
Act of 1905   Volume V

public, before whom the affidavits are sworn to, attaches his name and seal to each affidavit.

                Respectfully,

CTD-14.   Commissioner.
Env.

BIRTH AFFIDAVIT.

DEPARTMENT OF THE INTERIOR.
COMMISSION TO THE FIVE CIVILIZED TRIBES.

IN RE APPLICATION FOR ENROLLMENT, as a citizen of the Creek Nation, of Della May Looney, born on the 2nd day of December, 1903

Name of Father:	N. W. Looney	a citizen of the United States Nation.
Name of Mother:	Eller Looney	a citizen of the Creek Nation.

                Postoffice   Dustin, I.T.

AFFIDAVIT OF MOTHER.

UNITED STATES OF AMERICA, Indian Territory,
    Western   DISTRICT.

    I, Eller Looney, on oath state that I am 20 years of age and a citizen by blood, of the Creek Nation; that I am the lawful wife of N. W. Looney, who is a citizen, ~~by~~ *(blank)* of the United States ~~Nation~~; that a female child was born to me on 2nd day of December, 1903, that said child has been named Della May Looney, and was living March 4, 1905.

                                            Eller Looney

Witnesses To Mark:
{

    Subscribed and sworn to before me this 4th day of August, 1905.

                                  Horace Wilson
My Com Exp Mch 5th 1907   Notary Public.

AFFIDAVIT OF ATTENDING PHYSICIAN OR MID-WIFE.

UNITED STATES OF AMERICA, Indian Territory,
    Western   DISTRICT.

    I, J. W. Robertson, a physician, on oath state that I attended on Mrs. Eller Looney, wife of N. W. Looney on the 2nd day of December, 1903 ; that there was

Applications for Enrollment of Creek Newborn
Act of 1905 Volume V

born to her on said date a female child; that said child was living March 4, 1905, and is said to have been named Della May Looney

J.W. Robertson

Witnesses To Mark:

{

Subscribed and sworn to before me this 3rd day of August, 1905.

My Com Exp Mch 5th 1907

Horace Wilson
Notary Public.

BIRTH AFFIDAVIT.

DEPARTMENT OF THE INTERIOR.
COMMISSION TO THE FIVE CIVILIZED TRIBES.

IN RE APPLICATION FOR ENROLLMENT, as a citizen of the Creek Nation, of Della Looney, born on the 2 day of December, 1903

Name of Father: Newton Looney   a citizen of the United States Nation.
Name of Mother: Ella Looney (nee Smith)   a citizen of the   Creek   Nation.

Postoffice   Dustin, I.T.

AFFIDAVIT OF MOTHER.

UNITED STATES OF AMERICA, Indian Territory, ⎫
    Western   DISTRICT.   ⎬

I, Ella Looney, on oath state that I am 20 years of age and a citizen by blood, of the Creek Nation; that I am the lawful wife of Newton Looney, who is a citizen, ~~by~~ (blank) of the United States ~~Nation~~; that a female child was born to me on 2 day of December, 1903, that said child has been named Della Looney, and was living March 4, 1905. That the physician (Dr. Robertson) who attended me at the birth of the child has left the country.

Eller Looney

Witnesses To Mark:

{

Subscribed and sworn to before me this 20 day of March, 1905.

Drennan C Skaggs
Notary Public.

Applications for Enrollment of Creek Newborn
Act of 1905   Volume V

BIRTH AFFIDAVIT.

DEPARTMENT OF THE INTERIOR.
COMMISSION TO THE FIVE CIVILIZED TRIBES.

IN RE APPLICATION FOR ENROLLMENT, as a citizen of the Creek Nation, of Della May Looney, born on the 2 day of Dec, 1903

Name of Father: N. W. Looney   a citizen of the United States Nation.
Name of Mother: Ella Looney   a citizen of the Creek Nation.

Postoffice   Dustin, I.T.

AFFIDAVIT OF MOTHER.

UNITED STATES OF AMERICA, Indian Territory,
    Western   DISTRICT.

I, Ella Looney, on oath state that I am 20 years of age and a citizen by birth, of the Creek Nation; that I am the lawful wife of N. W. Looney, who is a citizen, by birth of the United States ~~Nation~~: that a girl child was born to me on 2 day of December, 1903, that said child has been named Della May Looney, and was living March 4, 1905.

Eller Looney

Witnesses To Mark:

Subscribed and sworn to before me this 9 day of April, 1905.

Com Expires 5/20 1907   E.E. Lewis
                                        Notary Public.

AFFIDAVIT OF ATTENDING PHYSICIAN OR MID-WIFE.

UNITED STATES OF AMERICA, Indian Territory,
    Western   DISTRICT.

I, J. W. Robertson, a Physician, on oath state that I attended on Mrs. Ella Looney, wife of N. W. Looney on the 2 day of April, 1903; that there was born to her on said date a female child; that said child was living March 4, 1905, and is said to have been named Della May

J.W. Robertson M.D.

Witnesses To Mark:

Subscribed and sworn to before me this 9 day of April, 1905.

Applications for Enrollment of Creek Newborn
Act of 1905   Volume V

Com Expires 5/20 1907

E.E. Lewis
Notary Public.

BIRTH AFFIDAVIT.

Department of the Interior,
COMMISSION TO THE FIVE CIVILIZED TRIBES.

IN RE *Application for Enrollment,* as a citizen of the Creek Nation, of Suthie Bell, born on the 3^d day of May, 1904

Name of Father: Eli Bell   a citizen of the Creek Nation.
Name of Father: Silby Bell   a citizen of the Creek Nation.

Post-office   Henry Oklahoma Teritory[sic]

AFFIDAVIT OF MOTHER.

UNITED STATES OF AMERICA,
INDIAN TERRITORY,
Western   District.

I, Silby Bell, on oath state that I am 30 years of age and a citizen by blood, of the Creek Nation; that I am the lawful wife of Eli Bell, who is a citizen, by blood of the Creek Nation; that a male child was born to me on 3^d day of May, 1904, that said child has been named Suthie Bell, and is now living.

WITNESSES TO MARK:
 Legus C. Perryman
 Chas. E. Stewart

her
Silby x Bell
mark

Subscribed and sworn to before me this 20 day of March, 1905.

(Name Illegible)
Notary Public.

Applications for Enrollment of Creek Newborn
Act of 1905   Volume V

AFFIDAVIT OF ATTENDING PHYSICIAN OR MID-WIFE.

UNITED STATES OF AMERICA,
   INDIAN TERRITORY,
  Western   District.

I, Lizzy Enriques, a midwife, on oath state that I attended on Mrs. Silby Bell, wife of Eli Bell on the 3^d day of May, 1904; that there was born to her on said date a *(blank)* child; that said child is now living and is said to have been named Suthie Bell

                            her
                      Lizzie x Enriques
                          mark

WITNESSES TO MARK:
    Legus C. Perryman
    Chas. E. Steward

Subscribed and sworn to before me this 20 day of March, 1905.

                          (Name Illegible)
My Commission Expires July 10, 1906.   Notary Public.
BIRTH AFFIDAVIT.

DEPARTMENT OF THE INTERIOR.
COMMISSION TO THE FIVE CIVILIZED TRIBES.

IN RE APPLICATION FOR ENROLLMENT, as a citizen of the Creek Nation, of Thompson Bell, born on the 22^d day of September, 1902

Name of Father:	Eli Bell	a citizen of the Creek	Nation.
Name of Mother:	Silby Bell	a citizen of the Creek	Nation.

                    Postoffice   Henry Oklahoma Teritory[sic]

AFFIDAVIT OF MOTHER.

UNITED STATES OF AMERICA, Indian Territory,
    Western   DISTRICT.

I, Silby Bell, on oath state that I am 30 years of age and a citizen by blood, of the Creek Nation; that I am the lawful wife of Eli Bell, who is a citizen, by blood of the Creek Nation; that a male child was born to me on 22^d day of September, 1902, that said child has been named Thompson Bell, and was living March 4, 1905.

                            her
                        Silby x Bell
                          mark

Applications for Enrollment of Creek Newborn
Act of 1905   Volume V

Witnesses To Mark:
{ Legus C Perryman
{ Jesus Enriques

    Subscribed and sworn to before me this 20th day of March, 1905.

(Name Illegible)
Notary Public.

AFFIDAVIT OF ATTENDING PHYSICIAN OR MID-WIFE.

UNITED STATES OF AMERICA, Indian Territory,
    Western   DISTRICT.

    I, Sordie Gooden, a midwife, on oath state that I attended on Mrs. Silby Bell, wife of Eli Bell on the 22^d day of September, 1902; that there was born to her on said date a male child; that said child was living March 4, 1905, and is said to have been named Thompson Bell

                        her
                    Sordie x Gooden
Witnesses To Mark: mark
{ Legus C Perryman
{ Jesus Enriques

    Subscribed and sworn to before me this 20th day of March, 1905.

(Name Illegible)
Notary Public.

BIRTH AFFIDAVIT.

DEPARTMENT OF THE INTERIOR.
COMMISSION TO THE FIVE CIVILIZED TRIBES.

    IN RE APPLICATION FOR ENROLLMENT, as a citizen of the Creek Nation, of Tony Lucus, born on the 22 day of April, 1903

Name of Father:	Nenie Lucus	a citizen of the United States Nation.
Name of Mother:	Lucy Lucus	a citizen of the Creek Nation.

                  Postoffice   Wetumka, Ind. Ter.

Applications for Enrollment of Creek Newborn
Act of 1905   Volume V

AFFIDAVIT OF MOTHER.

UNITED STATES OF AMERICA, Indian Territory, }
  Western   DISTRICT.

    I, Lucy Lucus , on oath state that I am about 21 years of age and a citizen by blood , of the Creek Nation; that I am the lawful wife of Nenie Lucus , who is a citizen, ~~by~~ *(blank)* of the United States Nation; that a male child was born to me on 22 day of April , 1903 , that said child has been named Tony Lucus , and was living March 4, 1905.

                                        her
                               Lucy x Lucus
Witnesses To Mark: mark
   { Alex Posey
     D C Skaggs

    Subscribed and sworn to before me 22 day of March , 1905.

                            Drennan C Skaggs
                                Notary Public.

AFFIDAVIT OF ATTENDING PHYSICIAN OR MID-WIFE.

UNITED STATES OF AMERICA, Indian Territory, }
  Western   DISTRICT.

    I, Martha Lucus , a midwife , on oath state that I attended on Mrs. Lucy Lucus, wife of Nenie Lucus on the 22 day of April , 1903 ; that there was born to her on said date a *(blank)* child; that said child was living March 4, 1905, and is said to have been named Tony Lucus

                                   her
                           Martha x Lucus
Witnesses To Mark: mark
   { Alex Posey
     D C Skaggs

    Subscribed and sworn to before me 22 day of March , 1905.

                            Drennan C Skaggs
                                Notary Public.

                                                     NC 389.

                    Muskogee, Indian Territory, June 3, 1905.

Lucy Lucus,
    Wetumka, Indian Territory.

Applications for Enrollment of Creek Newborn
Act of 1905 Volume V

Dear Madam:

    In the matter of the application for the enrollment of your minor child, Toney[sic] Lucus, you are advised that the Commission is unable to identify you on its rolls as a citizen of the Creek Nation.

    You are requested to furnish the Commission with your maiden name, the names of your parents, the Creek Indian Town to which you belong, and, if possible, the roll number as it appears on your deeds to land in the Creek Nation.

                                      Respectfully,

                                                          Commissioner in Charge.

N.C. 389   HGH (Copy)

DEPARTMENT OF.
COMMISSIONER TO THE FIVE CIVILIZED TRIBES.

                                Muskogee, Indian Territory, July 21, 1906.

Nenie Lucus,
    Wetumka, Indian Territory.

Dear Sir: In the matter of the application for the enrollment of your minor child, Toney Lucus, you are advised that this office is unable to identify your wife on its rolls as a citizen of the Creek Nation.

    You are requested to state her maiden name, the names of her parents, the Creek Indian Town to which she belongs, and if possible, the number which appears on her deeds to land in the Creek Nation.

                                      Respectfully,

                                  (signed) TAMS BIXBY
                                            Commissioner.

                              Wetumka, Ind. Ter., July 22ond[sic]. 1905

Dear Sir:

    Application for enrollment of Toney Lucus, a Male child of Nanie[sic] and Lucy Lucus, was made at Spokogee, I.T. some time in March 1905. where all the proff necessary was made,; as soon as the Enrollment is properly recognized I desire to apply for his Allotment.

                              Respectfully Yours
                          (signed)   NANIE LUCUS
                                        Wetumka, Ind. Ter.

Applications for Enrollment of Creek Newborn
Act of 1905   Volume V

NC-389

Muskogee, Indian Territory, July 26, 1905.

Nenie Lucus,
    Wetumka, Indian Territory.

Dear Sir:

In the matter of the application for the enrollment of your minor child, Tony Lucus, as a citizen of the Creek Nation, you are advised that without further information, it is impossible to identify you and Lucy Lucus, the mother of said child, as citizens of the Creek Nation.

You are requested to have your wife state her maiden name, the names of her parents, the Creek Indian Town to which she claims to belong, and, if possible, the roll number as same appears on her deeds to land in the Creek Nation, and also any other information which will help identify you and your wife, Lucy Lucus, as citizens of the Creek Nation.

This matter should receive your prompt attention.

Respectfully,

Commissioner.

Wetumka, Ind. Ter. Sept. 12th, 1905.

L.C. Gammill
Notary Public for
Western District, Indian Territory
N.C. No. 389

Hon. T.B. Needles,
    Acting Commissioner
        Muskogee, Ind. Ter.

In answer to yours of June 3rd 05 will say: Toney Lucus son of Nannie and Lucy Lucus, whose maiden name was Lucy Harjo, whose fathers[sic] name was Tubus Harjo, mothers[sic] name was Dinaer Harjo, or Sar-woch-koch-kah Harjo, whose Indian town was Ki-a-la-gy, the selection number appearing on my certificate of allotment if No. 10,587. I have not received my deed yet.

Trusting this answer will enable you to identify me on the Creek rolls, I am most respectfully yours

Applications for Enrollment of Creek Newborn
Act of 1905 Volume V

Address C of Box 296

Lucy Lucus
By L.C. Gammill

I am anxious to file on lands for Toney and wish to receive notification at your earliest convenience.

Lucy Lucus

N.C. 389

Muskogee, Indian Territory, September 13, 1905.

Lucy Lucus,
    Wetumka, Indian Territory.
Dear Madam:

    Receipt is acknowledged of your letter of September 12, 1905, containing information which enables this office to identify you on its roll of citizens of the Creek Nation.

    You state that you wish to receive notification as to when you can file on lands in the Creek Nation for your minor child, Toney Lucus.

    In reply you are advised that when the matter of the enrollment of said Toney Lucus has been finally approved, you will be given due notice in regard to filing.

Respectfully,

Acting Commissioner.

NC-390.

Muskogee, Indian Territory, August 2, 1905.

Mossie Morton,
    Okemah, Indian Territory.

Dear Sir:

    In the matter of the application for the enrollment of your minor son Claude S. Morton as a citizen by blood of the Creek Nation it will be necessary, before the rights of said child as such citizen can be finally determined, for your[sic] to file with this office

Applications for Enrollment of Creek Newborn
Act of 1905   Volume V

either the original or a certified copy of the marriage license and certificate between yourself and Josie A. Morton, the noncitizen mother of said child.

This office also requires your affidavit as to the birth of said child and a blank for that purpose properly filled out is inclosed[sic] herewith. Be careful to see that the notary public before whom the same is sworn to attaches both his name and seal to the affidavit.

                        Respectfully,

                                                          Commissioner.

CTD-15.
Env.

MARRIAGE LICENSE

United States of America, |
   Indian Territory,   (SS.   No. 931.
     Northern District. |

TO ANY PERSON AUTHORIZED BY LAW TO SOLEMNIZE MARRIAGE---GREETING:

      You are hereby commanded to solemnize the Rite and publish the Banns of Matrimony between Mr. Mossie M. Morton of Okmulgee, in the Indian Territory, aged 28 years, and Miss Josie A. Dean of Okmulgee, in the Indian Territory, aged 18 years, according to law, and do you officially sign and return this License to the parties therein named.
      WITNESS my hand and official seal at Muscogee[sic], Indian Territory, this 14" day of September, A. D. 1900.

          (SEAL)   Chas A Davidson
                                          Clerk of the U.S. Court.
By L A Winston
   Deputy.

CERTIFICATE OF MARRIAGE.

United States of America, |
    Indian Territory, (SS.
    Northern District. |

     I, A. M. Lusk, a Minister of the Gospel, DO HEREBY CERTIFY, that on the 16 day of Sept., A.D. 1900, I did duly and according to law as commanded in the foregoing License, solemnize the Rite and publish the Banns of Matrimony between the parties therein named.
     WITNESS my hand that 16 day of Sept., A. D. 1900.

Applications for Enrollment of Creek Newborn
Act of 1905 Volume V

  My credentials are recorded in the office of the Clerk of the United States Court, Indian Territory, Third Judicial Division, Book A, Page 138.

      signed. A. M. Lusk
           A Minister of the Gospel.

ENDORSEMENTS:
      CERTIFICATE OF RECORD.

United State of America. I
  Indian Territory, (SS.
  Northern District. I

  I, Charles A. Davidson, Clerk of the United States Court in the Northern District, Indian Territory, do hereby certify that the instrument hereto attached was filed for record in my office the 6 day of Oct 1900, at _____M., and duly recorded in Book J., Marriage Record, Page 119.

  WITNESS my hand and seal of said Court at Muscogee[sic], in said Territory this 5 day of Dec. A.D. 1900.

    Seal   Chas A. Davidson
               Clerk.

Northern Dist. Ind. Ter. Filed Oct. 6, 1900. Chas. A. Davidson, Clerk, U.S. Courts.

  I, D. C. Skaggs, on oath state that the above and foregoing is a full and complete copy of the original now on file in the office of the Commissioner to the Five Civilized Tribes at Muskogee, Indian Territory.

          D.C. Skaggs

Subscribed and sworn to before me this 3 day of August, 1905.

         Edw C Griesel
           Notary Public.
   My Commission expires Nov. 29-1908.

Applications for Enrollment of Creek Newborn
Act of 1905   Volume V

BIRTH AFFIDAVIT.

DEPARTMENT OF THE INTERIOR.
COMMISSION TO THE FIVE CIVILIZED TRIBES.

IN RE APPLICATION FOR ENROLLMENT, as a citizen of the Creek Nation, of Claude S. Morton, born on the 30th day of July, 1901

Name of Father: Mossie Morton   a citizen of the Creek Nation.
Name of Mother: Josie A. Morton   a citizen of the United StatesNation.

Postoffice   Okemah, I.T.

AFFIDAVIT OF MOTHER.

UNITED STATES OF AMERICA, Indian Territory,
Western   DISTRICT.

I, Mossie Morton, on oath state that I am 32 years of age and a citizen by blood, of the Creek Nation; that I am the lawful ~~wife~~ husband of Josie A. Morton, who is a citizen, ~~by~~ *(blank)* of the United States Nation; that a male child was born to ~~me~~ us on 30th day of July, 1901, that said child has been named Claude S. Morton, and was living March 4, 1905.

Mossie Morton

Witnesses To Mark:
{ WH Dill   Okemah I.T.
{ Geo. A. Harvison

Subscribed and sworn to before me this 5 day of August, 1905.

Creed T. Huddleston
My com. expires March 12-1909   Notary Public.

BIRTH AFFIDAVIT.

DEPARTMENT OF THE INTERIOR.
COMMISSION TO THE FIVE CIVILIZED TRIBES.

IN RE APPLICATION FOR ENROLLMENT, as a citizen of the Creek Nation, of Claude S. Morton, born on the 30 day of July, 1901

Name of Father: Mossie Morton   a citizen of the Creek Nation.
Name of Mother: Josie A. Morton   a citizen of the United StatesNation.

Postoffice   Okemah, I.T.

Applications for Enrollment of Creek Newborn
Act of 1905   Volume V

AFFIDAVIT OF MOTHER.

UNITED STATES OF AMERICA, Indian Territory, }
   Western   DISTRICT.

   I, Josie A. Morton , on oath state that I am 22 years of age and a citizen ~~by (blank)~~ , of the United States ~~Nation~~; that I am the lawful wife of Mossie Morton, who is a citizen, by blood of the Creek Nation; that a male child was born to me on the 30 day of July , 1901, that said child has been named Claude S. Morton , and is now living.

                                        Josie A Morton
Witnesses To Mark:
{

   Subscribed and sworn to before me this 8" day of March , 1905.

         (Seal)   Drennan C Skaggs
                                        Notary Public.

AFFIDAVIT OF ATTENDING PHYSICIAN OR MID-WIFE.

UNITED STATES OF AMERICA, Indian Territory, }
   Western   DISTRICT.

   I, W. M. Cott , a Physician , on oath state that I attended on Mrs. Josie A Morton , wife of Mossie Morton on the 30" day of July , 1901 ; that there was born to her on said date a male child; that said child is now living and is said to have been named Claude S. Morton

                                        W M Cott M.D.
Witnesses To Mark:
{

   Subscribed and sworn to before me this 13th day of March, 1905.

   My Com ex Apr. 24, 1907   E.T. Noble
                                        Notary Public.

BIRTH AFFIDAVIT.
DEPARTMENT OF THE INTERIOR.
COMMISSION TO THE FIVE CIVILIZED TRIBES.

   IN RE APPLICATION FOR ENROLLMENT, as a citizen of the Creek Nation, of Maude Morton , born on the 16 day of January , 1903

Applications for Enrollment of Creek Newborn
Act of 1905   Volume V

Name of Father: Mossie Morton   a citizen of the   Creek   Nation.
Name of Mother: Josie A. Morton   a citizen of the United StatesNation.

Postoffice   Okemah, I.T.

AFFIDAVIT OF MOTHER.

UNITED STATES OF AMERICA, Indian Territory, }
Western   DISTRICT.

I, Josie A. Morton, on oath state that I am 22 years of age and a citizen ~~by (blank)~~, of the United States Nation; that I am the lawful wife of Mossie Morton, who is a citizen, by blood of the Creek Nation; that a female child was born to me on the the 16" day of January, 1903, that said child has been named Maude Morton, and is now living.

Josie A Morton

Witnesses To Mark:
{

Subscribed and sworn to before me this 8" day of March, 1905.

(Seal)   Drennan C Skaggs
             Notary Public.

AFFIDAVIT OF ATTENDING PHYSICIAN OR MID-WIFE.

UNITED STATES OF AMERICA, Indian Territory, }
Western   DISTRICT.

I, Robert Allan, a Physician, on oath state that I attended on Mrs. Josie A Morton, wife of Mossie Morton on the 16" day of January, 1903 ; that there was born to her on said date a female child; that said child is now living and is said to have been named Maude Morton

Robert Allan

Witnesses To Mark:
{

Subscribed and sworn to before me this 8" day of March, 1905.

(Seal)   Drennan C Skaggs
             Notary Public.

(Note: Written along the border of the above Birth Affidavit was:
See D.A. - Died Jan 16. 1903 - Gr.)

Applications for Enrollment of Creek Newborn
Act of 1905 Volume V

DEPARTMENT OF THE INTERIOR.
COMMISSION TO THE FIVE CIVILIZED TRIBES.

In the matter of the death of Maude Morton a citizen of the Creek Nation, who formerly resided at or near Okemah , Ind. Ter., and died on the 16" day of January , 1903.

AFFIDAVIT OF RELATIVE.

UNITED STATES OF AMERICA, Indian Territory,
Western DISTRICT.

I, Mossie Morton , on oath state that I am 32 years of age and a citizen by blood , of the Creek Nation; that my postoffice address is Okemah , Ind. Ter.; that I am the father of Maude Morton who was a citizen, by blood , of the Creek Nation and that said Maude Morton died on the 16" day of January , 1903.

Mossie Morton

Witnesses To Mark:

Subscribed and sworn to before me this 8" day of March , 1905.

Seal

Drennan C Skaggs
Notary Public.

AFFIDAVIT OF ACQUAINTANCE.

UNITED STATES OF AMERICA, Indian Territory,
Western DISTRICT.

I, Robert Allan , on oath state that I am 28 years of age, and a citizen ~~by~~ ~~(blank)~~ of the United States ~~Nation~~; that my postoffice address is Okemah , Ind. Ter.; that I was personally acquainted with Maude Morton and was the attending physician at her death who was a citizen, by blood , of the Creek Nation; and that said Maude Morton died on the 16" day of January , 1903.

Robert Allan

Witnesses To Mark:

Subscribed and sworn to before me this 8" day of March , 1905.

Seal

Applications for Enrollment of Creek Newborn
Act of 1905   Volume V

Drennan C Skaggs
Notary Public.

NC 390   JLD

DEPARTMENT OF THE INTERIOR,
COMMISSIONER TO THE FIVE CIVILIZED TRIBES.

In the matter of the application for the enrollment of Maude Morton, deceased, as a citizen by blood of the Creek Nation.

STATEMENT AND ORDER.

The record in this case shows that on April 11, 1905, application was made, in affidavit form, for the enrollment of Maude Morton, deceased, as a citizen by blood of the Creek Nation, under the provisions of the act of Congress approved March 3, 1905.

It appears that the affidavit filed in this matter that said Maude Morton, deceased, was born January 16, 1903, and died January 16, 1903.

The act of Congress approved March 3, 1905, (33 Stats., 1048), provides:

"That the Commission to the Five Civilized Tribes is authorized for sixty days after the date of the approval of this act to receive and consider applications for enrollment, of children, born subsequent to May twenty-fifth, nineteen hundred and one, and prior to March fourth, nineteen hundred and five, and living on said latter date, to citizens of the Creek tribe of Indians whose enrollment has been approved by the Secretary of the Interior prior to the approval of this act; and to enroll and make allotments to such children."

It is, therefore, ordered that the application for the enrollment of Maude Morton, deceased, as a citizen by blood of the Creek Nation be, and the same is, hereby dismissed.

Tams Bixby Commissioner.

Muskogee, Indian Territory.
JAN 4 – 1907

Applications for Enrollment of Creek Newborn
Act of 1905 Volume V

NC 391.

Muskogee, Indian Territory, June 3, 1905.

Annie Roberson,
    Henryetta, Indian Territory.

Dear Madam:

    There is on file with the Commission an affidavit executed by the midwife in attendance at the birth of your minor child, Bertha Roberson; the date of the birth of said child is not given. You are advised if it is impossible to secure the affidavit of the midwife or physician in attendance at the birth of said child, the affidavits of two disinterested witnesses should be supplied.

    There are herewith enclosed two blank forms of birth affidavit. In having same executed, care should be taken to see that all blanks are properly filled, all names written in full, and in the event that the person signing the affidavit is unable to write, signatures by mark must be attested by two witnesses. Each affidavit must be executed before a Notary Public and the notarial seal and signature of the officer must be attached to each separate affidavit.

                Respectfully,

2 BA   Commissioner in Charge.

NC-391.

Muskogee, Indian Territory, August 2, 1905.

Annie Robinson[sic],
    Henryetta, Indian Territory.

Dear Madam:

    In the matter of the application for the enrollment of your minor children Nelson Robinson and Louisa Robinson, as citizens by blood of the Creek Nation, it will be necessary for you to furnish this office with properly verified affidavits as to the birth of said children and two blanks for proof of birth, which have been filled out, are inclosed[sic] herewith.

    You are requested to have the same properly executed before a notary public and return to this office in the inclosed[sic] envelope. In case any signature is by mark the same must be attested by two disinterested witnesses. Be careful to see that the notary public, before whom the affidavits are sworn to, attaches his name and seal to each affidavit.

Applications for Enrollment of Creek Newborn
Act of 1905 Volume V

Respectfully,

CTD-16
Env.

Commissioner.

BIRTH AFFIDAVIT.

DEPARTMENT OF THE INTERIOR.
COMMISSION TO THE FIVE CIVILIZED TRIBES.

IN RE APPLICATION FOR ENROLLMENT, as a citizen of the Creek Nation, of Louisa Roberson, born on the 27 day of March, 1904

Name of Father: Dave Roberson   a citizen of the   Creek   Nation.
Name of Mother: Annie Roberson   a citizen of the   Creek   Nation.

Postoffice   Henryetta, Ind. Ter.

AFFIDAVIT OF MOTHER.

UNITED STATES OF AMERICA, Indian Territory, }
    Western   DISTRICT.

I, Annie Roberson, on oath state that I am about 28 years of age and a citizen by blood, of the Creek Nation; that I am the lawful wife of Dave Roberson, who is a citizen, by adoption of the Creek Nation; that a female child was born to me on 27 day of March, 1904, that said child has been named Louisa Roberson, and was living March 4, 1905.

                                    her
                          Annie x Roberson
Witnesses To Mark: mark
  { Alex Posey
  { DC Skaggs

Subscribed and sworn to before me this 20 day of March, 1905.

Drennan C Skaggs
Notary Public.

AFFIDAVIT OF ATTENDING PHYSICIAN OR MID-WIFE.

UNITED STATES OF AMERICA, Indian Territory, }
    Western   DISTRICT.

I, Hannah Roberson, a midwife, on oath state that I attended on Mrs. Annie Roberson, wife of Dave Roberson ~~on the day of~~ March, 1904; that there was born

Applications for Enrollment of Creek Newborn
Act of 1905   Volume V

to her on said date a *(blank)* child; that said child was living March 4, 1905, and is said to have been named   Louisa Roberson

Witnesses To Mark:
{ Alex Posey
  DC Skaggs

Hannah x Roberson
her   mark

Subscribed and sworn to before me this 20 day of March , 1905.

Drennan C Skaggs
Notary Public.

BIRTH AFFIDAVIT.

DEPARTMENT OF THE INTERIOR.
COMMISSION TO THE FIVE CIVILIZED TRIBES.

IN RE APPLICATION FOR ENROLLMENT, as a citizen of the Creek Nation, of Louisa Robinson , born on the 27th day of March , 1904

Name of Father: Dave Robinson   a citizen of the   Creek   Nation.
Name of Mother: Annie Robinson   a citizen of the   Creek   Nation.

Postoffice   Henryetta, I.T.

AFFIDAVIT OF MOTHER.

UNITED STATES OF AMERICA, Indian Territory,
     Western   DISTRICT.

I, Annie Robinson , on oath state that I am about 38[sic] years of age and a citizen by blood , of the Creek   Nation; that I am the lawful wife of Dave Robinson , who is a citizen, by adoption of the Creek   Nation; that a female   child was born to me on 27th day of March , 1904 , that said child has been named   Louisa Robinson , and was living March 4, 1905.

Annie Robinson x
her   mark

Witnesses To Mark:
{ T. A. Medlen
  M. F. Graham

Subscribed and sworn to before me this 25th day of August , 1905.

M. F. Graham
Notary Public.

Commission Ex Oct 9-1907

Applications for Enrollment of Creek Newborn
Act of 1905   Volume V

AFFIDAVIT OF ATTENDING PHYSICIAN OR MID-WIFE.

UNITED STATES OF AMERICA, Indian Territory,
  Western   DISTRICT.

I, Hannah Robinson, a mid-wife, on oath state that I attended on Mrs. Annie Robinson, wife of Dave Robinson on the 27th day of March, 1904; that there was born to her on said date a female child; that said child was living March 4, 1905, and is said to have been named Louisa Robinson

Han nah Robison[sic]

Witnesses To Mark:

Subscribed and sworn to before me this 29 day of Aug, 1905.

My Com expires Aug 30 1906

Olin W Meacham
Notary Public.

BIRTH AFFIDAVIT.

DEPARTMENT OF THE INTERIOR.
COMMISSION TO THE FIVE CIVILIZED TRIBES.

IN RE APPLICATION FOR ENROLLMENT, as a citizen of the Creek Nation, of Nelson Roberson, born on the 23 day of February, 1902

Name of Father: Dave Roberson   a citizen of the   Creek   Nation.
Name of Mother: Annie Roberson   a citizen of the   Creek   Nation.

Postoffice   Henryetta, Ind. Ter.

AFFIDAVIT OF MOTHER.

UNITED STATES OF AMERICA, Indian Territory,
  Western   DISTRICT.

I, Annie Roberson, on oath state that I am about 28 years of age and a citizen by blood, of the Creek Nation; that I am the lawful wife of Dave Roberson, who is a citizen, by adoption of the Creek Nation; that a male child was born to me on 23 day of February, 1902, that said child has been named Nelson Roberson, and was living March 4, 1905.

her
Annie x Roberson
mark

Witnesses To Mark:
  Alex Posey
  DC Skaggs

Applications for Enrollment of Creek Newborn
Act of 1905 Volume V

Subscribed and sworn to before me this 20 day of March, 1905.

                                        Drennan C Skaggs
                                        Notary Public.

AFFIDAVIT OF ATTENDING PHYSICIAN OR MID-WIFE.

UNITED STATES OF AMERICA, Indian Territory,
    Western   DISTRICT.

I, Hannah Roberson, a midwife, on oath state that I attended on Mrs. Annie Roberson, wife of Dave Roberson ~~on the (blank) day of (blank), 1~~; that there was born to her on said date a male child; that said child was living March 4, 1905, and is said to have been named Nelson Roberson

                                        her
                            Hannah x Roberson
Witnesses To Mark: mark
  { Alex Posey
    DC Skaggs

Subscribed and sworn to before me this 22 day of March, 1905.

                                        Drennan C Skaggs
                                        Notary Public.

BIRTH AFFIDAVIT.

DEPARTMENT OF THE INTERIOR.
COMMISSION TO THE FIVE CIVILIZED TRIBES.

IN RE APPLICATION FOR ENROLLMENT, as a citizen of the Creek Nation, of Nelson Robinson, born on the 23rd day of February, 1902

Name of Father:	Dave Robinson	a citizen of the	Creek	Nation.
Name of Mother:	Annie Robinson	a citizen of the	Creek	Nation.

                            Postoffice   Henryetta, Ind. Ter.

AFFIDAVIT OF MOTHER.

UNITED STATES OF AMERICA, Indian Territory,
    Western   DISTRICT.

I, Annie Robinson, on oath state that I am about 28 years of age and a citizen by blood, of the Creek Nation; that I am the lawful wife of Dave Robinson, who is a citizen, by adoption of the Creek Nation; that a male child was born to me on 23rd

Applications for Enrollment of Creek Newborn
Act of 1905   Volume V

day of February, 1902, that said child has been named Nelson Robinson, and was living March 4, 1905.

Witnesses To Mark:
{ T. A. Medlen
{ M. F. Graham

                 her
            Annie Robinson x
                  mark

  Subscribed and sworn to before me this 25th day of August, 1905.

                M. F. Graham
                  Notary Public.
      Commission Expires Oct 9-1907

AFFIDAVIT OF ATTENDING PHYSICIAN OR MID-WIFE.

UNITED STATES OF AMERICA, Indian Territory, }
  Western   DISTRICT.   }

  I, Hannah Robinson, a mid-wife, on oath state that I attended on Mrs. Annie Robinson, wife of Dave Robinson on the 23rd day of February, 1902: that there was born to her on said date a male child; that said child was living March 4, 1905, and is said to have been named Nelson Robinson

                 Han nah Robison[sic]

Witnesses To Mark:
{
{ Subscribed and sworn to before me this 29 day of Aug, 1905.

              Olin W Meacham
  My Com expires Aug 30 1906   Notary Public.

        Department of the Interior,

      Commission to the Five Civilized Tribes.

         -----oOo-----

  In re Application for Enrollment, as a citizen of the Creek Nation of Cora Harris, born on the 2nd day of March, 1904. Name of Father, Charley Harris a citizen of the United States Nation. Name of Mother, Polly Barnett (Harris) a citizen of the Creek Nation.

        Post office Weleetka, Ind. Ter.

Applications for Enrollment of Creek Newborn
Act of 1905 Volume V

Affidavit of Mother.

United States of America,   )
Western District of the Indian Territory,) SS.

    I, Polly Harris (nee Barnett), on my oath state that I am 24 years of age and a citizen by Birth of the Muskogee (Creek) Nation; that I am the lawful wife of Charley Harris, who is a citizen by Birth of the United States of America Nation; that a female child was born to me on March[sic] 2nd day of March 2nd[sic], 1904; that said child was named Cora Harris, and was living on March 4, 1905.

                                        Polly Harris

Witness to Mark:

Subscribed and sworn to before me this 21" day of March, 1905.

MY COMMISSION EXPIRES FEBY. 29, 1906.   John B Patterson
                                                      Notary Public.

Affidavit of attending Physician or Midwife.

United States of America,   )
Western District of the Indian Territory,) SS.

    I, Elizabeth Barnett a Midwife on my oath state that I attended on Mrs. Polly Harris (nee Barnett) wife of Charley Harris on the 2nd day of March 1904, that there was born to her on said date a Female child; that said child was living on March 4, 1905, and is said to have been named Cora Harris.
                                                      her
                                    Elizabeth x Barnett
                                           mark

Witness [sic] Mark   Scipio Barnett
                              Charley Harris
                              Rachell Barnett

Subscribed and sworn to before me this 21st day of March, 1905.

        MY COMMISSION EXPIRES FEBY. 29, 1906.   John B Patterson
                                                          Notary Public.

Applications for Enrollment of Creek Newborn
Act of 1905   Volume V

N.C. 393

Muskogee, Indian Territory, August 3, 1905.

Mina Scott,
    Care Sandy Watson,
        Weleetka, Indian Territory.

Dear Madam:

    March 24, 1905 there was filed at this office an affidavit executed by you relative to the birth of your child, Dave Watson, a citizen by blood of the Creek Nation. You state that the father of said child is Sandy Watson.

    This office cannot identify you on its rolls of citizens of the Creek Nation and you are requested to state your maiden name, the names of your parents, the Creek Indian town to which you belong and if possible the numbers which appear on your deeds to land in the Creek Nation.

    This matter should receive your prompt attention.

        Respectfully,

                Commissioner.

DEPARTMENT OF THE INTERIOR,
COMMISSIONER TO THE FIVE CIVILIZED TRIBES.
Muskogee, Indian Territory, December 13, 1905.

    In the matter of the application for the enrollment of Dave Watson as a Creek citizen.

    Lambert Scott, being duly sworn, testified as follows through Jesse McDermott official interpreter.

Q What is your name? A Lambert Scott.
Q What is your age? A I am over 70 years old.
Q What is your post office address? A Weleetka.
Q Are you a citizen of the Creek Nation? A Yes, sir
Q Do you know a minor child name Dave Watson? A The mother of the child lives at my house.
Q Is it your grand-child? A Yes, sir.
Q What is the name of the mother of the child? A Mina.
Q What as the name of Mina's mother? A Wicey Scott.
Q Was Mina ever married? A She was once married to a man named William Larney
Q So your name was Mina Larney once was it? A Yes, sir

Applications for Enrollment of Creek Newborn
Act of 1905   Volume V

Q   Do you know how to spell that first name, Mina? A   No, sir
Q   Do you think it could be Maner? A   Possibly her name was interpreted that way when she was enrolled. I am not positive but I think she was arbitrarily allotted.
Q   Do you know if this William Larney was ever known by any other name? A   Sometimes they called him in the neighborhood Billy Larney, since they parted he has married another woman.
Q   Mina, your daughter, wasn't married to Sandy Watson when Dave was born was she? A   They lived together about a year before they child was born and since then he hardly ever comes around any more. They were not married according to the United States laws.

   I, Anna Garrigues, on oath state that the above and foregoing is a true and correct copy of my stenographic notes taken in said case on said date.

                              Anna Garrigues
Subscribed and sworn to before me this
16 day of December 1905.

                              J. McDermott
                                 Notary Public.

DEPARTMENT OF THE INTERIOR,
COMMISSIONER TO THE FIVE CIVILIZED TRIBES.
Dustin, I.T., May 16, 1906.

   In the matter of the application for the enrollment of David Watson as a citizen by blood of the Creek Nation.

           MINNIE LARNEY, being duly sworn, testified as follows:

   Through Alex Posey official interpreter:

BY THE COMMISSIONER:
Q   What is your name? A   Minnie Larney.
Q   How old are you? A   About 28.
Q   What is your post office address? A   Weleetka.
Q   Are you a citizen of the Creek Nation? A   Yes, sir.
Q   To what town do you belong? A   Artusse.
Q   Have you a child you desire to make application for? A   Yes, sir.
Q   What is the child's name? A   David Watson.
Q   Is the child living? A   Yes, sir.
Q   When was the child born? A   February 4, 1905.
Q   Have you heretofore mae application for the enrollment of your minor child, you are advised that the Commission requires further evidence as to the birth of said child. of this child? A   I had a white man at Weleetka to make out some papers for me about the child. I do not know whether the Commission ever received the papers or not--I never heard and do not think my child is enrolled.

Applications for Enrollment of Creek Newborn
Act of 1905   Volume V

Q Who is the father of the child? A Sandy Watson.
Q Is he your lawful husband? A No, sir, I was never married to him.
Q This then is an illegitimate child? A Yes, sir.
Q Is Sandy Watson a citizen of the Creek Nation? A Yes, sir.
Q To what town does he belong? A Okchiye.
Q Does he recognize the child as his own? A I learn that he dis-claims the child but he does not dis-claim the child to me.

---oooOOOooo---

I, D. C. Skaggs, on oath state that the above and foregoing is a full and true transcript of my stenographic notes as taken in said cause on said date.

DC Skaggs

Subscribed and sworn to before me this 16th day of May, 1906.

Alex Posey
Notary Public.

DEPARTMENT OF THE INTERIOR,
COMMISSIONER TO THE FIVE CIVILIZED TRIBES.
Wetumka, Indian Territory.
July 18, 1906.

In the matter of the application for the enrollment , [sic] as citizens of the Creek Nation, of minor children born to duly enrolled citizens members of the so called Snake faction.

D.W. Fields, being duly sworn, testified as follows:
Through Official Interpreter, Alex Posey.

Q What is your name? A DW. Fields.
Q What is your age? A Twenty-seven.
Q What is your post office address? A Henryetta.
Q Are you a citizen of the Creek Nation? A Yes sir.
Q To what Creek Indian town do you belong? A Huthechuppa.
Q Do you know of any minor children in your town or neighborhood for whose enrollment application has not been made? A Billy West and Louisa his wife, have a child, a girl but I don't know its name.
Q Is the child living? A Yes sir.
Q To what Creek Indian town do the parents belong? A Billy West belongs to Kialigee and Louisa to Thlopthlocco.
Q What is the post office address of the parents? A Weleetka.
(Note: Notation on the page indicates the number 434 for this party)

Applications for Enrollment of Creek Newborn
Act of 1905 Volume V

Sun Thloppa an old woman living at Hutchechuppa has an illegitimate child of Joe Brown and Betsey Barnett; the child is two years old and is a girl. I don't know its name.
Q What is the post office address of the parents? A Dustin.
Q To what Creek Indian towns do they belong? A Joe Brown belongs to Okchiye and Betsey Barnett belongs to Hutchechuppa.

Little Tommy Johnson of Nuyaka and his wife Arlie Johnson, also of Nuyaka, have a girl about two years old but I don't know its name.
Q What is the post office address of the parents? A Henryetta.
Q Is little Tommy Johnson known by any other name? A That is the only name by which I know him.
Little Tommy Johnson is identified opposite Creek Indian Roll No. 5372 as Little Tom Johnson and Arlie Johnson is identified opposite No. 5373 as Ellie Johnson.
Q Is the child living? A Yes sir.
(Note: Notation on the page indicates the number 435 for this party)

Nannie Scott of Artussee has a child, a boy, about a year and a half old; I don't know its name. The father is said to be Sandy Watson of Okchiye. The child is living.
Q What is the post office address of the parents? A Weleetka.
(Note: Notation for this party is NB (Mar. 3.05) Card #393)

McDaniel Watson of Hutchechuppa and Louisa Watson his wife have a boy child about a year and a half old. I don't know the child's name or the town of its mother. The post office address of the parents is Dustin. The mother's maiden name was Louisa Bird.
Q Is the child living? A Yes sir.

Sandy Wildcat and Losanna Wildcat, both of Thlewarthle town, have a child between two and three years old. It is a boy. I don't know its name. The post office address of the parents is Bryant.

Sandy and Losanna Wildcat are identified opposite Creek Indian roll Nos. 5072 and 5073.

Cotchoche and is wife Lucinda have four children. I don't think any of them are enrolled as the father is a strong snake sympathizer and much opposed to the work of the Dawes Commission among the Indians. I don't know the names of any of the children or what their ages are. I three[sic] three[sic] girls and one a boy. Cotchoche belongs to Thlewathle town but I don't know to what town his wife belongs. Lucinda is probably enrolled as Lucinda Mitchell as that was her maiden name. The post office of the parents is Henryetta.
Q Are all these children living? A Yes sir.

Lumsey West of Kialigee town and Emma West of the same town have three children; one boy and two girls that are probably not enrolled but I don't know the

Applications for Enrollment of Creek Newborn
Act of 1905   Volume V

children's names or ages. The post office address of the parents is Bryant. The children are all living.

        Lumsey West is identified opposite Creek Indian roll No. 4944.

        Sam Lowe of Cussehta has one child. I think it is a boy. I don't know the name of the mother nor to what town she belongs.

Q What is the post office address of the parents? A Schulter.
Q What is the post office address of the parents? A Schulter.[sic]
Q Is the child living? A Yes sir.

        Sam Lowe is identified opposite No. 8343 as Samuel Lowe.

Q You don't think that application has been made for the enrollment of any of the above children about whom you have given information? A No sir, because their parents all belong to the Snake faction.

        I, Alex Posey, on oath state that the above and foregoing is a true and correct transcript of my notes as taken in said cause on said date.

SEAL   (Signed) Alex Posey
Subscribed and sworn to before me this 1 day of August, 1906.

                        (Signed) Edward Merrick,
                                  Notary Public.

        Lona Merrick, being duly sworn, states that she copied the above and foregoing and that the same is a correct copy of the original testimony.

                                  Lona Merrick

Subscribed and sworn to before me this 6th day of August, 1906.

                                  Edward Merrick
                                  Notary Public.

AFFIDAVIT OF DISINTERESTED WITNESSES.

United States of America,
      Western District,
      Indian Territory.

        We, the undersigned, on oath state that we are personally acquainted with Minnie Larney not the wife of Sandy Watson; that there was born to her a male child on or about 4 day of February, 1905; that the said child has been named David Watson and was living March 4, 1905.

        We further state that we have no interest in this case.

Applications for Enrollment of Creek Newborn
Act of 1905 Volume V

his
John x Chupco
mark
his
Johnson x Barnett
mark

Subscribed and sworn to before me this 16 day of May 1906.

Witness   Alex Posey
                                                        Notary Public.
        Alex Posey
        D C Skaggs

Department of the Interior,

Commission to the Five Civilized Tribes.

-----oOo-----

In re Application for Enrollment, as a citizen of the Creek Nation of Dave Watson, born on the 4th day of February, 1905, Name of Father, Sandy Watson a citizen of the Creek Nation, Name of Mother, Mina Scott a citizen of the *(blank)* Nation.

Post office Weleetka, Ind. Ter.

Affidavit of Mother.

United States of America,   )
Western District of the Indian Territory ,) SS.

    I, Mina Scott , on my oath state that I am 27 years of age and a citizen by Birth of the Muskogee (Creek) Nation; that I am the ~~lawful~~ Creek wife of Sandy Watson, who is a citizen by Birth of the Muskogee (Creek) Nation and am the daughter of Lambert Scott a Creek citizen by Birth; that a male child was born to me on 4th day of February , 1905; that said child was named Dave Watson, and was living on March 4, 1905.

her
Mina x Scott
mark

Witness to Mark:
        T.W. Blackman   Subscribed and sworn to before
        E W James   me this 21" day of March, 1905.

MY COMMISSION EXPIRES FEBY. 29, 1906.   John B Patterson
                                                              Notary Public.

Applications for Enrollment of Creek Newborn
Act of 1905   Volume V

Affidavit of attending Physician or Midwife.

United States of America.   )
Western District of the Indian Territory .) SS.

  I, Phoeba Barnett a Midwife on my oath state that I attended on Mrs. Mina Scott Creek wife of Sandy Watson on the 4th day of February 1905, that there was born to her on said date a male child; that said child was living on March 4, 1905, and is said to have been named Dave Watson

            Phoeba Barnett
            Midwife

Witness Mark
  T.W. Blackman
  E.W. James

Subscribed and sworn to before me this 21 day of March, 1905.

  MY COMMISSION EXPIRES FEBY. 29, 1906. John B Patterson
                Notary Public.

BIRTH AFFIDAVIT.

DEPARTMENT OF THE INTERIOR,
COMMISSIONER TO THE FIVE CIVILIZED TRIBES.

ENROLLMENT OF MINORS.   ACT OF CONGRESS, APPROVED APRIL 26, 1906.

  IN RE APPLICATION FOR ENROLLMENT, as a citizen of the Creek Nation, of David Watson , born on the 4   day of February , 1905

Name of Father: Santy[sic] Watson (Roll No 7659) a citizen of the   Creek   Nation.
Name of Mother: Minnie Larney (Roll No 75)   a citizen of the   Creek   Nation.

Tribal enrollment of father   Okchiye   Tribal enrollment of mother   Artussee

         Postoffice   Weleetka Indian Territory

AFFIDAVIT OF MOTHER.

UNITED STATES OF AMERICA, Indian Territory, }   child present
 Western   District.

  I, Minnie Larney , on oath state that I am about 28   years of age and a citizen by blood , of the Creek Nation; that I am not the lawful wife of Santy Watson , who is a citizen, by blood of the Creek Nation; that a male   child was born to me on   4   day

Applications for Enrollment of Creek Newborn
Act of 1905 Volume V

of February , 1905 , that said child has been named David Watson , and was living March 4, 1906.

WITNESSES TO MARK:
{ Alex Posey
DC Skaggs

her
Minnie x Larney
mark

Subscribed and sworn to before me this 16 day of May , 1906.

Alex Posey
Notary Public.

BIRTH AFFIDAVIT.

DEPARTMENT OF THE INTERIOR.
COMMISSION TO THE FIVE CIVILIZED TRIBES.

IN RE APPLICATION FOR ENROLLMENT, as a citizen of the CREEK Nation, of Flossie McNac , born on the 23^d day of August , 1902

Name of Father: Fred McNac   a citizen of the   Creek   Nation.
Name of Mother: Annie McNac nee Greenleaf   a citizen of the   Creek   Nation.
                          Postoffice   *(Illegible)* Hill, Indian Ter.

AFFIDAVIT OF MOTHER.

UNITED STATES OF AMERICA, Indian Territory,
WESTERN   DISTRICT.

I, Annie McNac nee Greenleaf , on oath state that I am twenty five years of age and a citizen by blood , of the Creek Nation; that I am the Common Law lawful wife of Fred McNac , who is a citizen, by blood of the Creek Nation; that a female child was born to me on 23^d day of August , 1902 , that said child has been named Flossie McNac , and is now living.

Annie McNac (nee Greenleaf)

Witnesses To Mark:
{

Subscribed and sworn to before me this 20th day of March , 1905.

My Commission Expires July 1, 1906.   JB Morrow
Notary Public.

Applications for Enrollment of Creek Newborn
Act of 1905 Volume V

AFFIDAVIT OF ATTENDING PHYSICIAN OR MID-WIFE.

UNITED STATES OF AMERICA, Indian Territory,
    WESTERN DISTRICT.

I, Sarah Greenleaf, a mid wife, on oath state that I attended on Mrs. Annie McNac, nee Greenleaf, wife of Fred McNac on the 23^d day of August, 1902; that there was born to her on said date a female child; that said child is now living and is said to have been named Flossie McNac

                                          her
                                Sarah x Greenleaf
Witnesses To Mark: mark
    JB Morrow Checotah I.T.
    (Name Illegible)   "   "

Subscribed and sworn to before me this 20th day of March, 1905.

My Commission Expires July 1, 1906.   JB Morrow
                                        Notary Public.

                                    Cr BA-1080-B

                    Muskogee, Indian Territory, May 31, 1905.

Alex Posey,
    Dustin, Indian Territory.

Dear Sir:

    There is herewith enclosed birth affidavit in the matter of the application for the enrollment of William H. Wills as a citizen of the Creek Nation. D. C. Skaggs is the only person who signed as witness to the mark of Amelia Hutton, the midwife in the case, and the year has been omitted in the affidavit of said midwife.

    If you witnessed the signature of the said, you are requested to put your name as witness to her affidavit, and to also see that the year is inserted in same.

                                Respectfully,

                                        Chairman.

JYM-31-1

Applications for Enrollment of Creek Newborn
Act of 1905 Volume V

BIRTH AFFIDAVIT.

DEPARTMENT OF THE INTERIOR.
COMMISSION TO THE FIVE CIVILIZED TRIBES.

IN RE APPLICATION FOR ENROLLMENT, as a citizen of the Creek Nation, of William H. Wills, born on the 11 day of July, 1901

Name of Father: John J. Wills   a citizen of the Creek Nation.
Name of Mother: Ollie Ann Wills   a citizen of the United States Nation.

Postoffice   Dustin, I.T.

AFFIDAVIT OF MOTHER.

UNITED STATES OF AMERICA, Indian Territory,
 Western   DISTRICT.

I, Ollie Ann Wills, on oath state that I am 33 years of age and a citizen by *(blank)*, of the United States ~~Nation~~; that I am the lawful wife of John J. Wills, who is a citizen, by blood of the Creek Nation; that a male child was born to me on 11 day of July, 1901, that said child has been named William H. Wills, and was living March 4, 1905.

Ollie Ann Wills

Witnesses To Mark:
{

Subscribed and sworn to before me this 22 day of March, 1905.

Drennan C Skaggs
Notary Public.

AFFIDAVIT OF ATTENDING PHYSICIAN OR MID-WIFE.

UNITED STATES OF AMERICA, Indian Territory,
 Western   DISTRICT.

I, Amelia Hutton, a mid - wife, on oath state that I attended on Mrs. Ollie Ann Wills, wife of John J. Wills on or about the 11 day of July, 1901; that there was born to her on said date a male child; that said child was living March 4, 1905, and is said to have been named William H. Wills

 her
Amelia x Hutton
 mark

Witnesses To Mark:
{ DC Skaggs
  Alex Posey

Applications for Enrollment of Creek Newborn
Act of 1905   Volume V

Subscribed and sworn to before me this 22 day of March . 1905.

                                                 Drennan C Skaggs
                                                        Notary Public.

(The above Birth Affidavit given again, minus Alex Posey's signature and the year the child was born)

NC-396

                                         Muskogee, Indian Territory, August 2, 1905.

Robert Bruner,
        Carson, Indian Territory.

Dear Sir:

        On March 22, 1905 you appeared before the Commission to the Five Civilized Tribes and made application for the enrollment of Lillie Washington, born June 13, 1902, as a citizen by blood of the Creek Nation and at that time submitted your affidavit relative to the birth of said child on said date. You stated that her father's name was Colbert Washington and that her mother's name was Polly Washington, deceased.

        This office has been unable to identify the said Polly Washington upon the final roll of citizens by blood of the Creek Nation and you are, therefore, requested to state the name under which she was enrolled, the names of her parents and other members of her family, the Creek town to which she belonged and if possible to give her final roll number as the same appears upon her allotment certificate and deed.

        In the matter of the application for the enrollment of said child it will also be necessary that this office be supplied with the affidavit of Colbert Washington, the father of said child, relative to her birth and the affidavit of the attending physician or midwife and a blank for that purpose is inclosed[sic] herewith.

        In having the same executed be careful to see that all blank spaces are properly filled, all names written in full and that the notary public before whom the affidavits are acknowledged, attaches his name and seal to each affidavit. In case any signature is by mark it must be attested by two disinterested witnesses.

        If there was no attending physician or midwife when said child was born you should furnish in lieu of the affidavit of said attending physician or midwife the affidavit of some disinterested person who is acquainted with said child, knows when she was born, the names of her parents and whether or not she was living on March 4, 1905.

Applications for Enrollment of Creek Newborn
Act of 1905   Volume V

This matter should have prompt attention.

Respectfully,

Commissioner.

B-C
ENV.

BIRTH AFFIDAVIT.

DEPARTMENT OF THE INTERIOR.
COMMISSION TO THE FIVE CIVILIZED TRIBES.

IN RE APPLICATION FOR ENROLLMENT, as a citizen of the Creek Nation, of Lillie Washington, born on the 13 day of June, 1902

Name of Father: Colbert Washington   a citizen of the   Creek   Nation.
Name of Mother: Polly Jones (nee Washington)   a citizen of the   Creek   Nation.

Postoffice   Carson I.T.

AFFIDAVIT OF ATTENDING PHYSICIAN OR MID-WIFE.

UNITED STATES OF AMERICA, Indian Territory,
     Western   DISTRICT.

I, Sucky Washington, a Midwife, on oath state that I attended on Mrs. Polly Jones (nee Washington), wife of Colbert Washington on the 13 day of June, 1902; that there was born to her on said date a female child; that said child was living March 4, 1905, and is said to have been named Lillie Washington

                     her
               Sucky x Washington
Witnesses To Mark: mark
  { J.H. Alexander
    J.M. Shipp

Subscribed and sworn to before me this 9th day of Sept, 1905.

Com Ex Sept 4-06.   Barney C Robison
                                       Notary Public.

Applications for Enrollment of Creek Newborn
Act of 1905   Volume V

AFFIDAVIT OF ATTENDING PHYSICIAN OR MID-WIFE.

UNITED STATES OF AMERICA, Indian Territory,
Western   DISTRICT.

know
I, Hannah Jones , a Witness , on oath state that I ~~attended on~~ Mrs. Polly Jones (Washington) , wife of Colbert Washington on the 13   day of June , 1902 ; that there was born to her on said date a female child; that said child was living March 4, 1905, and is said to have been named Lillie Washington

            her
           Hannah x Jones
Witnesses To Mark: mark
 { J.H. Alexander
   J.M. Shipp

Subscribed and sworn to before me this 9th day of Sept. 1905.

Com Ex Sept 4-06.   Barney C Robison
            Notary Public.

BIRTH AFFIDAVIT.
DEPARTMENT OF THE INTERIOR.
COMMISSION TO THE FIVE CIVILIZED TRIBES.

IN RE APPLICATION FOR ENROLLMENT, as a citizen of the Creek Nation, of   Lillie Washington, born on the 13 day of June , 1902

Name of Father: Colbert Washington a citizen of the Creek Nation.
Name of Mother: Polly Washington   a citizen of the Creek Nation.

         Postoffice Carson Ind. Ter.

         Town Chief
AFFIDAVIT OF ~~MOTHER~~.

UNITED STATES OF AMERICA, Indian Territory,
Western   DISTRICT.

I, Robert Bruner , on oath state that I am about 40 years of age and a citizen by blood , of the   Creek   Nation; that I am ~~the lawful wife~~ a townsman of   Polly Washington , who ~~is~~ was a citizen, by   blood   of the   Creek   Nation; that a female child was born to ~~me~~ her on 13   day of June , 1902 , that said child has been named Lillie Washington , and was living March 4, 1905.

           Robert Bruner

Applications for Enrollment of Creek Newborn
Act of 1905   Volume V

Witnesses To Mark:
{

Subscribed and sworn to before me this 22 day of March, 1905.

Drennan C Skaggs
Notary Public.

DEPARTMENT OF THE INTERIOR.
COMMISSION TO THE FIVE CIVILIZED TRIBES.

In the matter of the death of Polly Washington a citizen of the Creek Nation, who formerly resided at or near Carson , Ind. Ter., and died ~~on~~ in the fall ~~day~~ of *(blank)* , 1903.

AFFIDAVIT OF ACQUAINTANCE.

UNITED STATES OF AMERICA, Indian Territory,
Western   DISTRICT. }

I, Robert Bruner , on oath state that I am about 40 years of age, and a citizen by blood of the Creek Nation; that my postoffice address is Carson , Ind. Ter.; that I was personally acquainted with Polly Washington who was a citizen, by blood , of the Creek Nation; and that said Polly Washington died ~~on~~ in the ~~day~~ fall of , 1903.

Robert Bruner

Witnesses To Mark:
{

Subscribed and sworn to before me this 22 day of March, 1905.

Drennan C Skaggs
Notary Public.

Applications for Enrollment of Creek Newborn
Act of 1905   Volume V

C
#5- 1024

(Copy)   Cr 2449-B

DEPARTMENT OF THE INTERIOR.
COMMISSION TO THE FIVE CIVILIZED TRIBES.
Near Weleetka, I.T. April 25, 1905.

In the matter of the application for new born children concerning whose enrollment no affidavits could be obtained in time.

James Spaniard, being duly sworn, testified as follows through Alex Posey, Official Interpreter:

Examination by the Commission:
Q What is your name? A James Spaniard.
Q How old are you? A About 42.
Q What is your post office address? A Carson.

Statement: Tommie Lott of Cheyarhar Town and Tena Lott of Tulmochuss Town, have two children both girls, the oldest Lucy and the other Jennie. They are both living. I don't know their ages exactly, but they are new borns. Their post office is Carson.

Ceasar Johnson, of Tookpufka and Eliza Johnson, probably of Eufaula Canadian, have two children. I don't know their names or ages, but they are new borns. Both are living and boys. Their Post office is Carson, and I think the oldest is named Wesley and the youngest Hotulke.

Boley and Kizzie---of Thlewarthle and Tulmochuss respectively I just know they have a child, whose name or sex I am unfamiliar with. Don't know its age. It's a young child something over a year old I think.

Dave Hullie of Tookpufka and Eliza Hullie, deceased, of Kialigee, have a boy about three or under and living, named Tarpie. Their post office is Carson.

Thomas Wilson of Hickory Ground and Bettie Wilson of Tulmochuss have two children both girls. The oldest is named Wisey and the youngest Minnie. Wisey is three or nearly so and Minnie is about two years old. Both living. Post office, Carson.

Timmie Stidham of Cheyarhar, and Liza Stidham of Weogufky, have two children. The oldest a girl named Mattie and the youngest a boy, don't know the name. Both living, the youngest about a year old and the other over two years old. Post office, Carson.

Applications for Enrollment of Creek Newborn
Act of 1905 Volume V

Henry G. Hains, being duly sworn, on his oath, states that the above and foregoing is a true and correct transcript of his stenographic notes as taken in said cause on said date.

(signed) HENRY G. HAINS

Subscribed and sworn to before me this 10th day of May, 1905.

(signed) DRENNAN C SKAGGS.
(SEAL) Notary Public.

INDIAN TERRITORY, Western District.

I, J. Y. Miller, a stenographer in the office of the Commissioner to the Five Civilized Tribes, do hereby certify that the above and foregoing is a true and correct copy of its original, to be found in the records of the aforesaid office.

JY Miller

Sworn to and subscribed before
me this 18th day of July, 1905

Edw C Griesel
Notary Public.

2449 B.
DEPARTMENT OF THE INTERIOR,
COMMISSION TO THE FIVE CIVILIZED TRIBES.
Carson, I.T June 9, 1905

In the matter of the application for the enrollment of Wicey and Minnie Wilson as citizens by blood of the Creek Nation.

Charley Wilson, being duly sworn, testified as follows:

Through Alex Posey Official Interpreter.

By Commission.

Q What is your name? A Charley Wilson.
Q How old are you? A Between 32 and 33 years old.
Q What is your post office address? A Carson.
Q Are you a citizen of the Creek Nation? A Yes, sir.
Q What town do you belong to? A Hickory Ground.
Q Are you acquainted with Thomas and Bettie Wilson? A Yes, sir
Q What relation are they to you? A Thomas is my brother.
Q Do you know their children Wicey and Minnie? A Yes, sir
Q Do you know when Wicey was born? A On or about the 23rd day of March 1902.
Q Were you present when the child was born? A The child was born on the highway between here and Calvin and I was not present.

Applications for Enrollment of Creek Newborn
Act of 1905   Volume V

Q Did you make a record of the birth of the child? A No, sir, but the parents have a record. (The parents were approached this day but refused to give any information in regard to their children.)
Q Was there any one else present? A There was no one present except the father.
Q Do you know when Minnie was born? A On the 7th or 8th of January 1903.
Q Who was present when Minnie was born? A Hannah Jones, I think was present at the birth of the child.
Q Are you positive that Wicey was born on or about the 23rd day of March 1902, and that Minnie was born on the 7th or 8th day of January 1903? A Yes, sir.

I, D.C. Skaggs, on oath state that the above and foregoing is a full and true transcript of my stenographic notes as taken in said cause on said date.

D.C. Skaggs

Subscribed and sworn to before me this 5th day of August 1905.

Edw C Griesel
Notary Public.

DEPARTMENT OF THE INTERIOR,
COMMISSION TO THE FIVE CIVILIZED TRIBES.
Carson, I.T June 9, 1905

In the matter of the application for the enrollment of Wicey and Minnie Wilson as citizens by blood of the Creek Nation.

CHARLEY WILSON, being duly sworn, testified as follows:

Through Alex Posey Official Interpreter.

BY COMMISSION.

Q What is your name? A Charley Wilson.
Q How old are you? A Between 32 and 33.
Q What is your post office address? A Carson.
Q Are you a citizen of the Creek Nation? A Yes, sir.
Q What town do you belong to? A Hickory Ground.
Q Are you acquainted with Thomas and Bettie Wilson? A Yes, sir. Thomas is my brother.
Q Do you know their children, Wicey and Minnie? A Yes, sir
Q Do you know when Wicey was born? A On or about the 23 day of March, 1902.
Q Were you present when the child was born? A The child was born on the highway between here and Calvin, and I was not present.

Applications for Enrollment of Creek Newborn
Act of 1905 Volume V

Q Did you make a record of the birth of the child? A No, sir, but the parents have a record. (the parents of said children were approached and an effort made to secure their testimony, which they refused, being members of the Snake Faction.)
Q Was there any one else present? A There was no one present except the father.
Q Do you know when Minnie was born? A On the 7th or 8th of January, 1903.
Q Who was present when Minnie was born? A Hannah Jones, I think, was present at the birth of the child.
Q Are you positive that Wicey was born on or about the 23rd day of March, 1902, and that Minnie was born on the 7th or 8th dat[sic] of January, 1903? A Yes, sir.

I, D. C. Skaggs, on oath state that the above and foregoing is a full and true transcript of my stenographic notes as taken in said cause on said date.

D.C. Skaggs

Subscribed and sworn to before me this *(blank)* day of JUL 17 1905 1905.

Edw C Griesel
Notary Public.

BIRTH AFFIDAVIT.
DEPARTMENT OF THE INTERIOR.
COMMISSION TO THE FIVE CIVILIZED TRIBES.

IN RE APPLICATION FOR ENROLLMENT, as a citizen of the Creek Nation, of Minnie Wilson, born on the (blank) day of January, 1903

Name of Father:	Thomas Wilson	a citizen of the	Creek	Nation.
Name of Mother:	Bettie Wilson	a citizen of the	Creek	Nation.

Postoffice   Carson, Ind. Ter

Town Chief
AFFIDAVIT OF MOTHER.

UNITED STATES OF AMERICA, Indian Territory, ⎤
    Western   DISTRICT.   ⎦

I, Robert Bruner , on oath state that I am about 40 years of age and a citizen by blood , of the Creek Nation; that I am the lawful wife a townsman of Bettie Wilson , who is a citizen, by blood of the Creek who, with her husband, refuses to make application for the enrollment of your minor child, you are advised that the Commission requires further evidence as to the birth of said child. of their children Nation; that a

Applications for Enrollment of Creek Newborn
Act of 1905   Volume V

female child was born to ~~me~~ her on *(blank)* ~~day of~~ January, 1903, that said child has been named Minnie Wilson, and was living March 4, 1905.

                                                        Robert Bruner

Witnesses To Mark:
{

    Subscribed and sworn to before me this 22 day of March, 1905.

                                                Drennan C Skaggs
                                                     Notary Public.

BIRTH AFFIDAVIT.

DEPARTMENT OF THE INTERIOR.
COMMISSION TO THE FIVE CIVILIZED TRIBES.

    IN RE APPLICATION FOR ENROLLMENT, as a citizen of the Creek Nation, of Wisey Wilson, born on the 27 day of March, 1902

Name of Father: Thomas Wilson   a citizen of the   Creek   Nation.
Name of Mother: Bettie Wilson   a citizen of the   Creek   Nation.

                                     Postoffice   Carson, Ind. Ter

---

                                                      Town Chief
                          AFFIDAVIT OF ~~MOTHER~~.

UNITED STATES OF AMERICA, Indian Territory, }
    Western   DISTRICT.

    I, Robert Bruner, on oath state that I am about 40 years of age and a citizen by blood, of the Creek Nation; that I am ~~the lawful wife~~ a townsman of Bettie Wilson, who is a citizen, by blood of the Creek who, with her husband, refuses to make application for the enrollment of your minor child, you are advised that the Commission requires further evidence as to the birth of said child. of their children Nation; that a female child was born to ~~me~~ her on 27 day of March, 1902, that said child has been named Wisey Wilson, and was living March 4, 1905.

                                                    Robert Bruner

Witnesses To Mark:
{

    Subscribed and sworn to before me this 22 day of March, 1905.

                                                Drennan C Skaggs
                                                  Notary Public.

Applications for Enrollment of Creek Newborn
Act of 1905 Volume V

NC 397.

Muskogee, Indian Territory, June 5, 1905.

Robert Bruner,
    Carson, Indian Territory.

Dear Sir:

    In the matter of the application for the enrollment of ~~your~~ minor Wisey and Minnie Wilson, as citizens of the Creek Nation, you are advised that the Commission requires the affidavits of the mother and midwife or physician in attendance at the birth of said child.

    There are herewith enclosed two blank forms of birth affidavit and in executing same care should be exercised to see that all blanks are properly filled, all names written in full, and in the event that the persons signing the affidavits are unable to write, signatures by mark must be attested by two witnesses. Each affidavit must be executed before a Notary Public and the notarial seal and signature of the officer must be attached to each separate affidavit.

    In order to identify Bettie Wilson, the mother of said children, You are requested to furnish this office with her maiden name, the names of her parents, the Creek Indian Town to which she belong, and if possible, the numbers on her deeds to land in the Creek Nation.

                                      Respectfully,

2 BA   Commissioner in Charge.

Dustin, Indian Territory, June 13, 1905.

Commission to the Five Civilized Tribes,
    Muskogee, Indian Territory.

Gentlemen:

    There is enclosed herewith testimony in the matter of the application for enrollment of Wicey and Minnie Wilson, No. 2449-B., as citizens by blood of the Creek Nation. No information could be obtained from the parents as to when these two children were born; nor could further evidence be secured from relatives and neighbors.

                                       Respectfully,
                                            Alex Posey
                              Clerk in Charge Creek Field Party.

Applications for Enrollment of Creek Newborn
Act of 1905   Volume V

NC-397.

Muskogee, Indian Territory, August 2, 1905.

Thomas Wilson,
Carson, Indian Territory.

Dear Sir:

On March 22, 1905 Robert Bruner appeared before the Commission to the Five Civilized Tribes and made application for the enrollment of your minor children Wisey Wilson and Minnie Wilson as citizens by blood of the Creek Nation.

You are advised that before the matter of the enrollment of said children can receive further consideration it will be necessary for you to file with this office the affidavits of the mother of said children and the attending physician or midwife at their birth and two blanks for that purpose are inclosed[sic] herewith.

In having the same executed be careful to see that all blanks are properly filled, all names written in full and that the notary public, before whom the affidavits are sworn to, attaches his name and seal to each affidavit. In case any signature is by mark it must be attested by two disinterested witnesses.

Respectfully,

2 B C
Env.

Commissioner.

BA- 1202 & 1203- B.

DEPARTMENT OF THE INTERIOR,
COMMISSION TO THE FIVE CIVILIZED TRIBES.
MUSKOGEE, INDIAN TERRITORY, March 27, 1905.

-ooOoo-

In the matter of the application for the enrollment of Newman Lietka and Richard Lietka, as citizens by blood of the Creek Nation.

RICHARD LIETKA, being duly sworn, testified as follows:

EXAMINATION BY COMMISSION:
Q What is your name? Richard Lietka.
Q How old are you? A About 32.

Applications for Enrollment of Creek Newborn
Act of 1905 Volume V

Q What is your postoffice address? A Fry.
Q Have you any new-born children? A Yes.
Q Who are they? A Newman.
Q And who else? A Richard.
Q When was Newman born? A November 10, 1902.
Q Is he living? A Yes.
Q When was Richard born? A February 10.
Q What year? A 1905.
Q Is he living? A No.
Q When did he die? A February 13, 1905.
Q You are a citizen of the Seminole Nation, are you not? A Yes.
Q Your wife, Martha, is a citizen of the Creek Nation? A Yes.

Records of the Commission examined and the name of Martha Lietka is identified on Creek Indian Card, Field Number 444, and her name is contained in the partial list of citizens by blood, approved by the Secretary of the Interior March 13, 1902, Roll Number 1448,

Q In the event that it should be found that your children have rights in both the Seminole and Creek Nation, in which Nation do you elect to have them enrolled and receive their allotment of land? A The Creek Nation.

MARTHA LIETKA, being duly sworn, testified as follows:

Q What is your name? A Martha Lietka.
Q How old are you? A 29.
Q What is your postoffice address? A Fry.
Q You have two new-born children, have you not? A Yes.
Q What are their names? A Newman and Richard.
Q Is Richard living? A No, he died last February 13th.
Q Is Newman living? A Yes, he is her. (Child is present).
Q In the event that it should be found that your children have rights in both the Seminole Nation and the Creek Nation, in which Nation do you elect to have them enrolled and receive their allotment of land? A In the Creek Nation.

Zera Ellen Parrish, being sworn on her oath states that as a stenographer to the Commission to the Five Civilized Tribes she reported the above case and that this is a full, true and correct transcript of her stenographic notes in same.

Zera Ellen Parrish

Subscribed and sworn to before me this 30th day of March, 1905.

Edw C Griesel
Notary Public.

Applications for Enrollment of Creek Newborn
Act of 1905   Volume V

BIRTH AFFIDAVIT.

DEPARTMENT OF THE INTERIOR.
COMMISSION TO THE FIVE CIVILIZED TRIBES.

IN RE APPLICATION FOR ENROLLMENT, as a citizen of the CREEK Nation, of Richard Litka[sic], born on the 10 day of Feb. 1905

Name of Father:	Richard Litka	a citizen of the	Seminole Nation.
Name of Mother:	Martha "	a citizen of the Creek	Nation.

Postoffice   Fry, I.T.

AFFIDAVIT OF MOTHER.

UNITED STATES OF AMERICA, Indian Territory,
WESTERN   DISTRICT.

I, Martha Litka, on oath state that I am 29 years of age and a citizen by blood, of the Creek Nation; that I am the lawful wife of Richard Litka, who is a citizen, by blood of the Seminole Nation; that a male child was born to me on 10 day of Feb, 1905, that said child ~~has been named~~ died Feb 13-1905, ~~and is now living~~.

Martha Litka

Witnesses To Mark:

Subscribed and sworn to before me this 27 day of March, 1905.

J McDermott
Notary Public.

NC 398   JLD

DEPARTMENT OF THE INTERIOR,
COMMISSIONER TO THE FIVE CIVILIZED TRIBES.
. . . .

In the matter of the application for the enrollment of Richard Litka, deceased, as a citizen by blood of the Creek Nation.

. . . .

STATEMENT AND ORDER.

The record in this case shows that on March 27, 1905, application was made, in affidavit form, supplemented by sworn testimony, for the enrollment of Richard Litka,

Applications for Enrollment of Creek Newborn
Act of 1905 Volume V

deceased, as a citizen by blood of the Creek Nation, under the provisions of the act of Congress approved March 3, 1905.

It appears from the evidence filed in this matter that said Richard Litka, deceased, was born February 10, 1905, and died February 13, 1905.

The Act of Congress approved March 3, 1905, (33 Stats., 1048), provides:

"That the Commission to the Five Civilized Tribes is authorized for sixty days after the date of the approval of this act to receive and consider applications for enrollment, <u>of children, born subsequent to May twenty-fifth, nineteen hundred and one, and prior to March fourth, nineteen hundred and five, and living on said latter date,</u> to citizens of the Creek tribe of Indians whose enrollment has been approved by the Secretary of the Interior prior to the approval of this act; and to enroll and make allotments to such children."

It is, therefore, ordered that the application for the enrollment of Richard Litka, deceased, as a citizen by blood of the Creek Nation, be, and the same is hereby dismissed.

Tams Bixby Commissioner.

Muskogee, Indian Territory.
JAN 15 1907

BIRTH AFFIDAVIT.

DEPARTMENT OF THE INTERIOR.
COMMISSION TO THE FIVE CIVILIZED TRIBES.

IN RE APPLICATION FOR ENROLLMENT, as a citizen of the Creek Nation, of Newman Litka[sic], born on the 10 day of November, 1902

Name of Father:	Dick Litka	a citizen of the Seminole	Nation.
Name of Mother:	Martha Litka	a citizen of the Creek	Nation.

Postoffice Frye, I.T.

AFFIDAVIT OF ATTENDING PHYSICIAN OR MID-WIFE.

UNITED STATES OF AMERICA, Indian Territory,
Western DISTRICT.

I, Malinda Litka , a Mid Wife , on oath state that I attended on Mrs. Martha Litka , wife of Dick Litka on the 10th day of November , 1902 ; that there was born to her on said date a male child; that said child is now living and is said to have been named Newman Litka

            her
          Malinda x Litka
            mark

Witnesses To Mark:
{ Josie Smith
{ J C Johnson

Applications for Enrollment of Creek Newborn
Act of 1905   Volume V

Subscribed and sworn to before me this 29th day of April, 1905.

                              J C Johnson
                                    Notary Public.

BIRTH AFFIDAVIT.

DEPARTMENT OF THE INTERIOR.
COMMISSION TO THE FIVE CIVILIZED TRIBES.

IN RE APPLICATION FOR ENROLLMENT, as a citizen of the CREEK Nation, of Newman Litka[sic], born on the 10 day of Nov, 1902

| Name of Father: | Richard Litka | a citizen of the Seminole Nation. |
| Name of Mother: | Martha " | a citizen of the Creek Nation. |

                             Postoffice   Fry, I.T.

Child Present MAR 27 1905 Gr.

AFFIDAVIT OF MOTHER.

UNITED STATES OF AMERICA, Indian Territory,
    WESTERN   DISTRICT.

    I, Martha Litka , on oath state that I am 29 years of age and a citizen by blood , of the Creek Nation; that I am the lawful wife of Richard Litka , who is a citizen, by blood of the Seminole Nation; that a male child was born to me on 10 day of Nov. 1902 , that said child has been named Newman Litka , and is now living.

                            Martha Litka

Witnesses To Mark:

Subscribed and sworn to before me this 27" day of Mar. , 1905.

                            J. McDermott
                            Notary Public.

                                       NC. 398.

                     Muskogee, Indian Territory, July 14, 1905.

Commissioner to the Five Civilized Tribes,
    Seminole Enrollment Division,
        Muskogee, Indian Territory.

Applications for Enrollment of Creek Newborn
Act of 1905 Volume V

Gentlemen:

March 27, 1905, application was made to the Commission to the Five Civilized Tribes for the enrollment of Newman Litka, born November 10, 1902, and Richard Litka, born February 10, 1905, as citizens by blood of the Creek Nation. It is stated in said application that the father of said children is Richard Litka, a citizen of the Seminole Nation, and that the mother is Martha Litka, a citizen of the Creek Nation.

You are requested to inform the Creek Enrollment Division as to whether application has been made for the enrollment of said children as citizens of the Seminole Nation, and if so, what disposition has been made of the same.

Respectfully,

Commissioner.

DEPARTMENT OF THE INTERIOR.
COMMISSION TO THE FIVE CIVILIZED TRIBES.

Muskogee, Indian Territory, July 19, 1905.

Chief Clerk,
    Creek Enrollment Division.

Dear Sir:

Receipt is acknowledged of your letter of July 14, 1905 (NC-398) stating that application was made to the Commission to the Five Civilized Tribes for the enrollment of Newman Litka, born November 10, 1902, and Richard Litka, born February 10, 1905, children of Richard Litka, a citizen of the Seminole Nation, and Martha Litka, a citizen of the Creek Nation, as citizens by blood of the Creek Nation and requesting to be informed as to whether application has been made for the enrollment of said children as citizens of the Seminole Nation.

In reply to your letter you are advised that it does not appear from an examination of the records of this office that any application was made to the Commission to the Five Civilized Tribes for the enrollment of said Newman Litka and Richard Litka as a citizen of the Seminole Nation.

Respectfully,

Tams Bixby   Commissioner.

Applications for Enrollment of Creek Newborn
Act of 1905 Volume V

Muskogee, Indian Territory, November 12, 1906.

Chief Clerk,
    Seminole Enrollment Division,
        General Office.

Dear Sir:

    You are hereby advised that the name of Newman Litka, born November 10, 1902, to Richard Litka, an alleged citizen of the Seminole Nation, and Martha Litka, a citizen by blood of the Creek Nation, is contained in a schedule of New Born citizens of the Creek Nation, approved by the Secretary of the Interior September 27, 1905, opposite Roll No. 409.

                Respectfully,

                        Commissioner.

            Muskogee, Indian Territory, January 16, 1907.

Martha Litka,
    c/o Richard Litka,
        Fry, Indian Territory.

Dear Madam:

    There is herewith enclosed one copy of the Statement and Order of the Commissioner to the Five Civilized Tribes, dated January 15, 1907, dismissing the application made by you for the enrollment of your minor child, Richard Litka, as a citizen of the Creek Nation.

                Respectfully,

                        Commissioner.

LM-67.

Applications for Enrollment of Creek Newborn
Act of 1905   Volume V

NC 399.

Muskogee, Indian Territory, June 3, 1905.

Lizzie Wilson,
    Carson, Indian Territory.

Dear Madam:

    In the matter of the application for the enrollment of your minor child, Bennie Wilson, you are advised that the Commission requires the affidavits of two disinterested witnesses as to the birth of said child.

    There are herewith enclosed two blank forms of birth affidavit, and in executing same care should be taken to see that all blanks are properly filled, all names written in full, and in the event that either of the persons signing the affidavits is unable to write, signatures by mark must be attested by two witnesses. Each affidavit must be executed before a Notary Public and the notarial seal and signature of the officer must be attached to each separate affidavit.

                                        Respectfully,

2 BA   Commissioner in Charge.

BIRTH AFFIDAVIT.

DEPARTMENT OF THE INTERIOR.
COMMISSION TO THE FIVE CIVILIZED TRIBES.

    IN RE APPLICATION FOR ENROLLMENT, as a citizen of the Creek Nation, of Bennie Wilson , born on the 16 day of May , 1902

Name of Father:	Charley Wilson	a citizen of the	Creek	Nation.
Name of Mother:	Lizzie Wilson	a citizen of the	Creek	Nation.

                      Postoffice   Carson, Ind. Ter.

AFFIDAVIT OF MOTHER.

UNITED STATES OF AMERICA, Indian Territory, ⎫
    Western   DISTRICT.   ⎬

    I, Lizzie Wilson , on oath state that I am about 30 years of age and a citizen by blood , of the Creek Nation; that I am the lawful wife of Charley Wilson , who is a citizen, by blood of the Creek Nation; that a male child was born to me on 16 day of May , 1902 , that said child has been named Bennie Wilson , and was living March

Applications for Enrollment of Creek Newborn
Act of 1905   Volume V

4, 1905. That no one attended on me as midwife or physician in attendance at the birth of the child.

Witnesses To Mark:
{ Alex Posey
{ DC Skaggs

her
Lizzie x Wilson
mark

Subscribed and sworn to before me 22 day of March, 1905.

Drennan C Skaggs
Notary Public.

Acquaintance
AFFIDAVIT OF ~~ATTENDING PHYSICIAN OR MID-WIFE~~.

UNITED STATES OF AMERICA, Indian Territory, }
Western   DISTRICT.

Child present

am acquainted with
I, Tommie Lott, ~~a (blank)~~, on oath state that I ~~attended on~~ Mrs. Lizzie Wilson, wife of Charley Wilson ~~on the (blank) day of (blank), 190~~; that there was born to her on said date a male child; that said child was living March 4, 1905, and is said to have been named Bennie Wilson

his
Tommie x Lott
mark

Witnesses To Mark:
{ DC Skaggs
{ Alex Posey

Subscribed and sworn to before me this 10 day of June, 1905.

Drennan C Skaggs
Notary Public.

Acquaintance
AFFIDAVIT OF ~~ATTENDING PHYSICIAN OR MID-WIFE~~.

UNITED STATES OF AMERICA, Indian Territory, }
Western   DISTRICT.

am acquainted with
I, Peter Fish, ~~a (blank)~~, on oath state that I ~~attended on~~ Mrs. Lizzie Wilson, wife of Charley Wilson ~~on the (blank) day of (blank), 190~~; that there was born to her on or about May 17, 1902 ~~said date~~ a male child; that said child was living March 4, 1905, and is said to have been named Bennie Wilson

his
Peter x Fish
mark

Witnesses To Mark:
{ DC Skaggs
{ Alex Posey

Applications for Enrollment of Creek Newborn
Act of 1905   Volume V

Subscribed and sworn to before me this 10 day of June, 1905.

           Drennan C Skaggs
           Notary Public.

BIRTH AFFIDAVIT. (Child Present)

DEPARTMENT OF THE INTERIOR.
COMMISSION TO THE FIVE CIVILIZED TRIBES.

IN RE APPLICATION FOR ENROLLMENT, as a citizen of the CREEK Nation, of Mahala Frank, born on the ----- day of Sept, 1903

Name of Father:	Short Frank	a citizen of the	Creek	Nation.
Name of Mother:	Betty "	a citizen of the	"	Nation.

      Postoffice Mounds

AFFIDAVIT OF MOTHER.

UNITED STATES OF AMERICA, Indian Territory,
  Western   DISTRICT.

  I, Betty Frank, on oath state that I am 26 years of age and a citizen by blood, of the Creek Nation; that I am the lawful wife of Short Frank, who is a citizen, by blood of the Creek Nation; that a female child was born to me on ----- day of Sept, 1903, that said child has been named Mahala Frank, and is now living.

           her
         Betty x Frank
Witnesses To Mark: mark
  { Irwin Donovan
   Jesse McDermott

  Subscribed and sworn to before me this 27" day of March, 1905.

           J. McDermott
           Notary Public.

Applications for Enrollment of Creek Newborn
Act of 1905 Volume V

AFFIDAVIT OF ATTENDING PHYSICIAN OR MID-WIFE.

UNITED STATES OF AMERICA, Indian Territory, }
    Western   DISTRICT.

I, Eliza Beaver , a midwife , on oath state that I attended on Mrs. Betty Frank , wife of Short Frank on the ----- day of Sept , 1903 : that there was born to her on said date a female child: that said child is now living and is said to have been named Mahala Frank

                              her
                        Eliza x Beaver
Witnesses To Mark: mark
   { Irwin Donovan
     Jesse McDermott

Subscribed and sworn to before me this 27" day of March, 1905.

                        J. McDermott
                            Notary Public.

        Child Present

BIRTH AFFIDAVIT.
DEPARTMENT OF THE INTERIOR.
COMMISSION TO THE FIVE CIVILIZED TRIBES.

IN RE APPLICATION FOR ENROLLMENT, as a citizen of the CREEK Nation, of Neddie Frank , born on the ----- day of Dec , 1901

Name of Father: Short Frank   a citizen of the   Creek   Nation.
Name of Mother: Betty "   a citizen of the   "   Nation.

                    Postoffice   Mounds

AFFIDAVIT OF MOTHER.

UNITED STATES OF AMERICA, Indian Territory, }
    Western   DISTRICT.

I, Betty Frank , on oath state that I am 26 years of age and a citizen by blood , of the Creek Nation; that I am the lawful wife of Short Frank , who is a citizen, by blood of the Creek Nation: that a male child was born to me on ----- day of Dec. , 1901 , that said child has been named Neddie Frank , and is now living.

                              her
                        Betty x Frank
Witnesses To Mark: mark
   { Irwin Donovan
     Jesse McDermott

Applications for Enrollment of Creek Newborn
Act of 1905   Volume V

Subscribed and sworn to before me this 27" day of March, 1905.

J. McDermott
Notary Public.

AFFIDAVIT OF ATTENDING PHYSICIAN OR MID-WIFE.

UNITED STATES OF AMERICA, Indian Territory, }
  Western   DISTRICT.

I, Eliza Beaver , a midwife , on oath state that I attended on Mrs. Betty Frank , wife of Short Frank on the ----- day of Dec , 1901 ; that there was born to her on said date a male child; that said child is now living and is said to have been named Neddie Frank
                                                    her
                                            Eliza x Beaver
Witnesses To Mark: mark
 { Irwin Donovan
   Jesse McDermott

Subscribed and sworn to before me this 27" day of March, 1905.

J. McDermott
Notary Public.

N.C. 401.

DEPARTMENT OF THE INTERIOR,
COMMISSIONER TO THE FIVE CIVILIZED TRIBES.
Dustin, I.T., May 14, 1906.

In the matter of the application for the enrollment of Willie Bruner as a citizen by blood of the Creek Nation.

ILSEY BRUNER, being duly sworn, testified as follows:

Through Alex Posey official interpreter:

BY THE COMMISSIONER:
Q What is your name? A Ilsey Bruner.
Q How old are you? A About twenty-five.
Q What is your post office address? A Carson.
Q Are you a citizen of the Creek Nation? A Yes, sir.

Applications for Enrollment of Creek Newborn
Act of 1905 Volume V

Q To what town do you belong? A Tulmochusse.
Q Have you a child named Willie Bruner? A Yes, sir. The child is now dead.
Q When did he die? A August 5, 1905.
Q When was he born? A July 2, 1904.
Q How old was the child when he died? The child was a little over a year old and was beginning to walk.
Q Who is the father of the child? A David Bruner.
Q Is he a Creek citizen? A Yes, sir.
Q To what town does he belong? A Tulmochusse.
Q Is David Bruner your lawful husband? A He was formerly my husband but we have separated.
Q Have you married again? A Yes, sir, to Robert Bruner.
Q We have an affidavit executed by Charlie Wilson and Loney McGirt, stating that the child was born July 2, 1905? A That is not correct. The child was born the year before that--in 1904.
Q We have two affidavits executed by you. In one you sign your name as Elsie Bruner and in the other as Ilsey Bruner. In one you state that you are the wife of David Bruner and in the other you state you are the wife of Robert Bruner and he corroborates your affidavit? A My name is Ilsey Bruner. David Bruner was my former husband but we have separated and I have married Robert Bruner.

Witness is identified as Ilsey Bruner, opposite Creek Indian Roll No. 7186.

---oooOOOooo---

I, D. C. Skaggs, on oath state that the above and foregoing is a full and true transcript of my stenographic notes as taken in said cause on said date.

D. C. Skaggs

Subscribed and sworn to before me this 14th day of May, 1906.

Alex Posey
Notary Public.

AFFIDAVIT OF DISINTERESTED WITNESSES.

United States of America,
Western District,
Indian Territory.

We, the undersigned, on oath state that we are personally acquainted with Ilsey Bruner formerly the wife of David Bruner; that there was born to her a male child on or about 2 day of July , 1904; that the said child has been named Willie Bruner and was living March 4, 1905 and died August 5, 1905.

Applications for Enrollment of Creek Newborn
Act of 1905 Volume V

We further state that we have no interest in this case.

Anne Cowe
h??
Cogee x King
mark

Subscribed and sworn to before me this 14 day of May 1906.

Alex Posey
Notary Public.

Witnesses
    Alex Posey

    D. C. Skaggs

DEPARTMENT OF THE INTERIOR.
COMMISSION TO THE FIVE CIVILIZED TRIBES.

In the matter of the death of Willie Bruner a citizen of the Creek Nation, who formerly resided at or near Carson , Ind. Ter., and died on the 5 day of August , 1905.

AFFIDAVIT OF RELATIVE.

UNITED STATES OF AMERICA, Indian Territory,
Western DISTRICT.

I, Ilsey Bruner , on oath state that I am about 25 years of age and a citizen by blood , of the Creek Nation; that my postoffice address is Carson , Ind. Ter.; that I am mother of Willie Bruner who was a citizen, by blood , of the Creek Nation and that said Willie Bruner died on the 5 day of August , 1905

her
Ilsey x Bruner
mark

Witnesses To Mark:
  { Alex Posey
    DC Skaggs

Subscribed and sworn to before me this 14 day of May, 190*(blank)*.

Alex Posey
Notary Public.

Applications for Enrollment of Creek Newborn
Act of 1905   Volume V

BIRTH AFFIDAVIT.

DEPARTMENT OF THE INTERIOR.
COMMISSION TO THE FIVE CIVILIZED TRIBES.

IN RE APPLICATION FOR ENROLLMENT, as a citizen of the Creek Nation, of Willie Bruner, born on the 2 day of July, 1904

Name of Father:	Dave Bruner	a citizen of the	Creek	Nation.
Name of Mother:	Ilsey Bruner	a citizen of the	Creek	Nation.

Postoffice   Carson I.T.

AFFIDAVIT OF MOTHER.

UNITED STATES OF AMERICA, Indian Territory,
   Western   DISTRICT.

I, Ilsey Bruner, on oath state that I am 24 years of age and a citizen by Blood, of the Creek Nation; that I am the lawful wife of Dave Bruner, who is a citizen, by Blood of the Creek Nation; that a male child was born to me on 2nd day of July, 1905, that said child has been named Willie Bruner, and was living March 4, 1905.

Ilsey Bruner

Witnesses To Mark:

Subscribed and sworn to before me this 11 day of Sept, 1905.

Barney C Robison
Notary Public.

AFFIDAVIT OF ATTENDING PHYSICIAN OR MID-WIFE.

UNITED STATES OF AMERICA, Indian Territory,
   Western   DISTRICT.

I, Robert Bruner, a Husband, on oath state that I attended on Mrs. Ilsey Bruner, wife of Dave Bruner on the 2nd day of July, 1905 ; that there was born to her on said date a male child; that said child was living March 4, 1905, and is said to have been named Willie Bruner

Robert Bruner

Witnesses To Mark:

Applications for Enrollment of Creek Newborn
Act of 1905   Volume V

Subscribed and sworn to before me this 11 day of Sept, 1905.

Barney C Robison
Notary Public.

Com Ex Sept 4-06

AFFIDAVIT OF ATTENDING PHYSICIAN OR MID-WIFE.

UNITED STATES OF AMERICA, Indian Territory, ⎫
    Western   DISTRICT.   ⎬

visited

I, Chlie[sic] Wilson   Loney McGirt , a Witness , on oath state that I ~~attended on~~ Mrs. Ilsey Bruner , wife of Dave Bruner on the 2nd day of July , 1905 ; that there was born to her on said date a male child; that said child was living March 4, 1905, and is said to have been named   Willie Bruner

Charley Wilson

Witnesses To Mark: Loney McGirt
{

Subscribed and sworn to before me this 11 day of Sept , 1905.

Barney C Robison
Notary Public.

BIRTH AFFIDAVIT.
DEPARTMENT OF THE INTERIOR,
COMMISSIONER TO THE FIVE CIVILIZED TRIBES.

ENROLLMENT OF MINORS.   ACT OF CONGRESS, APPROVED APRIL 26, 1906.

IN RE APPLICATION FOR ENROLLMENT, as a citizen of the Creek Nation, of Willie Bruner , born on the 2 day of July , 1904

Name of Father: David Bruner (Roll No 7125)   a citizen of the   Creek   Nation.
Name of Mother: Ilsey Bruner (Roll No 7126)   a citizen of the   Creek   Nation.

Tribal enrollment of father Tulmochussee Tribal enrollment of mother   Tulmochussee

Postoffice   Carson Indian Territory

Applications for Enrollment of Creek Newborn
Act of 1905   Volume V

AFFIDAVIT OF MOTHER.

UNITED STATES OF AMERICA, Indian Territory,
Western   District.

I, Ilsey Bruner, on oath state that I am about 25 years of age and a citizen by blood, of the Creek Nation; that I was formerly ~~am~~ the lawful wife of David Bruner, who is a citizen, by blood of the Creek Nation; that a male child was born to me on 2 day of July, 1904, that said child has been named Willie Bruner, and was living March 4, 190~~6~~.5 and died August 5, 1905

             her
           Ilsey x Bruner

WITNESSES TO MARK: mark
 Alex Posey
 DC Skaggs

Subscribed and sworn to before me this 14 day of May, 1906.

          Alex Posey
            Notary Public.

BIRTH AFFIDAVIT.

DEPARTMENT OF THE INTERIOR.
COMMISSION TO THE FIVE CIVILIZED TRIBES.

IN RE APPLICATION FOR ENROLLMENT, as a citizen of the Creek Nation, of Willie Bruner, born on the 2 day of July, 1904

Name of Father:	Dave Bruner	a citizen of the	Creek	Nation.
Name of Mother:	Elsie Bruner	a citizen of the	Creek	Nation.

       Postoffice Carson Ind. Ter.

AFFIDAVIT OF MOTHER.

UNITED STATES OF AMERICA, Indian Territory,
Western   DISTRICT.

I, Elsie Bruner, on oath state that I am 24 years of age and a citizen by blood, of the Creek Nation; that I am not the lawful wife of Dave Bruner, who is a citizen, by blood of the Creek Nation; that a male child was born to me on 2 day of July, 1904, that said child has been named Willie Bruner, and was living March 4, 1905. That no one attended on me as midwife or physician at the birth of child

            her
          Elsie x Bruner
            mark

Applications for Enrollment of Creek Newborn
Act of 1905   Volume V

Witnesses To Mark:
{ Alex Posey
{ DC Skaggs

Subscribed and sworn to before me this 22 day of March, 1905.

Drennan C Skaggs
Notary Public.

NC-401.

Muskogee, Indian Territory, August 3, 1905.

Elsie Bruner,
Carson, Indian Territory.

Dear Madam:

In the matter of the application for the enrollment of your son Willie Bruner, born July 2, 1904, as a citizen by blood of the Creek Nation you are advised that it will be necessary for you to furnish this office with the affidavits of two disinterested persons who are acquainted with said child, know when he was born, the names of his parents and whether or not he was living on March 4, 1905.

Inasmuch as this office has been unable to identify you upon the final roll of Creek citizens by blood you are requested to immediately inform this office as to the name under which you were finally enrolled, the names of your parents and other members of your family, the Creek town to which you belong and if you have received your allotment certificate and deed your final roll number as the same appears thereon.

This matter should have your prompt attention.

Respectfully,

Commissioner.

NC-401

Muskogee, Indian Territory, December 12, 1905.

Elsie Bruner,
Care of Dave Bruner,
Carson, Indian Territory.

Dear Madam:

Applications for Enrollment of Creek Newborn
Act of 1905   Volume V

In the matter of the application for the enrollment of your minor child, Willie Bruner, as a citizen by blood of the Creek Nation, you are advised that it will be necessary for you to appear at this office with the midwife or physician who attended you at the birth of said child for the purpose of being examined under oath. In the event there was no midwife or physician present at the birth of said child, it will be necessary for you to bring with you two disinterested witnesses who know the exact date of the birth of said child, the names of its parents and whether or not it was living March 4, 1905.

Respectfully,

Acting Commissioner.

NC-402

6

Muskogee, Indian Territory, June 5, 1905.

Marcy Morrow,
Okemah, Indian Territory.

Dear Madam:

In the matter of the application for the enrollment of your minor child, Alice Morrow, as a citizen of the Creek Nation, there is herewith enclosed a blank form of death affidavit, and you are requested to fill out and execute before an officer authorized to administer oaths, and return it to the Commission in the enclosed envelope.

Respectfully,

Commissioner in Charge.

I D A

N C 402.

Muskogee, Indian Territory, January 16, 1907.

Marcy Morrow,
Okemah, Indian Territory.

Dear Madam:

There is herewith enclosed one copy of the Statement and Order of the Commissioner to the Five Civilized Tribes, dated January 15, 1907, dismissing the application made by you for the enrollment of your minor child, Alice Morrow, deceased, as a citizen by blood of the Creek Nation.

Applications for Enrollment of Creek Newborn
Act of 1905 Volume V

Respectfully,

Commissioner.

LM-54.

NC-402

DEPARTMENT OF THE INTERIOR,
COMMISSION TO THE FIVE CIVILIZED TRIBES.

Muskogee, Indian Territory, May 27, 1905.

In the matter of the application for the enrollment of Alice Morrow as a citizen of the Creek Nation.

Jesse McDermott, being duly sworn, testified as follows:

EXAMINATION BY THE COMMISSION:
Q What is your name, age and postoffice? A Jesse McDermott; age 25; Muskogee.
Q Do you know Marcy Morrow? A She is my half sister.
Q Do you know a couple of new-born children of hers named Elva and Alice?
A Yes sir.
Q When were they born? A I don't know the exact date; sometime in July, 1904.
Q Are they living? A Yes, one is; one of them is dead; Alice is dead.
Q Do you know when Alice died? A Her mother wrote me that she died on the 27th of last February.
Q What time did you receive this letter? A About two weeks after the child died.

INDIAN TERRITORY, Western District.
I, J. Y. Miller, a stenographer to the Commission to the Five Civilized Tribes, do hereby certify that the above and foregoing is a true and complete translation of my notes as same appear in my stenographic report of this case.

J.Y. Miller

Sworn to and subscribed before me
this the 17 day of June, 1905

Edw C Griesel
Notary Public.

Applications for Enrollment of Creek Newborn
Act of 1905   Volume V

DEPARTMENT OF THE INTERIOR.
COMMISSION TO THE FIVE CIVILIZED TRIBES.

In the matter of the death of   Alice Morrow   a citizen of the CREEK ~~NATION~~ Nation, who formerly resided at or near   Okemah, Creek Nation   , Ind. Ter., and died on the 27th day of February , 1905

AFFIDAVIT OF RELATIVE.

UNITED STATES OF AMERICA, Indian Territory, }
Western Judicial   DISTRICT.

   I, Marcy Morrow , on oath state that I am 20 years of age and a citizen by Blood , of the CREEK Nation: that my postoffice address is Okemah, Creek Nation , Ind. Ter.; that I am Mother   of Alice Morrow   who was a citizen, by Blood , of the Creek   Nation and that said   Alice Morrow   died on the 27th   day of February , 1905

                                     Marcy Morrow
Witnesses To Mark:
{

   Subscribed and sworn to before me this 30th day of June, 1905, 190*(blank)*

My Commission Expires Sept 6th 1906.   John H. Phillips
                                     Notary Public.

AFFIDAVIT OF ACQUAINTANCE.

UNITED STATES OF AMERICA, Indian Territory, }
Western Judicial   DISTRICT.

   I, N.L. Morrow , on oath state that I am 48 years of age, and a citizen by *(blank)* of the United States ~~Nation~~; that my postoffice address is Okemah, Creek Nation , Ind. Ter.; that I was personally acquainted with Alice Morrow   who was a citizen, by Blood , of the CREEK   Nation; and that said   Alice Morrow   died on the 27th   day of February, 1905   , I*(blank)*.

                                     N.L. Morrow
Witnesses To Mark:
{

262

Applications for Enrollment of Creek Newborn
Act of 1905   Volume V

Subscribed and sworn to before me this 30th day of June, 1905, 190*(blank)*

My Commission Expires Sept 6th 1906.   John H. Phillips
                                             Notary Public.

BIRTH AFFIDAVIT.

DEPARTMENT OF THE INTERIOR.
COMMISSION TO THE FIVE CIVILIZED TRIBES.

  IN RE APPLICATION FOR ENROLLMENT, as a citizen of the Creek Nation, of Alice Morrow (d), born on the 28th day of   July, 1904

Name of Father:	Alfred Morrow	a citizen of the	United	~~Nation~~.
Name of Mother:	Marcy Morrow	a citizen of the	Creek	Nation.

                    Postoffice   Okemah, I.T.

AFFIDAVIT OF MOTHER.

UNITED STATES OF AMERICA, Indian Territory, ⎫
   Western Judicial   DISTRICT.   ⎭

   I, Marcy Morrow , on oath state that I am 20 years of age and a citizen by Blood , of the Muskokee[sic] or Creek   Nation; that I am the lawful wife of Alfred Morrow, U.S. Ci~~tizen   , who is a citizen, by   (blank) of the~~   *(blank)* Nation; that a Female child was born to me on 28th day of July , 1904 , that said child has been named   ~~Alice Morrow, and was living~~ March 4, 1905.

                              Marcy Morrow
Witnesses To Mark:

{

Subscribed and sworn to before me this 20th day of March, 1905 , 190*(blank)*

My Commission Expires Sept 6th 1906.   John H. Phillips
                                            Notary Public.

AFFIDAVIT OF ATTENDING PHYSICIAN OR MID-WIFE.

UNITED STATES OF AMERICA, Indian Territory, ⎫
   Western Judicial   DISTRICT.   ⎭

   I, Dr. B. Watts , a PHYSICIAN   , on oath state that I attended on Mrs. Marcy Morrow , wife of Alfred Morrow on the 28th day of July , 1904 ; that there was born

Applications for Enrollment of Creek Newborn
Act of 1905 Volume V

to her on said date a Female child; ~~that said child was living March 4, 1905~~, and is said to have been named Alice Morrow

B. Watts M.D.

Witnesses To Mark:
{

Subscribed and sworn to before me this 20th day of March, 1905 , 190*(blank)*

My Commission Expires Sept 6th 1906.

John H. Phillips
Notary Public.

NC 402 JLD

DEPARTMENT OF THE INTERIOR,
COMMISSIONER TO THE FIVE CIVILIZED TRIBES.

. . . .

In the matter of the application for the enrollment of Alice Morrow, deceased, as a citizen by blood of the Creek Nation.

. . . .

The record in this case shows that on March 24, 1905, application was made, in affidavit form, supplemented by sworn testimony taken May 27, 1905, for the enrollment of Alice Morrow, deceased, as a citizen by blood of the Creek Nation, under the provisions of the act of Congress approved March 3, 1905.

It appears from the evidence filed in this matter that said Alice Morrow, deceased, was born July 28, 1904, and died February 27, 1905.

The act of Congress approved March 3, 1905 (33 Stats., 1048), provides:

"That the Commission to the Five Civilized Tribes is authorized for sixty days after the date of the approval of this Act to receive and consider applications for enrollments of children born subsequent to May twenty five, nineteen hundred and one, and prior to March fourth, nineteen hundred and five, and living on said latter date, to citizens of the Creek tribe of Indians whose enrollment has been approved by the Secretary of the Interior prior to the date of approval of this act; and to enroll and make allotments to such children."

It is, therefore, ordered that the application for the enrollment of said Alice Morrow, deceased, as a citizen by blood of the Creek Nation, be, and the same is hereby dismissed.

Tams Bixby Commissioner.

Muskogee, Indian Territory.
JAN 15 1907

Applications for Enrollment of Creek Newborn
Act of 1905   Volume V

BIRTH AFFIDAVIT.

DEPARTMENT OF THE INTERIOR.
COMMISSION TO THE FIVE CIVILIZED TRIBES.

IN RE APPLICATION FOR ENROLLMENT, as a citizen of the Creek Nation, of Elva Morrow, born on the 28th day of   July, 1904

Name of Father: Alfred Morrow   a citizen of the   United   ~~Nation~~.
Name of Mother: Marcy Morrow   a citizen of the   Creek   Nation.

Postoffice   Okemah, I.T.

AFFIDAVIT OF MOTHER.

UNITED STATES OF AMERICA, Indian Territory,
Western Judicial   DISTRICT.

I, Marcy Morrow , on oath state that I am 20   years of age and a citizen by Blood , of the Muskokee[sic] or Creek   Nation; that I am the lawful wife of Alfred Morrow, U.S. C~~itizen   , who is a citizen, by   (blank) of the~~ *(blank)* Nation; that a Male child was born to me on 28th day of July , 1904 , that said child has been named Elva Morrow , and was living March 4, 1905.

Marcy Morrow

Witnesses To Mark:
{

Subscribed and sworn to before me this 20th day of March, 1905 , 190*(blank)*

My Commission Expires Sept 6th 1906.   John H. Phillips
                                             Notary Public.

AFFIDAVIT OF ATTENDING PHYSICIAN OR MID-WIFE.

UNITED STATES OF AMERICA, Indian Territory,
Western Judicial   DISTRICT.

I, Dr. B. Watts , a PHYSCIAN[sic]   , on oath state that I attended on Mrs. Marcy Morrow , wife of Alfred Morrow on the 28th day of July , 1904 ; that there was born to her on said date a Male child; that said child was living March 4, 1905, and is said to have been named Elva Morrow

B. Watts M.D.

Witnesses To Mark:
{

265

Applications for Enrollment of Creek Newborn
Act of 1905   Volume V

Subscribed and sworn to before me this 20th day of July, 1905 , 190*(blank)*

My Commission Expires Sept 6th 1906.

John H. Phillips
Notary Public.

BIRTH AFFIDAVIT.

DEPARTMENT OF THE INTERIOR.
COMMISSION TO THE FIVE CIVILIZED TRIBES.

IN RE APPLICATION FOR ENROLLMENT, as a citizen of the Creek Nation, of George Baker, born on the 10th day of Dec, 1903

Name of Father:	Leslie Baker	a citizen of the	Creek	Nation.
Name of Mother:	Anna Baker	a citizen of the	Creek	Nation.

Postoffice   Weleetka, Ind. Ter.

AFFIDAVIT OF MOTHER.

UNITED STATES OF AMERICA, Indian Territory,
Western Judicial   DISTRICT.

I, Anna Baker , on oath state that I am 32 years of age and a citizen by birth , of the Creek Nation; that I am the lawful wife of Leslie Baker , who is a citizen, by birth of the Creek Nation; that a Male child was born to me on 10th day of Dec, 1903 , that said child has been named George Baker , and was living March 4, 1905.

Witnesses To Mark:
{ Nat. Williams
{ Chas. Coachman

her
Anna Baker x
mark

Subscribed and sworn to before me this 22nd day of July , 1905.

My Commission Expires Aug 15, 1906

B.H. Mills
Notary Public.

Applications for Enrollment of Creek Newborn
Act of 1905 Volume V

AFFIDAVIT OF ATTENDING PHYSICIAN OR MID-WIFE.

UNITED STATES OF AMERICA, Indian Territory,
Western Judicial DISTRICT.

    I, Chas Coachman & Sinda McGilbra , a Witnesses , on oath state that I attended on Mrs. Anna Baker , wife of Leslie Baker on the 10th day of Dec , 1903 ; that there was born to her on said date a Male child; that said child was living March 4, 1905, and is said to have been named George Baker

                          Chas Coachman

Witnesses To Mark:
{ Nat. Williams
  Chas Coachman

                                  her
                        Sinda McGilbra x
                                  mark

Subscribed and sworn to before me this 22nd day of July , 1905.

My Commission Expires Aug 15, 1906   B.H. Mills
                                            Notary Public.

BIRTH AFFIDAVIT.

DEPARTMENT OF THE INTERIOR.
COMMISSION TO THE FIVE CIVILIZED TRIBES.

    IN RE APPLICATION FOR ENROLLMENT, as a citizen of the Creek Nation, of George Baker, born on the 10th day of December, 1903

Name of Father: Lasley Baker   a citizen of the   Creek   Nation.
Name of Mother: Anna Baker (Coachman)   a citizen of the   Creek   Nation.

                        Postoffice   Weleetka, Ind. Tery.

AFFIDAVIT OF MOTHER.

UNITED STATES OF AMERICA, Indian Territory,
Western Judicial DISTRICT.

    I, Anna Baker , on oath state that I am 32 years of age and a citizen by birth , of the Creek Nation; that I am the lawful wife of Lasley Baker , who is a citizen, by birth of the Creek Nation; that a male child was born to me on the 10th day of December, 1903 , that said child has been named George Baker , and was living March 4, 1905. And I also state that I had neither physician nor mid-wife to assist me at the birth of said child

                                      Anna Baker her x mark

Applications for Enrollment of Creek Newborn
Act of 1905   Volume V

Witnesses To Mark:
- Bernard B. Mooney
- Chas. Coachman

Subscribed and sworn to before me this 21st day of Mch , 1905.

(Name Illegible)
Notary Public.

BIRTH AFFIDAVIT.

DEPARTMENT OF THE INTERIOR.
COMMISSION TO THE FIVE CIVILIZED TRIBES.

IN RE APPLICATION FOR ENROLLMENT, as a citizen of the CREEK Nation, of Albert K. Smith , born on the 2 day of Dec , 1902

Name of Father: Thomas M Smith   a citizen of the   Creek   Nation.
Name of Mother: Adeline Smith   a ^non citizen of the   *(blank)*   Nation.

Postoffice   Grayson, I.T.

AFFIDAVIT OF MOTHER.

UNITED STATES OF AMERICA, Indian Territory,
WESTERN   DISTRICT.

I, Adeline Smith , on oath state that I am 35 years of age and a citizen by none, of the *(blank)* Nation; that I am the lawful wife of Thomas M Smith , who is a citizen, by Blood of the Creek Nation; that a male child was born to me on 2 day of Dec , 1903 , that said child has been named Albert K Smith , and was living March 4, 1905.

Adeline Smith

Witnesses To Mark:

Subscribed and sworn to before me this 21 day of Mar , 1905.

My Commission expires 11/17/06   M H Harrison
Notary Public.

Applications for Enrollment of Creek Newborn
Act of 1905 Volume V

AFFIDAVIT OF ATTENDING PHYSICIAN OR MID-WIFE.

UNITED STATES OF AMERICA, Indian Territory, }
Western District DISTRICT.

  I, Emerline lucus[sic] , a Midwife , on oath state that I attended on Mrs. Adeline Smith , wife of Thomas M Smith on the 2 day of Dec , 1903 ; that there was born to her on said date a male child; that said child was living March 4, 1905, and is said to have been named Albert K. Smith

                    her
               Emerline x Lucus
Witnesses To Mark: mark
{ James R Smith
 Minnie Smith

  Subscribed and sworn to before me this 21 day of Mar , 1905.

  My Commission expires 11/17/06 M H Harrison
                   Notary Public.

BIRTH AFFIDAVIT.

DEPARTMENT OF THE INTERIOR.
COMMISSION TO THE FIVE CIVILIZED TRIBES.

  IN RE APPLICATION FOR ENROLLMENT, as a citizen of the CREEK Nation, of Stere J. Smith , born on the 16 day of Feb , 1902

Name of Father:	Thomas M Smith	a citizen of the	Creek	Nation.
Name of Mother:	Adeline Smith	a non citizen of the	(blank)	Nation.

       Postoffice Grayson, I.T.

AFFIDAVIT OF MOTHER.

UNITED STATES OF AMERICA, Indian Territory, }
 WESTERN DISTRICT.

  I, Adeline Smith , on oath state that I am 35 years of age and a citizen by non, of the *(blank)* Nation; that I am the lawful wife of Thomas M Smith , who is a citizen, by Blood of the Creek Nation; that a male child was born to me on 16 day of Feb , 1902 , that said child has been named Stere J Smith , and was living March 4, 1905.

               Adeline Smith
Witnesses To Mark:
{

Applications for Enrollment of Creek Newborn
Act of 1905   Volume V

Subscribed and sworn to before me this 21 day of Mar, 1905.

My Commission expires 11/17/06   M H Harrison
                                                                    Notary Public.

AFFIDAVIT OF ATTENDING PHYSICIAN OR MID-WIFE.

UNITED STATES OF AMERICA, Indian Territory,
    Western   DISTRICT.

I, Emerline Lucus, a Midwife, on oath state that I attended on Mrs. Adeline Smith, wife of Thomas M Smith on the 16 day of Feb, 1902; that there was born to her on said date a male child; that said child was living March 4, 1905, and is said to have been named Stere J. Smith
                                                                    her
                                                        Emerline x Lucus
Witnesses To Mark: mark
    James R Smith
    Minnie Smith

Subscribed and sworn to before me this 21 day of Mar, 1905.

My Commission expires 11/17/06   M H Harrison
                                                                    Notary Public.

N.C. 405.

                                    Muskogee, Indian Territory, August 3, 1905.

Katie Barnett,
        Care of Tucker Barnett,
                Weleetka, Indian Territory.
Dear Madam:

March 25, 1905, there was filed in this office an affidavit, executed by you, relative to your minor child, Rosanna Barnett; you state that said child was born January 19, 1904, and that the name of her father is Tucker Barnett.

You are advised that this office cannot identify you on its roll of citizens of the Creek Nation, and you are requested to state your maiden name, the names of your parents, the Creek Indian Town to which you belong, and, if possible, the numbers which appear on your deeds to land in the Creek Nation.

Applications for Enrollment of Creek Newborn
Act of 1905   Volume V

This matter should receive your prompt attention.

Respectfully,

Commissioner.

DCS.

NC-405

Muskogee, Indian Territory, December 12, 1905.

Katie Barnett,
    Care of Tucker Barnett,
        Weleetka, Indian Territory.

Dear Madam:

    March 25, 1905, there was filed in this office an affidavit, executed by you, relative to the birth of your minor child, Rosanna Barnett; born January 19, 1904.

    You are advised that this office cannot identify you on its rolls of citizens by blood of the Creek Nation. You are requested to write this office at an early date, giving your maiden name, the names of your parents and other members of your family, the Creek Indian Town to which you belong, and if possible, your name and roll number as same appear on your allotment certificate or deeds to land in the Creek Nation.

    This matter should receive your prompt attention.

Respectfully,

Acting Commissioner.

No. 57238

Copy   N.C. 405

W.R. Blake Agent,
    Weleetka, I.T.   12/28/05

U.S. Commissioner,
    Muskogee, I.T.

Dear Sir:- In reply to NC-405 I would say that my maiden name was Katie Canard. My mother's name was Rosanna Canard, & my father's name is Billy Canard.

My Roll number 4965 & my deed was delivered to me on January 3 1905. Filed for record Mar 7 1904 at 4 o'clock P.M. in Book 22, Page 279. Commissioner File # 13430.

Applications for Enrollment of Creek Newborn
Act of 1905   Volume V

Yours truly,

(Signed) Katie Canard.

BIRTH AFFIDAVIT.

DEPARTMENT OF THE INTERIOR.
COMMISSION TO THE FIVE CIVILIZED TRIBES.

IN RE APPLICATION FOR ENROLLMENT, as a citizen of the Creek Nation, of Rosanna Barnett, born on the 19 day of January, 1904

Name of Father: Tucker Barnett   a citizen of the   Creek   Nation.
Name of Mother: Katie Barnett   a citizen of the   Creek   Nation.

Postoffice   Weleetka, Ind. Ter.

AFFIDAVIT OF MOTHER.

UNITED STATES OF AMERICA, Indian Territory,
     Western   DISTRICT.

I, Katie Barnett, on oath state that I am 20 years of age and a citizen by blood, of the Creek Nation; that I am the lawful wife of Tucker Barnett, who is a citizen, by blood of the Creek Nation; that a female child was born to me on 19 day of January, 1904, that said child has been named Rosanna Barnett, and was living March 4, 1905.

                              her
                    Katie x Barnett
                              mark

Witnesses To Mark:
   Alex Posey
   DC Skaggs

Subscribed and sworn to before me this 20 day of March, 1905.

Drennan C Skaggs
Notary Public.

AFFIDAVIT OF ATTENDING PHYSICIAN OR MID-WIFE.

UNITED STATES OF AMERICA, Indian Territory,
     Western   DISTRICT.

I, Kizzie Canard, a midwife, on oath state that I attended on Mrs. Katie Barnett, wife of Tucker Barnett on the 19 day of January, 1904 : that there was born

Applications for Enrollment of Creek Newborn
Act of 1905   Volume V

to her on said date a female child; that said child was living March 4, 1905, and is said to have been named   Rosanna Barnett

            her
          Kizzie x Canard
Witnesses To Mark: mark
 { Alex Posey
   DC Skaggs

  Subscribed and sworn to before me this 20 day of March , 1905.

           Drennan C Skaggs
           Notary Public.

NC-406.

        Muskogee, Indian Territory, August 3, 1905.

Sophia Berryhill,
 Fentress, Indian Territory.

Dear Madam:

  In the matter of the application for the enrollment of your minor son Clent Berryhill, born January 9, 1902, as a citizen by blood of the Creek Nation, you are advised that it will be necessary for you to furnish this office with the affidavit of the attending physician or midwife at the birth of said child or, in case there was no attending physician or midwife, with the affidavits of two disinterested persons who are acquainted with said child, know when he was born, the names of his parents and whether or not he was living on March 4, 1905.

  A blank for proof of birth is inclosed[sic] herewith.

       Respectfully,

           Commissioner.
B C
Env.

       Acquaintanted
    AFFIDAVIT OF ~~ATTENDING PHYSICIAN OR MID-WIFE~~.

UNITED STATES OF AMERICA, Indian Territory, ⎫
 Western Judicial DISTRICT. ⎭

              We acquainted
  We, William Field and Foster Field , acquainted , on oath state that ~~I attended~~ on Mrs. Sophia Berryhill , wife of Sam Berryhill on the 9 day of January , 1902 ; that

Applications for Enrollment of Creek Newborn
Act of 1905   Volume V

there was born to her on said date a male child; that said child was living March 4, 1905, and is said to have been named Clent Berryhill

         L.P. Caldwell   To mark   William x Field
Witnesses To Mark: Tupper Dunn   mark
 { L.P. Caldwell   his
   Tupper Dunn   Foster x Field
                  mark

  Subscribed and sworn to before me this 24 day of Aug, 1905.

my Com Exp Aug 19" 1908   Tupper Dunn
                 Notary Public.

BIRTH AFFIDAVIT.

DEPARTMENT OF THE INTERIOR.
COMMISSION TO THE FIVE CIVILIZED TRIBES.

  IN RE APPLICATION FOR ENROLLMENT, as a citizen of the Creek Nation, of Clent Berryhill, born on the 9 day of January, 1902

Name of Father: Sam Berryhill   a citizen of the   Creek   Nation.
Name of Mother: Sophia Berryhill   a citizen of the   Creek   Nation.

         Postoffice   Fentress Ind. Ter.

AFFIDAVIT OF MOTHER.

UNITED STATES OF AMERICA, Indian Territory, }
   Western   DISTRICT.

  I, Sophia Berryhill, on oath state that I am 27 years of age and a citizen by blood, of the Creek Nation; that I am the lawful wife of Sam Berryhill, who is a citizen, by blood of the Creek Nation; that a male child was born to me on 9 day of January, 1902, that said child has been named Clent Berryhill, and was living March 4, 1905.
                her
             Sophia x Berryhill
               mark

Witnesses To Mark:
 { E.D. Miles
   RA Dill

  Subscribed and sworn to before me this 15 day of March, 1905.

my Com Exp Aug 19" 1908   Tupper Dunn
                 Notary Public.

Applications for Enrollment of Creek Newborn
Act of 1905   Volume V

N.C. 407.

DEPARTMENT OF THE INTERIOR,
COMMISSIONER TO THE FIVE CIVILIZED TRIBES.
Castle, Indian Territory, September 28, 1906.

In the matter of the application for the enrollment of Nora Harjage as a citizen by blood of the Creek Nation.
FRANK HARJAGE, being duly sworn, testified as follows: (through Jesse McDermott of official interpreter)

BY COMMISSIONER:
Q What is your name? A Frank Harjage, sometimes the Indians call me Pin Harjogee but my right name is Frank.
Q What is your age? A About twenty eight.
Q What is your postoffice address? A Castle.
Q Are you a Creek citizen? A Yes.
Q Have you filed on your land? A Arbitrarily I have.
Q Have you the deeds to your allotment? A No, Hulbutta had them but he told me that he had lot them.
Q To which Creek Indian tow do you belong? A Hutchechuppa.
Q What is the name of your mother? A I don't know.
Q What is the name of your father? Liyerwiney.
Q Have you a child that you named Roller by Daley? A Yes, I have one I call Nora.

There is an application which purports to be an affidavit on file at the office of the Commissioner to the Five Civilized Tribes signed by Daley on March 17, 1905, in the presence of H.G. Malot and Tupper Dunn in which she gives the name of the child as Roller.

Q Is that the correct name of the child? A No, her name is Nora.
Q When was Nora born? A Sometime in April.
Q Of what year? A I don't know.
Q How old will she be next April? A She will be three.
Q Are you and Daley lawfully married? A Married according to the Indian custom.
Q This is the child here about whom you are testifying is it? A Yes.

(The child is present and appears to be about the age as stated in the preceding testimony.)

------------- --------

Applications for Enrollment of Creek Newborn
Act of 1905   Volume V

    I, Jesse McDermott, on oath state that the above and foregoing is a full and true transcript of my notes as taken in said cause on said date.

                                Jesse McDermott

Subscribed and sworn to before me this 14th day of November, 1906.

                                J H Swofford
                                Notary Public.
My Com Exp. 2/26/1910

BIRTH AFFIDAVIT.
DEPARTMENT OF THE INTERIOR.
COMMISSION TO THE FIVE CIVILIZED TRIBES.

    IN RE APPLICATION FOR ENROLLMENT, as a citizen of the Creek Nation, of Roller Harjo , born on the 29" day of April, 1904

Name of Father: Frank Harjo (Pin Harjo)   a citizen of the   Creek   Nation.
Name of Mother: Daley Harjo (nee Fixico)   a citizen of the   Creek   Nation.

                          Postoffice   Castle, I.T.

AFFIDAVIT OF MOTHER.

UNITED STATES OF AMERICA, Indian Territory,
    Western   **DISTRICT.**

    I, Daley Harjo (nee Fixico) , on oath state that I am 18 years of age and a citizen by blood , of the Creek Nation; that I am the lawful wife of Frank Harjo (Pin Harjo) , who is a citizen, by blood of the Creek Nation; that a female child was born to me on 29 day of April , 1904 , that said child has been named Roller Harjo , and was living March 4, 1905.

                                  her
                        Daley x Harjo (nee Fixico)
Witnesses To Mark: mark
   { W H Dill Okemah I.T.
     Tupper Dunn Okemah I.T.
   Subscribed and sworn to before me this 10 day of October , 1905.

My com exp Aug 19-1908   Tupper Dunn
                                      Notary Public.

Applications for Enrollment of Creek Newborn
Act of 1905 Volume V

AFFIDAVIT OF ATTENDING PHYSICIAN OR MID-WIFE.

UNITED STATES OF AMERICA, Indian Territory, }
Western DISTRICT.

I, Sallie Fixico , a midwife , on oath state that I attended on Mrs. Daley Harjo , wife of Frank Harjo (Pin Harjo) on the 29" day of April , 1904 ; that there was born to her on said date a *(blank)* child; that said child was living March 4, 1905, and is said to have been named Roller Harjo

                                                             her
                                                         Sallie x Fixico

Witnesses To Mark: mark
{ W H Dill Okemah I.T.
  Tupper Dunn Okemah I.T.

Subscribed and sworn to before me this 10 day of October , 1905.

My com exp Aug 19-1908   Tupper Dunn
                                                    Notary Public.

BIRTH AFFIDAVIT.

DEPARTMENT OF THE INTERIOR.
COMMISSION TO THE FIVE CIVILIZED TRIBES.

IN RE APPLICATION FOR ENROLLMENT, as a citizen of the Creek Nation, of Roller Harjo , born on the 29th day of April, 1904

| Name of Father: | Pin Harjo | a citizen of the | Creek | Nation. |
| Name of Mother: | Daley Harjo (nee Fixico) | a citizen of the | Creek | Nation. |

                                 Postoffice   Castle, I.T.

AFFIDAVIT OF MOTHER.

UNITED STATES OF AMERICA, Indian Territory, }
Western DISTRICT.

I, Daley Harjo (nee Fixico) , on oath state that I am 18 years of age and a citizen by blood , of the Creek Nation; that I am the lawful wife of Pin Harjo , who is a citizen, by blood of the Creek Nation; that a female child was born to me on 29th day of April , 1904 , that said child has been named Roller Harjo , and was living March 4, 1905.

Witnesses To Mark:

Applications for Enrollment of Creek Newborn
Act of 1905   Volume V

Subscribed and sworn to before me this   day of   , 1905.

                                          Notary Public.

AFFIDAVIT OF ATTENDING PHYSICIAN OR MID-WIFE.

UNITED STATES OF AMERICA, Indian Territory,
    Western   DISTRICT.

I, Sallie Fixico , a midwife , on oath state that I attended on Mrs. Daley Harjo , wife of Pin Harjo on the 29" day of April , 1904 ; that there was born to her on said date a *(blank)* child; that said child was living March 4, 1905, and is said to have been named Roller Harjo

                                                         his
                                                     Pin Harjo x
Witnesses To Mark: mark
    W H Linton
    M H Fixico

Subscribed and sworn to before me this 6th day of Oct , 1905.

My Commission Expires June 19th, 1909.   J. E. Eastman
                                                          Notary Public.

BIRTH AFFIDAVIT.
DEPARTMENT OF THE INTERIOR.
COMMISSION TO THE FIVE CIVILIZED TRIBES.

IN RE APPLICATION FOR ENROLLMENT, as a citizen of the Creek Nation, of Roller Harjochee , born on the 29 day of April, 1904

Name of Father: Pin Harjochee   a citizen of the   Creek   Nation.
Name of Mother: Dela Fixico nee Harjochee   a citizen of the   Creek   Nation.

                                Postoffice   Castle, Ind. Ter.

AFFIDAVIT OF MOTHER.

UNITED STATES OF AMERICA, Indian Territory,
    Western   DISTRICT.

I, Dela Fixico nee Harjochee , on oath state that I am 18 years of age and a citizen by blood , of the Creek Nation; that I am the lawful wife of Pin Harjochee , who is a citizen, by blood of the Creek Nation; that a female child was born to me

Applications for Enrollment of Creek Newborn
Act of 1905   Volume V

on 29 day of April, 1904, that said child has been named Roller Harjo chee, and was living March 4, 1905.

her
Dela Fixico x nee Harjochee
mark

Witnesses To Mark:
{ H.G. Malot
{ Tupper Dunn

Subscribed and sworn to before me this 17 day of March, 1905.

(No Signature)
Notary Public.

AFFIDAVIT OF ATTENDING PHYSICIAN OR MID-WIFE.

UNITED STATES OF AMERICA, Indian Territory, }
Western   DISTRICT.

I, Sallie Fixico, a midwife, on oath state that I attended on Mrs. Dela Fixico nee Harjochee, wife of Pin Harjochee on the 29 day of April, 1904; that there was born to her on said date a female child; that said child was living March 4, 1905, and is said to have been named Roller Harjochee

her
Sallie x Fixico
mark

Witnesses To Mark:
{ H.G. Malot
{ Tupper Dunn

Subscribed and sworn to before me this 17 day of March, 1905.

(No Signature)
Notary Public.

BIRTH AFFIDAVIT.

DEPARTMENT OF THE INTERIOR.
COMMISSION TO THE FIVE CIVILIZED TRIBES.

IN RE APPLICATION FOR ENROLLMENT, as a citizen of the Creek Nation, of Nora Harjage, born on the 29" day of April, 1904

Name of Father: Frank Harjage   a citizen of the   Creek   Nation.
Name of Mother: Daley Harjage (nee Fixico)   a citizen of the   Creek   Nation.
   Roll # 6695

Postoffice   Castle, Ind. Ter.

Applications for Enrollment of Creek Newborn
Act of 1905   Volume V

AFFIDAVIT OF MOTHER.

UNITED STATES OF AMERICA, Indian Territory, }
Western DISTRICT.

I, Daley Harjage (nee Fixico), on oath state that I am 19 years of age and a citizen by blood, of the Creek Nation; that I am the lawful wife of Frank Harjage, who is a citizen, by blood of the Creek Nation; that a female child was born to me on 29" day of April, 1904, that said child has been named Nora Harjage, and was living March 4, 1905.

                                                her
                                    Daley x Harjage

Witnesses To Mark: mark
  { Jesse McDermott
  { *(Name Illegible)*

Subscribed and sworn to before me this 28" day of Sept, 1906.
My Commission
Expires July 25" 1907   J. McDermott
                                          Notary Public.

AFFIDAVIT OF ATTENDING PHYSICIAN OR MID-WIFE.

UNITED STATES OF AMERICA, Indian Territory, }
Western DISTRICT.

I, Sallie Fixico, a midwife, on oath state that I attended on Mrs. Daley Harjage, wife of FrankHarjage on the 29" day of April, 1904 ; that there was born to her on said date a *(blank)* child; that said child was living March 4, 1905, and is said to have been named Nora Harjage

                                           her
                                  Sallie x Fixico

Witnesses To Mark: mark
  { Jesse McDermott
  { *(Name Illegible)*

Subscribed and sworn to before me this 28" day of Sept, 1906.
My Commission
Expires July 25" 1907   J. McDermott
                                          Notary Public.

BIRTH AFFIDAVIT.

DEPARTMENT OF THE INTERIOR.
COMMISSION TO THE FIVE CIVILIZED TRIBES.

IN RE APPLICATION FOR ENROLLMENT, as a citizen of the Creek Nation, of Roller Harjo, born on the 29th day of April, 1904

Applications for Enrollment of Creek Newborn
Act of 1905   Volume V

Name of Father: Pin Harjo   a citizen of the   Creek   Nation.
Name of Mother: Daley Harjo (nee Fixico)   a citizen of the   Creek   Nation.

                        Postoffice   Castle, I.T.

AFFIDAVIT OF MOTHER.

UNITED STATES OF AMERICA, Indian Territory, ⎫
    Western   DISTRICT.   ⎭

I, Daley Harjo (nee *Illegible*) , on oath state that I am 10[sic] years of age and a citizen by blood , of the Creek Nation; that I am the lawful wife of Pin Harjo , who is a citizen, by blood of the Creek Nation; that a female child was born to me on 29th day of April , 1904 , that said child has been named Roller Harjo , and was living March 4, 1905.

Witnesses To Mark:
{ ....
  ....

Subscribed and sworn to before me this ...... day of ...., 1905.

                                        ....
                                                  Notary Public.

AFFIDAVIT OF ATTENDING PHYSICIAN OR MID-WIFE.

UNITED STATES OF AMERICA, Indian Territory, ⎫
    Western   DISTRICT.   ⎭

I, Sallie Fixico , a midwife , on oath state that I attended on Mrs. Daley Harjo , wife of Pin Harjo on the 29" day of April , 1904 ; that there was born to her on said date a female child; that said child was living March 4, 1905, and is said to have been named Roller Harjo
                                                              her
                                       Sallie Fixico   x
Witnesses To Mark: mark
  { W H Linton
    M H. Fixico

Subscribed and sworn to before me this 6th day of Oct , 1905.

                (signed)   J E Eastman
                                Notary Public.
My Commission Expires June 10th 1909

Applications for Enrollment of Creek Newborn
Act of 1905 Volume V

REFER IN REPLY TO THE FOLLOWING:	
NC-407.	

HGH

DEPARTMENT OF THE INTERIOR,
COMMISSIONER TO THE FIVE CIVILIZED TRIBES.

Muskogee. Indian Territory. August 3, 1905.

Daley Harjo,
    c/o Pin Harjo,
        Castle, Indian Territory.

Dear Madam:

    In the matter of the application for the enrollment of your minor daughter Roller it will be necessary for you to furnish this office with new affidavits as to her birth inasmuch as the notary public, before whom your affidavit and the affidavit of Sallie Fixico were sworn to, neglected to affix his seal to said affidavits. There also appears a discrepancy as to your name and the name of your husband. Your said husband is identified upon the final roll of citizens of the Creek Nation as Pin Harjo, while his name appears in said affidavits as Pin Harjochee. You aver in your affidavit that you are the lawful wife of said Pin Harjochee and your name is signed to said affidavit by mark Dela Fixico, nee Harjochee.

    A blank for proof which has been filled out showing the necessary corrections is inclosed[sic] herewith and you are requested to have the same properly executed. Be careful to sign your name to your affidavit as the same appears in the body thereof and to see that the notary public before whom the affidavits are sworn to attaches his name and seal to each affidavit. Signatures by mark must be attested by two witnesses attested by two disinterested witnesses.

                      Respectfully,

                              Tams Bixby
                              Commissioner.

CTD-19
Env.

NC-407

Muskogee, Indian Territory, December 12, 1906.

Dailey Harjo,
    Care of Frank (or Pin) Harjo,
        Castle, Indian Territory.

Dear Madam:

Applications for Enrollment of Creek Newborn
Act of 1905   Volume V

In the matter of the application for the enrollment of your minor child, Roler Harjo, born April 29, 1904, as a citizen by blood of the Creek Nation, this office is unable to identify Frank (or Pin) Harjo, the father of said child, on its final roll of citizens by blood of the Creek Nation.

You are requested to write this office at an early date giving the names of the parents of said Frank (or Pin) Harjo, the Creek Indian Town to which he belongs, and, if possible, his name and roll number as same appear on hi allotment certificate or deeds to land in the Creek Nation.

You are also requested to advise this Office whether or not the correct name of Frank (or Pin) Harjo is Frank Harjoge If the name of the father of said child is in fact Frank Harjoge it necessarily follows that your name if Dailey Harjoge, and not Dailey Harjo, and the name of said child is Roller Harjoge and not Roller Harjo.

There is herewith enclosed a blank form of birth affidavit, and in the event the name of the father of said child is Frank Harjoge, or any name other than Frank (or Pin) Harjo, it will be necessary for you to execute same before a notary public, giving your correct name, the correct name of said child, and the correct name of the father of said child. You will then return said affidavit to this office in the enclosed envelover.

This matter should receive your prompt attention.

Respectfully,

Acting Commissioner.

1-BA.

N.C. 408.

DEPARTMENT OF THE INTERIOR,
COMMISSIONER TO THE FIVE CIVILIZED TRIBES,
Wewoka, Indian Territory, November 5, 1906.

In the matter of the application for the enrollment of Herford Barnett as a citizen by blood of the Creek Nation.

RACHEL BARNETT, being duly sworn testified as follows:

BY COMMISSIONER:

Q What is your name? A Rachel Barnett.
Q What is your age? A I am twenty seven.

Applications for Enrollment of Creek Newborn
Act of 1905   Volume V

Q What is your postoffice address? A Wewoka c/o Charley Carolina
Q Are you a Creek citizen? A No sir, I am a Seminole. My husband was a Creek citizen.
Q Was he a citizen by blood of the Creek Nation? A I don't know.
Q Have you a child named Herford? A Did have.
Q When was he born? A In 1903 July the first.
Q Isn't he living? A No sir.
Q When did he die? A Why, Herford died when it was about a week old I guess. He was a twin with this boy here. (Indicating a little boy who she calls Jeff) I made application for him in the Seminole but never did hear anything more about it.

There is an affidavit on file at the office of the Commissioner to the Five Civilized Tribes signed by you on March 21, 1905, before John B. Patterson stating that your child Herford was living March 4, 1905.

Q Do you remember signing such affidavit? A Yes sir.
Q Was Herford living on March 4, 1905, as stated in that affidavit? A No sir.
Q Well, what made you sign that affidavit? A My husband caused me to sign it. He said it would be allright for me to sign it. He said he'd have Herford enrolled with him and this boy with me in the Seminole.
Q Are you sure that your child Herford was not a month old when he died are you? A Yes sir, I am. Dick Barnett and them knows all about it.
Q Where does he live? A Near Weleetka. He raised me.
Q Were lawfully married to Dock Barnett when this child that dies was born? A We was married by the bible. I guess you'd called that lawfully.
Q What is the name of the minister who married you? A John Grayson.
Q When was it? A In 1898 I believe.

---oooOOOooo---

I, Jesse McDermott, on oath state that the above and foregoing is a full and true transcript of my notes as taken in said cause on said date.

Jesse McDermott

Subscribed and sworn to before me this 6th day of November, 1906.

Frank J. Smith
Notary Public.

Applications for Enrollment of Creek Newborn
Act of 1905 Volume V

BIRTH AFFIDAVIT.

DEPARTMENT OF THE INTERIOR.
COMMISSION TO THE FIVE CIVILIZED TRIBES.

IN RE APPLICATION FOR ENROLLMENT, as a citizen of the Creek Nation, of Herford Barnett, born on the 1st day of July, 1903

Name of Father:	Dock Barnett	a citizen of the	Creek	Nation.
Name of Mother:	Rachel Barnett	a citizen of the	Creek	Nation.

Postoffice   Weleetka Ind. Ter.

AFFIDAVIT OF MOTHER.

UNITED STATES OF AMERICA, Indian Territory, }
  Western   DISTRICT.

I, Rachel Barnett, on oath state that I am 27 years of age and a citizen by Birth, of the Muskogee (Creek) Nation; that I am the lawful wife of Dock Barnett, who is a citizen, by Birth of the Muskogee (Creek) Nation; that a male child was born to me on 1st day of July, 1903, that said child has been named Herford Barnett, and ~~is now~~ was living. March 4, 1905

(Signed) Rachel Barnett

Witnesses To Mark:
{

Subscribed and sworn to before me this 21st day of March, 1905.
(Signed) John B Patterson
Notary Public.

AFFIDAVIT OF ATTENDING PHYSICIAN OR MID-WIFE.

UNITED STATES OF AMERICA, Indian Territory, }
  Western   DISTRICT.

I, Elizabeth Barnett, a midwife, on oath state that I attended on Mrs. Rachel Barnett, wife of Dock Barnett on the 1st day of July, 1903; that there was born to her on said date a male child; that said child ~~is now~~ was living March 4, 1905 and is said to have been named Herford Barnett

  her
Elizabeth x Barnett
  mark

Witnesses To Mark:
 { Polly Harris
   Charley Harris

Applications for Enrollment of Creek Newborn
Act of 1905 Volume V

Subscribed and sworn to before me this 21st day of March, 1905.

                     (Signed) John B Patterson
                                 Notary Public.

N.C. 408/   F.H.W.
DEPARTMENT OF THE INTERIOR.
COMMISSIONER TO THE FIVE CIVILIZED TRIBES.

In the matter of the application for the enrollment of Herford Barnett, deceased, as a citizen by blood of the Creek Nation.

DECISION.

The record in this case shows that on March 24, 1905, an application was made, in affidavit form, for the enrollment of Herford Barnett as a citizen by blood of the Creek Nation, under the provisions of the Act of Congress approved March 3, 1905. Further proceedings were had at Wewoka, Indian Territory, before a Creek enrollment field party, on November 5, 1906.

It appears in evidence that the said Herford Barnett was born July 1, 1903.

The evidence is contradictory as to the date of death of said applicant but the weight of evidence establishes said date as about July 8, 1903.

The act of Congress approved March 3, 1905, (33 Stats., 1048), provides in part as follows:

"That the Commission to the Five Civilized Tribes is authorized for sixty days after the date of the approval of this Act to receive and consider applications for enrollments of children born subsequent to May twenty five, nineteen hundred and one, and prior to March fourth, nineteen hundred and five, and living on said latter date, to citizens of the Creek tribe of Indians whose enrollment has been approved by the Secretary of the Interior prior to the date of approval of this Act; and to enroll and make allotments to such children."

It is therefore, ordered and adjudged that under the provisions of the law above quoted said Herford Barnett, deceased, is not entitled to be enrolled as a citizen by blood of the Creek Nation and the application for his enrollment as such is accordingly denied.

                                   Tams Bixby   Commissioner.

Muskogee, Indian Territory.
JAN 25 1907

Applications for Enrollment of Creek Newborn
Act of 1905 Volume V

NC 408

Muskogee, Indian Territory, June 5, 1905.

Rachel Barnett,
    Weleetka, Indian Territory.

Dear Madam:

    In the matter of the application for the enrollment of your minor child, Herford Barnett, as a citizen of the Creek Nation, you are advised that the Commission is unable to identify you on its rolls.

    You are requested to furnish the Commission with your maiden name, the names of your parents, the Creek Indian Town to which you belong, and, if possible, the numbers on your deeds to land in the Creek Nation.

                  Respectfully,

                                    Commissioner in Charge.

NC 408

Muskogee, Indian Territory, December 12, 1905.

Rachel Barnett,
    Care of Dock Barnett,
        Weleetka, Indian Territory.

Dear Madam:

    In the matter of the application for the enrollment of your minor child, Herford Barnett, born July 1, 1903, as a citizen by blood of the Creek Nation, you are advised that this office is unable to identify you on its rolls of citizens of the Creek Nation.

    You are requested to write this office at an early date giving your maiden name, the names of your parents, and other members of your family, the Creek Indian Town to which you belong, and, if possible, your name and roll number as same appear on your allotment certificate and deeds to land in the Creek Nation.

                  Respectfully,

                                    Acting Commissioner.

Applications for Enrollment of Creek Newborn
Act of 1905 Volume V

NC 408.

Muskogee, Indian Territory, January 28, 1907.

Rachel Barnett,
    Care of Charley Carolina,
        Wewoka, Indian territory.

Dear Madam:

    There is herewith inclosed[sic] one copy of the decision of the Commissioner to the Five Civilized Tribes in the matter of the application for the enrollment of Herford Barnett as a citizen by blood of the Creek Nation, denying said application.

    The decision, with a copy of the proceedings had in the case, is this day transmitted to the Secretary of the Interior for his review and decision. The final decision of the Secretary will be made known to you as soon as the Commissioner is informed of t the same.

                Respectfully,

Register.   Commissioner.
CM-28-30

NC 408

Muskogee, Indian Territory, January 28, 1907.

M. L. Mott,
    Attorney for the Creek Nation,
        Muskogee, Indian Territory.

Dear Sir:

    There is inclosed[sic] herewith one copy of the decision of the Commissioner to the Five Civilized Tribes in the matter of the application for the enrollment of Herford Barnett as a citizen by blood of the Creek Nation.
    The decision with a copy of the proceedings had in the case is this day transmitted to the Secretary of the Interior for his review and decision. The final decision of the Secretary will be made known to you as soon as the Commissioner is informed of the same.

                Respectfully,

Inc. CM-23-31   Commissioner.

Applications for Enrollment of Creek Newborn
Act of 1905 Volume V

NC 408

Muskogee, Indian Territory, January 28, 1907.

The Honorable,
    The Secretary of the Interior,

Sir:

    There is herewith transmitted the record of proceedings in the matter of the application for the enrollment of Herford Barnett, deceased, as a citizen by blood of the Creek Nation, including the decision of the Commissioner dated January 25, 1907.

                  Respectfully,

                                  Commissioner.

Through the Commissioner
    of Indian Affairs.
CM-28-32

Refer in reply to the following:
    Land 10244-1907.

COPY

                DEPARTMENT OF THE INTERIOR,
                  OFFICE OF INDIAN AFFAIRS,
                        WASHINGTON.

                              February 25, 1907.

The Honorable,
    The Secretary of the Interior.

Sir:

    I have the honor to transmit herewith a communication from the Commissioner to the Five Civilized Tribes, dated January 28, 1907, enclosing the record in the matter of the enrollment of Herford Barnett, deceased, as a citizen by blood of the Creek Nation, including the decision of the Commissioner, dated January 26, 1907.

    It is shown by the record herein that an application in affidavit form was filed on March 24, 1905, for the enrollment of Herford Barnett as a citizen by blood of the Creek Nation, under the provisions of the Act of Congress approved March 3, 1905. Further proceedings were had before a Creek field party at Wewoka, Indian Territory, on November 5, 1906. The applicant was born July 1, 1903. The testimony of the mother is that he was a twin and lived only about a week and consequently died about July 8, 1903.

Applications for Enrollment of Creek Newborn
Act of 1905   Volume V

The Act under which application was made provides for enrollment of children born subsequent to May 25, 1901, and prior to March 3, 1905, "and living on said latter date."

The office is of the opinion that the Commissioner's decision denying the application for the enrollment of Herford Barnett, deceased, as a citizen by blood of the Creek Nation is correct and it is recommended that it be affirmed.

Very respectfully,

C. F. Larrabee,

Acting Commissioner.

EWE-C

LRS   WASHINGTON.   FHE.

I.T.D. 4850, 4890, 4904, 4960, 4962-07,
        4964, 5082, 5166, 5202, 5328- "   March 1, 1907.
        5342, 5374, 5376, 5378, 5380- "
        ~~5396~~, 5398, 5400, 5402, 5404- "
        5410, ~~5416~~, 5418, 5424, 5428- "
        5466, 5488, 5498, 5548,   - "
D.C.   12430-1907.
DIRECT.

Commissioner to the Five Civilized Tribes,
        Muskogee, Indian Territory.

Sir:

Your decisions in the following Creek citizenship cases adverse to the applicants are hereby affirmed, viz:

Title of case.	Date of your letter of transmittal.
Rhoda Walker,	December 19, 1906
Josiah McIntosh	January 18, 1907
Tony Harlings,	January 18, 1907
George Allen, (Freedman)	January 28, 1907
Henry Edwards, (Freedman)	January 28, 1907
Lewis Davis, deceased,	January 28, 1907
Robert Scott, deceased,	October 19, 1906

Applications for Enrollment of Creek Newborn
Act of 1905 Volume V

Tom and Mattie Jeffries, deceased,	February 8, 1907
Emma Dodge, (Freedman)	February 8, 1907
Georgia Davis, deceased, (Freedman)	February 7, 1907
Thelma Maud Gibson,	February 7, 1907
Magie Nola Poe, (Freedman)	January 28, 1907
Nelson McIntosh,	January 19, 1907
Calley Ceasar, deceased,	January 28, 1907
Sarah Buck, deceased,	January 25, 1907
Willie Perryman, (Freedman)	January 28, 1907
Joshua Gentry et al.,	January 28, 1907
Dennis Taylor, (Freedman)	January 22, 1907
Paul and Pauline Bruner,	January 25, 1907
Gennie Sanders, (Freedman)	January 28, 1907
Eddie Levi, (Freedman)	January 28, 1907
Gabriel Hawkins, (Freedman)	January 28, 1907
Lottie Dickson, (Freedman)	January 29, 1907
Charles Tiger, deceased,	January 29, 1907
Herford Barnett, deceased,	January 28, 1907
Cebern Holt, (Freedman)	February 7, 1907
Marguerite Scott, deceased, (Freedman)	January 31, 1907

Copies of Indian Office letters submitting your reports and recommending that the decisions be approved, are inclosed[sic].

A copy hereof and all the papers in the above mentioned cases have been sent to the Indian Office.

Respectfully,
(Signed) Jesse E. Wilson,
Assistant Secretary.

27 inc. and 61 for Ind. Of.

AFMc
3-1-07

N C 408

JWH

Muskogee, Indian Territory, March 8, 1907.

Dock Barnett,
Weleetka, Indian Territory.

Dear Sir :--

You are hereby advised that under date of March 1, 1907, the Secretary of the Interior affirmed the decision of the Commissioner to the Five Civilized Tribes, denying

Applications for Enrollment of Creek Newborn
Act of 1905   Volume V

the application for the enrollment of your minor child, Herford Barnett, as a citizen by blood of the Creek Nation.

                        Respectfully,

                                      Commissioner.

NC-409.

                        Muskogee, Indian Territory, August 3, 1905.

Cogee Davis,
    c/o Joe Davis,
        Okfusky[sic], Indian Territory.

Dear Madam:

    In the matter of the application for the enrollment of your minor daughter Alice Davis, born March 22, 1904, as a citizen by blood of the Creek Nation, it will be necessary for you to furnish this office with the affidavit of the attending physician or midwife at the birth of said child, but if no physician or midwife attended you when said child was born it will be necessary for you to furnish this office, relative to the birth of said child, with the affidavits of two disinterested persons who are acquainted with said child, know when she was born, the names of her parents and whether or not she was living on March 4, 1905.

    A blank for proof of birth is inclosed[sic] herewith.

                      Respectfully,

                                   Commissioner.

B C
Env.

N.C. 409

                    Muskogee, Indian Territory, September 25, 1905.

Joe Davis,
    Okfuskee, Indian Territory.

Dear Sir:

    Receipt is acknowledged of your letter of September 13, 1905, in which you ask if the enrollment of your minor child, Alice Davis, is all right, and when you can file for her.

Applications for Enrollment of Creek Newborn
Act of 1905   Volume V

In reply you are advised that the matter of the enrollment of said child is pending before the Secretary of the Interior, and when same has been finally approved by him, you will be given due notice with regard to filing.

Respectfully,

Commissioner.

Affidavit of two disinterested persons.

United States of America, I.T.
Western District.

We, London Knight and Eli Heneha, on oath state that we know Mrs. Cogee Davis wife of Joe Davis; that the[sic] was born to her on *(illegible)* 1904 a female child; that said child was living March 4, 1905, and is said to have been named Alice & we are no kin to parties herein.

London Knight

Eli Heneha

Subscribed and sworn to before me this 10th day of August 1905.

Henry G. Hains
Notary Public.

BIRTH AFFIDAVIT.

DEPARTMENT OF THE INTERIOR.
COMMISSION TO THE FIVE CIVILIZED TRIBES.

IN RE APPLICATION FOR ENROLLMENT, as a citizen of the Creek Nation, of Alice Davis, born on the 22 day of March, 1904

Name of Father:	Joe Davis	a citizen of the Creek	Nation.
Name of Mother:	Cogee Davis	a citizen of the Creek	Nation.

Postoffice   Okfusky[sic]

Applications for Enrollment of Creek Newborn
Act of 1905   Volume V

AFFIDAVIT OF MOTHER.

UNITED STATES OF AMERICA, Indian Territory,
Western   DISTRICT.

I, Cogee Davis, on oath state that I am 27 years of age and a citizen by Blood, of the Creek Nation; that I am the lawful wife of Joe Davis, who is a citizen, by Blood of the Creek Nation; that a female child was born to me on 22 day of March, 1904, that said child has been named Alice, and was living March 4, 1905.

                                              her
                                 Cogee Davis x
Witnesses To Mark: mark
  London Knight
  Eli Heneha

Subscribed and sworn to before me this 10th day of August, 1905.

                                  Wesley M Dyson
                                      Notary Public.

AFFIDAVIT OF ATTENDING PHYSICIAN OR MID-WIFE.

UNITED STATES OF AMERICA, Indian Territory,
Western   DISTRICT.

We, LONDON KNIGHT AND. ~~a~~ ELI HENEHA, on oath state that ~~I~~ WE ~~attended on~~ KNOW Mrs. COGEE DAVIS, wife of JOE DAVIS ~~on the~~ *(blank)* ~~day of~~ *(blank)*, ~~1~~ *(blank)*; that there was born to her on said date a FEMALE child; that said child was living March 4, 1905, and is said to have been named Alice

                                  London Knight
Witnesses To Mark: Eli Heneha

Subscribed and sworn to before me this 10th day of Aug, 1905.

                                  Wesley M. Dyson
                                     Notary Public.

BIRTH AFFIDAVIT.

DEPARTMENT OF THE INTERIOR.
COMMISSION TO THE FIVE CIVILIZED TRIBES.

IN RE APPLICATION FOR ENROLLMENT, as a citizen of the CREEK Nation, of Alice Davis, born on the 22 day of March, 1904

Applications for Enrollment of Creek Newborn
Act of 1905   Volume V

Name of Father: Joe Davis   a citizen of the   Creek   Nation.
Name of Mother: Cogee "   a citizen of the   "   Nation.

Postoffice   Okfusky[sic]

Child present

AFFIDAVIT OF MOTHER.

UNITED STATES OF AMERICA, Indian Territory, }
   WESTERN   DISTRICT.

    I, Cogee Davis , on oath state that I am 27 years of age and a citizen by blood , of the Creek Nation; that I am the lawful wife of Joe Davis , who is a citizen, by blood of the Creek Nation; that a female child was born to me on 22 day of March, 1904 , that said child has been named Alice Davis , and is now living.

                                      Cogee Davis

Witnesses To Mark:
{

    Subscribed and sworn to before me this 24" day of March , 1905.

                                      J McDermott
                                      Notary Public.

AFFIDAVIT OF ATTENDING PHYSICIAN OR MID-WIFE.

UNITED STATES OF AMERICA, Indian Territory, }
   WESTERN   DISTRICT.

    I, Joe Davis , a husband , on oath state that I attended on Mrs. Cogee Davis , wife of myself on the 22 day of March , 1904 ; that there was born to her on said date a female child; that said child is now living and is said to have been named Alice Davis
                                      Joe Davis

Witnesses To Mark:
{

    Subscribed and sworn to before me this 24" day of March , 1905.

                                    J McDermott
                                      Notary Public.

Applications for Enrollment of Creek Newborn
Act of 1905   Volume V

NC 410.

Muskogee, Indian Territory, June 5, 1905.

Cotcha Fixico,
   Okemah, Indian Territory.

Dear Sir:

In the matter of the application for the enrollment of your minor child, Willie Fixico, as a citizen of the Creek Nation, you are advised that the Commission is unable to identify the mother of said child, Cinda Fixico.

You are requested to furnish the Commission with her maiden name, the names of her parents, the Creek Indian Town to which she belong[sic], and if possible, the numbers on her deeds to land in the Creek Nation.

Respectfully,

Commissioner in Charge.

BIRTH AFFIDAVIT.

DEPARTMENT OF THE INTERIOR.
COMMISSION TO THE FIVE CIVILIZED TRIBES.

IN RE APPLICATION FOR ENROLLMENT, as a citizen of the Creek Nation, of Willie Fixico, born on the 6th day of July, 1903

Name of Father: Katcher Fixico   a citizen of the   Creek   Nation.
Name of Mother: Cinda Fixico   a citizen of the   Creek   Nation.

Postoffice   Okemah, I.T.

AFFIDAVIT OF MOTHER.

UNITED STATES OF AMERICA, Indian Territory,
   Western Judicial   DISTRICT.

I, Cinda Fixico, on oath state that I am 30 years of age and a citizen by Blood, of the Muskogee or Creek Nation; that I am the lawful wife of Katcher Fixico, who is a citizen, by Blood of the Muskokee[sic] or Creek Nation; that a Male child was born to me on 6th day of July, 1903, that said child has been named Willie Fixico, and was living March 4, 1905.

Applications for Enrollment of Creek Newborn
Act of 1905 Volume V

              her
            Cinda x Fixico
Witnesses To Mark: mark
 { S.J. Haynes
  Henry Micco

  Subscribed and sworn to before me this 21th[sic] day of March, 1905.

My Commission Expires Sept 6th 1906.   John H. Phillips
               Notary Public.

AFFIDAVIT OF ATTENDING PHYSICIAN OR MID-WIFE.

UNITED STATES OF AMERICA, Indian Territory,
 Western Judicial   DISTRICT.

  I, Monayee, a Mid-Wife, on oath state that I attended on Mrs. Cinda Fixico, wife of Katcher Fixico on the 6th day of July, 1903; that there was born to her on said date a Male child; that said child was living March 4, 1905, and is said to have been named Willie Fixico
              her
            Monayee x
Witnesses To Mark: mark
 { S.J. Haynes
  Henry Micco

  Subscribed and sworn to before me this 21th[sic] day of March, 1905.

My Commission Expires Sept 6th 1906.   John H. Phillips
               Notary Public.

BIRTH AFFIDAVIT.

DEPARTMENT OF THE INTERIOR.
COMMISSION TO THE FIVE CIVILIZED TRIBES.

  IN RE APPLICATION FOR ENROLLMENT, as a citizen of the Creek Nation, of Bertha Storm, born on the 14th day of January, 1903

| Name of Father: | John Storm | a citizen of theUnited States | Nation. |
| Name of Mother: | Lori Storm | a citizen of the Creek | Nation. |

      Postoffice   Checotah Ind. Ter.

Applications for Enrollment of Creek Newborn
Act of 1905   Volume V

AFFIDAVIT OF MOTHER.

UNITED STATES OF AMERICA, Indian Territory,
Western   DISTRICT.

I, Lori Storm, on oath state that I am 28 years of age and a citizen by Blood, of the Creek Nation; that I am the lawful wife of John Storm, who is a citizen, by *(blank)* of the United States Nation; that a Female child was born to me on 14th day of January, 1903, that said child has been named Bertha Storm, and was living March 4, 1905.

                                        her
Witnesses To Mark: Lori x Storm
   A.A. Smith Checotah I.T.   mark
   Ben D. Gross

Subscribed and sworn to before me this 21st day of March, 1905.

My Commission Expires July 1, 1906.   JB Morrow
                                                   Notary Public.

AFFIDAVIT OF ATTENDING PHYSICIAN OR MID-WIFE.

UNITED STATES OF AMERICA, Indian Territory,
Western   DISTRICT.

I, Lydia Wells, a Midwife, on oath state that I attended on Mrs. Lori Storm, wife of John Storm on the 14th day of January, 1903; that there was born to her on said date a Female child; that said child was living March 4, 1905, and is said to have been named Bertha Storm

                                        her
Witnesses To Mark: Lydia x Wells
   A.A. Smith Checotah I.T.   mark
   Ben D. Gross

Subscribed and sworn to before me this 21st day of March, 1905.

My Commission Expires July 1, 1906.   JB Morrow
                                                   Notary Public.

BIRTH AFFIDAVIT.

DEPARTMENT OF THE INTERIOR.
COMMISSION TO THE FIVE CIVILIZED TRIBES.

IN RE APPLICATION FOR ENROLLMENT, as a citizen of the Creek Nation, of Pocahontas Storm, born on the 19th day of December, 1904

Applications for Enrollment of Creek Newborn
Act of 1905   Volume V

Name of Father: John Storm   a citizen of the United States Nation.
Name of Mother: Lori Storm   a citizen of the   Creek   Nation.

Postoffice   Checotah I.T.

AFFIDAVIT OF MOTHER.

UNITED STATES OF AMERICA, Indian Territory, }
   Western   DISTRICT.

    I, Lori Storm , on oath state that I am 28 years of age and a citizen by Blood , of the Creek   Nation; that I am the lawful wife of   John Storm , who is a citizen, by *(blank)* of the United States   Nation; that a Female   child was born to me on 19th day of December , 1904 , that said child has been named   Pocahontas Storm   , and was living March 4, 1905.

                                  her
Witnesses To Mark: Lori x Storm
  { A.A. Smith Checotah I.T.   mark
    Ben D. Gross

    Subscribed and sworn to before me this 21st day of March , 1905.

My Commission Expires July 1, 1906.   JB Morrow
                                         Notary Public.

AFFIDAVIT OF ATTENDING PHYSICIAN OR MID-WIFE.

UNITED STATES OF AMERICA, Indian Territory, }
   Western   DISTRICT.

    I,   Lydia Wells, a Midwife , on oath state that I attended on Mrs. Lori Storm , wife of John Storm on the 19th day of December , 1904 ; that there was born to her on said date a Female child; that said child was living March 4, 1905, and is said to have been named   Pocahontas Storm

                                  her
Witnesses To Mark: Lydia x Wells
  { A.A. Smith Checotah I.T.   mark
    Ben D. Gross

    Subscribed and sworn to before me this 21st day of March , 1905.

My Commission Expires July 1, 1906.   JB Morrow
                                         Notary Public.

Applications for Enrollment of Creek Newborn
Act of 1905   Volume V

NC-412

Muskogee, Indian Territory, December 12, 1905.

Rose Etta Miller,
    Care of Quint H. Miller,
        Oktaha, Indian Territory.

Dear Madam:

    In the matter of the application for the enrollment of your minor children, Malvin H. Miller, born January 3, 1903, and Cecil Miller, as citizens by blood of the Creek Nation, this Office is unable to identify you on its final rolls of citizens of the Creek Nation.

    You are requested to write this Office at an early date, giving your maiden name, the names of your parents and other members of your family, the Creek Indian Town to which you belong, and, if possible, your name and roll numbers as same appear on your allotment certificate or deeds to land in the Creek Nation.

    The affidavit on file in this Office relative to the birth of your child, Cecil Miller, is defective, inasmuch as you state in your affidavit executed March 25, 1905, that said Cecil Miller was born June 4, 1904, and A.J. Snelson, the physician in attendance at the birth of said child, states in his affidavit executed March 25, 1905, that said Cecil Miller was born June 4, 1905. The date given in the affidavit of the physician is obviously an error. There is herewith enclosed a blank form of birth affidavit, which you are requested to have executed by said physician, giving the correct date of the birth of said child, and return affidavit when executed to this Office in the enclosed envelope.

    This matter should receive your prompt attention.

        Respectfully,

I B A   Acting Commissioner.

NC-412   (Copy)

        Oktaha, I. T. Dec. 14, 1905.

Interior Department

    Sir:

Applications for Enrollment of Creek Newborn
Act of 1905   Volume V

My maiden name was Rose Marcum

" mother's "   "   Patsy Thompson

" sister's   "   are Sarah Marcum

                        Alice Thompson

                        Ellen Thompson

                        Eva Thompson

My brother[sic] name Albert Blackstone.

    The name of the town to which I belong is Lewalah it May not be spelt just exactly right but you will know which town

Roll Numbr 3513

    Name appears on deed as Rose Marcum

                      Yours Truly

                      (signed) ROSE E. MILLER

BIRTH AFFIDAVIT.

DEPARTMENT OF THE INTERIOR.
COMMISSION TO THE FIVE CIVILIZED TRIBES.

    IN RE APPLICATION FOR ENROLLMENT, as a citizen of the CREEK Nation, of Malvin H Miller, born on the 3rd day of January, 1903

Name of Father:	Quint H Miller	a citizen of the U.S.	~~Nation~~.
Name of Mother:	Rose Etta Miller	a citizen of the Creek	Nation.

                    Postoffice   Oktaha Ind Ter

AFFIDAVIT OF MOTHER.

UNITED STATES OF AMERICA, Indian Territory, ⎫
    WESTERN   DISTRICT. ⎭

    I, Rose Etta Miller, on oath state that I am 23 years of age and a citizen by Blood, of the Creek Nation; that I am the lawful wife of Quint H Miller, who is a citizen, by marriage of the Creek Nation; that a male child was born to me on 3rd

Applications for Enrollment of Creek Newborn
Act of 1905 Volume V

day of January, 1903, that said child has been named Malvin H Miller, and is now living.

                                              Rose Etta Miller

Witnesses To Mark:
{

Subscribed and sworn to before me this 25 day of March, 1905.

                                              W.A. Cain
                                              Notary Public.

AFFIDAVIT OF ATTENDING PHYSICIAN OR MID-WIFE.

UNITED STATES OF AMERICA, Indian Territory, }
      WESTERN   DISTRICT.

I, A. J. Snelson, a physicial, on oath state that I attended on Mrs. Rose Etta Miller, wife of Quint Miller on the 3rd day of Jan, 1903 : that there was born to her on said date a male child: that said child is now living and is said to have been named Malvin H Miller

                                              AJ Snelson M.D.

Witnesses To Mark:
{

Subscribed and sworn to before me this 25 day of March, 1905.

                                              W.A. Cain
                                             Notary Public.

BIRTH AFFIDAVIT.
DEPARTMENT OF THE INTERIOR.
COMMISSION TO THE FIVE CIVILIZED TRIBES.

      IN RE APPLICATION FOR ENROLLMENT, as a citizen of the Creek Nation, of Cecil Miller, born on the 4th day of June, 1904

Name of Father:	Quint H. Miller	a citizen of the United States Nation.
Name of Mother:	Rose Etta Miller	a citizen of the Creek Nation.

                                    Postoffice   Oktaha Ind. Ter.

Applications for Enrollment of Creek Newborn
Act of 1905 Volume V

AFFIDAVIT OF MOTHER.

UNITED STATES OF AMERICA, Indian Territory, }
Western DISTRICT.

I, Rose Etta Miller , on oath state that I am 24 years of age and a citizen by blood , of the Creek Nation; that I am the lawful wife of Quint H. Miller , who is a citizen, by *(blank)* of the United S~~tates~~ Nation; that a Male child was born to me on 4th day of June , 1904 , that said child has been named Cecil Miller , and is now living.

                                                Rose Etta Miller

Witnesses To Mark:
{ O.S. Somerville
  W.A. Wallace

Subscribed and sworn to before me this 15th day of December , 1905.

                                          A.M. Darling
                                          Notary Public.

AFFIDAVIT OF ATTENDING PHYSICIAN OR MID-WIFE.

UNITED STATES OF AMERICA, Indian Territory, }
Western DISTRICT.

I, A. J. Snelson , a physician , on oath state that I attended on Mrs. Rose Etta Miller , wife of Quint H. Miller on the 4th day of June , 1904 ; that there was born to her on said date a male child; that said child is now living and is said to have been named Cecil Miller

                                                A. J. Snelson

Witnesses To Mark:
{

Subscribed and sworn to before me this 15th day of December , 1905.

                                          A.M. Darling
                                          Notary Public.

BIRTH AFFIDAVIT.

DEPARTMENT OF THE INTERIOR.
COMMISSION TO THE FIVE CIVILIZED TRIBES.

IN RE APPLICATION FOR ENROLLMENT, as a citizen of the Creek Nation, of Cecil Miller , born on the 4th day of June , 1904

Applications for Enrollment of Creek Newborn
Act of 1905 Volume V

Name of Father: Quint H. Miller a citizen of the U.S. Nation.
Name of Mother: Rose Etta Miller a citizen of the Creek Nation.

Postoffice Oktaha I.T.

AFFIDAVIT OF MOTHER.

UNITED STATES OF AMERICA, Indian Territory,
Western DISTRICT.

I, Rose Etta Miller , on oath state that I am 23 years of age and a citizen by blood , of the Creek Nation: that I am the lawful wife of Quint H. Miller , who is a citizen, by marriage of the Creek Nation: that a male child was born to me on 4th day of June , 1904 , that said child has been named Cecil Miller , and is now living.

Rose Etta Miller

Witnesses To Mark:

Subscribed and sworn to before me this 25 day of March , 1905.

W.A Cain
Notary Public.

AFFIDAVIT OF ATTENDING PHYSICIAN OR MID-WIFE.

UNITED STATES OF AMERICA, Indian Territory,
Western DISTRICT.

I, A. J. Snelson , a physician , on oath state that I attended on Mrs. Rose Etta Miller , wife of Quint H. Miller on the 4th day of June , 1905[sic] : that there was born to her on said date a male child: that said child is now living and is said to have been named Cecil Miller

A. J. Snelson

Witnesses To Mark:

Subscribed and sworn to before me this 25 day of March , 1905.

W.A Cain
Notary Public.

Applications for Enrollment of Creek Newborn
Act of 1905   Volume V

NC-413.

Muskogee, Indian Territory, August 3, 1905.

Della A. Evans,
    c/o Richard Evans,
        Oktaha, Indian Territory.

Dear Madam:

    In the matter of the application for the enrollment of your minor daughter Nettie Evans as a citizen by blood of the Creek Nation you are advised that it will be necessary for you to file with this office either the original or a certified copy of the marriage license and certificate between you and your husband Richard Evans.

    It is also advisable for you to file with this office the affidavit of said Richard Evans as to the birth of said child and a blank for that purpose partially filled out is inclosed[sic] herewith.

                          Respectfully,

                                        Commissioner.

CTD-20.
Env.

BIRTH AFFIDAVIT.

DEPARTMENT OF THE INTERIOR.
COMMISSION TO THE FIVE CIVILIZED TRIBES.

    IN RE APPLICATION FOR ENROLLMENT, as a citizen of the Creek Nation, of Nettie Evans, born on the 31st day of Dec, 1905

| Name of Father: | Richard Evans | a citizen of the | Creek | Nation. |
| Name of Mother: | Della A. Evans | a citizen of the | U.S. | Nation. |

                        Postoffice   Oktaha Ind. Ter.

AFFIDAVIT OF MOTHER.

UNITED STATES OF AMERICA, Indian Territory, ⎫
    WESTERN   DISTRICT. ⎭

    I, Della A Evans , on oath state that I am 18 years of age and a citizen by marriage , of the Creek Nation; that I am the lawful wife of Richard Evans , who is a

Applications for Enrollment of Creek Newborn
Act of 1905   Volume V

citizen, by blood of the Creek Nation; that a Female child was born to me on 31st day of Dec, 1903, that said child has been named Nettie Evans, and is now living.

                                          Mrs. Della A Evans

Witnesses To Mark:

    Subscribed and sworn to before me this 25th day of March, 1905.

                                          W.A. Cain
                                                Notary Public.

AFFIDAVIT OF ATTENDING PHYSICIAN OR MID-WIFE.

UNITED STATES OF AMERICA, Indian Territory,
    WESTERN DISTRICT.

    I, A.J. Snelson, a physician, on oath state that I attended on Mrs. Della A Evans, wife of Richard Evans on the 31st day of Dec, 1903 : that there was born to her on said date a Female child; that said child is now living and is said to have been named Nettie Evans

                                          A J Snelson M.D.

Witnesses To Mark:

    Subscribed and sworn to before me this 25th day of March, 1905.

                                          W.A. Cain
                                              Notary Public.

BIRTH AFFIDAVIT.
DEPARTMENT OF THE INTERIOR.
COMMISSION TO THE FIVE CIVILIZED TRIBES.

    IN RE APPLICATION FOR ENROLLMENT, as a citizen of the Creek Nation, of Nettie Evans, born on the 31st day of December, 1903

Name of Father:	Richard Evans	a citizen of the	Creek	Nation.
Name of Mother:	Della A. Evans	a citizen of the	U.S.	Nation.

                              Postoffice   Oktaha Ind. Ter.

Applications for Enrollment of Creek Newborn
Act of 1905   Volume V

AFFIDAVIT OF MOTHER.

UNITED STATES OF AMERICA, Indian Territory,
　　Western　　　　　　　DISTRICT.

　　I, Richard Evans, on oath state that I am *(blank)* years of age and a citizen by blood, of the Creek Nation; that I am the lawful ~~wife~~ husband of Della A. Evans, who is a citizen, ~~by~~ *(blank)* of the United States ~~Nation~~; that a female child was born to ~~me~~ us on 31st day of December, 1903, that said child has been named Nettie Evans, and was living March 4, 1905.

Witnesses To Mark:
　{ ....
　　............................

　　Subscribed and sworn to before me this ...... day of ...., 1905.

　　　　　　　　　　　　　　　　　　..
　　　　　　　　　　　　　　　　　　　　　　　Notary Public.

CERTIFICATE OF RECORD.

United States of America,
　Indian Territory,　　} ss.
　Northern District.

　　I, *ROBERT P. HARRISON*, Clerk of the United States Court in the Western District, Indian Territory, do hereby certify that the instrument hereto attached was filed for record in my office the 14th day of Aug 1902 at ----- M., and duly recorded in Book N, Marriage Record, Page 159

　　　　WITNESS my hand and seal of said Court at Muscogee, in said Territory, this 14th day of Aug A. D. 1902

　　　　　　　　　　　　　　　　　　RP Harrison　　　　Clerk.
By　J L Peacock　Deputy.

MARRIAGE LICENSE.
•••••••

United States of America,
　Indian Territory,　　} ss.　　　　　　　　　No. **69**
　Northern District.

To Any Person Authorized by Law to Solemnize Marriage---Greeting:

Applications for Enrollment of Creek Newborn
Act of 1905 Volume V

You are Hereby Commanded to Solemnize the Rite and Publish the Banns of Matrimony between Mr.   Richard Evans   of   Oaktaha[sic] , in the Indian Territory, aged   17   years and Miss Della Agnes Morgan   of   Oaktaha in the Indian Territory aged   16   years according to law, and do you officially sign and return this License to the parties therein named.

WITNESS my hand and official seal at Muscogee Indian Territory this   26   day of   July   A.D. 190 2

                                 R.P. Harrison
                                   Clerk of the U.S. Court

By   C.E. (Illegible)   Deputy

CERTIFICATE OF MARRIAGE.

● ● ● ● ● ●

United States of America,
   Indian Territory,   } ss.
   Northern District.

I,   Jas. T Elam   , a Minister of the Gospel, DO HEREBY CERTIFY that on the 27   day of   July   A. D. 1902, I did duly and according to law as commanded in the foregoing License, solemnize the Rite and publish the Banns of Matrimony between the parties therein named.

WITNESS my hand this   27   day of   July   A. D. 1902

My credentials are recorded in the office of the Clerk of the United States Court, Indian Territory, Northern District, Book   C   , Page   33   .

                                   Jas. T. Elam
                                   A Minister of the Gospel

Note—This License and Certificate of Marriage must be returned to the Office of the Clerk of the United States Court in the Northern District, Indian Territory, from whence it was issued, within sixty days from the date thereof, or the party to whom the license was issued will be liable in the amount of the One Hundred Dollars ($100.00)

NC 414.

Muskogee, Indian Territory, June 5, 1905.

Hattie Wilson,
    Dustin, Indian Territory.

Applications for Enrollment of Creek Newborn
Act of 1905   Volume V

Dear Madam:

In the matter of the application for the enrollment of your minor children, Raymond and Sarah Jane Wilson, as citizens of the Creek Nation, you are advised that the Commission requires your affidavit as to the birth of said child[sic].

There is herewith enclosed a blank form of birth affidavit, and in executing same care should be exercised to see that all blanks are properly filled, all names written in full and in the event that you are unable to write, signature by mark must be attested by two witnesses. The affidavit must be executed before a Notary Public and the notarial seal and signature of the officer must be attached to the affidavit.

Respectfully,

1 BA   Commissioner in Charge.

NC 414.

Muskogee, Indian Territory, June 22, 1905.

Hattie Wilson,
    Dustin, Indian Territory.

Dear Madam:

In the matter of the application for the enrollment of your minor child, Raymond Wilson, as a citizen of the Creek Nation, you are advised that the Commission requires your affidavit as to the birth of said child.

There is herewith enclosed a blank form of birth affidavit, and in executing same care should be exercised to see that all blanks are properly filled, all names written in full and in the event that you are unable to write, signature by mark must be attested by two witnesses. The affidavit must be executed before a Notary Public and the notarial seal and signature of the officer must be attached to the affidavit.

Respectfully,

1 BA   Chairman.

Applications for Enrollment of Creek Newborn
Act of 1905   Volume V

BIRTH AFFIDAVIT.

DEPARTMENT OF THE INTERIOR.
COMMISSION TO THE FIVE CIVILIZED TRIBES.

IN RE APPLICATION FOR ENROLLMENT, as a citizen of the Creek Nation, of Raymond Wilson, born on the 16 day of October, 1903

Name of Father: R.B. Wilson　　　　　a citizen of the United States Nation.
Name of Mother: Hettie Wilson　　　　a citizen of the   Creek   Nation.

Postoffice   Dustin, I.T.

AFFIDAVIT OF ~~MOTHER~~. Father

UNITED STATES OF AMERICA, Indian Territory,　}
　　Western　　　DISTRICT.

I, R. B. Wilson, on oath state that I am 48 years of age and a citizen ~~by~~ *(blank)*, of the United States ~~Nation~~; that I am the lawful ~~wife~~ Husband of Hettie Wilson, who is a citizen, by blood of the Creek Nation; that a male child was born to ~~me~~ her on 16 day of October, 1903, that said child has been named Raymond Wilson, and was living March 4, 1905. That on account of sickness the mother of the child is unable to appear to make affidavit.

　　　　　　　　　　　　　　　　R. B. Wilson
Witnesses To Mark:
{

Subscribed and sworn to before me this 20 day of March, 1905.
　　　　　　　　　　　　Drennan C Skaggs
　　　　　　　　　　　　　　Notary Public.

AFFIDAVIT OF ATTENDING PHYSICIAN OR MID-WIFE.

UNITED STATES OF AMERICA, Indian Territory,　}
　　Western　　　DISTRICT.

I, Louisa Morrison, a Mid-wife, on oath state that I attended on Mrs. Hettie Wilson, wife of R. B. Wilson on the 16 day of October, 1903 ; that there was born to her on said date a male child; that said child was living March 4, 1905, and is said to have been named Raymond Wilson

　　　　　　　　　　　　　　Louisa Morrison
Witnesses To Mark:
{

Applications for Enrollment of Creek Newborn
Act of 1905 Volume V

Subscribed and sworn to before me this 20 day of March, 1905.

                                                Drennan C Skaggs
                                                Notary Public.

BIRTH AFFIDAVIT.

DEPARTMENT OF THE INTERIOR.
COMMISSION TO THE FIVE CIVILIZED TRIBES.

IN RE APPLICATION FOR ENROLLMENT, as a citizen of the Creek Nation, of Sarah Jane Wilson, born on the 15th day of Febry, 1902

| Name of Father: | R.B. Wilson | a citizen of the | U S | Nation. |
| Name of Mother: | Hettie Wilson | a citizen of the | Creek | Nation. |

                              Postoffice   Dustin, I.T.

AFFIDAVIT OF MOTHER.

UNITED STATES OF AMERICA, Indian Territory,
    Western   DISTRICT.

    I, Hettie Wilson, on oath state that I am 34 years of age and a citizen by birth, of the Creek Nation; that I am the lawful wife of R. B. Wilson, who is a citizen, by birth of the U S Nation; that a Female child was born to me on 15th day of Febry, 1902, that said child has been named Sarah Jane Wilson, and was living March 4, 1905.

                                                Hettie Wilson

Witnesses To Mark:

Subscribed and sworn to before me this 14th day of June, 1905.

                                                Horace Wilson
                                                Notary Public.
                                   My Com Exp Mar 5th 1907

BIRTH AFFIDAVIT.

DEPARTMENT OF THE INTERIOR.
COMMISSION TO THE FIVE CIVILIZED TRIBES.

IN RE APPLICATION FOR ENROLLMENT, as a citizen of the Creek Nation, of Sarah Jane Wilson, born on the 15 day of Feb, 1902

Applications for Enrollment of Creek Newborn
Act of 1905   Volume V

Name of Father: R.B. Wilson   a citizen of the United States Nation.
Name of Mother: Hettie Wilson   a citizen of the   Creek   Nation.

Postoffice   Dustin, I.T.

_____
Father
AFFIDAVIT OF ~~MOTHER~~.

UNITED STATES OF AMERICA, Indian Territory, }
    Western   DISTRICT.

I, R. B. Wilson , on oath state that I am 48 years of age and a citizen ~~by~~ *(blank)*, of the United States ~~Nation~~; that I am the lawful ~~wife of~~ Husband of Hettie Wilson , who is a citizen, by blood of the Creek Nation; that a female child was born to ~~me~~ her on 15 day of February . 1902 . that said child has been named Sarah Jane Wilson, and was living March 4, 1905. That on account of sickness the mother of the child is unable to appear to make affidavit.

R. B. Wilson

Witnesses To Mark:
{

Subscribed and sworn to before me this 20 day of March, 1905.

Drennan C Skaggs
Notary Public.

_____

AFFIDAVIT OF ATTENDING PHYSICIAN OR MID-WIFE.

UNITED STATES OF AMERICA, Indian Territory, }
    Western   DISTRICT.

I, Louisa Morrison , a mid-wife . on oath state that I attended on Mrs. Hettie Wilson , wife of R. B. Wilson on the 15 day of February , 1902 ; that there was born to her on said date a female child; that said child is now living and is said to have been named Sarah Jane Wilson

Louisa Morrison

Witnesses To Mark:
{

Subscribed and sworn to before me this 20 day of March, 1905.

Drennan C Skaggs
Notary Public.

Applications for Enrollment of Creek Newborn
Act of 1905 Volume V

BIRTH AFFIDAVIT.

DEPARTMENT OF THE INTERIOR.
COMMISSION TO THE FIVE CIVILIZED TRIBES.

IN RE APPLICATION FOR ENROLLMENT, as a citizen of the Creek Nation, of Raymond Wilson, born on the 16th day of Oct , 1903

Name of Father:	R.B. Wilson	a citizen of the	U S	Nation.
Name of Mother:	Hettie Wilson	a citizen of the	Creek	Nation.

Postoffice *(blank)*

AFFIDAVIT OF MOTHER.

UNITED STATES OF AMERICA, Indian Territory, ⎫
    Western   DISTRICT. ⎬

I, Hettie Wilson , on oath state that I am 34 years of age and a citizen by birth , of the Creek Nation; that I am the lawful wife of R. B. Wilson , who is a citizen, by birth of the U. S. Nation; that a Male child was born to me on 16th day of Oct , 1903 , that said child has been named Raymond Wilson , and was living March 4, 1905.

                                          Hettie Wilson

Witnesses To Mark:
{

Subscribed and sworn to before me this 26th day of June , 1905.

My Com Expires   Horace Wilson
Mar 5th 1907   Notary Public.

Birth Affidavit.
        Department of the Interior,
            Commission to the Five Civilized Tribes.

---------------O---------------

In re application for enrollment, as a citizen of the Creek Nation of Sophia Charles , born on the 20th day of December , 1904. Name of father Nero Charles , a citizen of the ~~Cherokee~~ Creek Nation. Name of mother: Ellen Charles a citizen of the Creek Nation.

                                    Coweta Indian Territory
                                            Postoffice.

Applications for Enrollment of Creek Newborn
Act of 1905   Volume V

Affidavit of Mother.

United States of America,, Indian Territory,   : ss.
Western District.   :

I, Ellen Charles, on my oath state that I am thirty years of age and a citizen by blood of the Creek Nation; that I am the lawful wife of Nero Charles, who is a citizen by blood of the Creek Nation and a Freedman; that a female child was born to me on 20th day of December, 1904; that said child was named Sophia Charles, and is now living.

                                                her
                                      Ellen x Charles
Witnesses to mark.   mark
  Shirly Wofford
  Eliza Childers

Subscribed and sworn to before me this 23rd day of March, 1905.

                                        B.J. Beavers
                                                Notary Public.
My commission expires Dec. 19th. 1908.

Affidavit of attending Physician or Midwife.

United States of America,, Indian Territory,   : ss.
Western District.   :

I, Ivy Abbot a midwife on my oath state that I attended on Mrs. Ellen Charles wife of Nero Charles on the 20th day of December, 1904, that there was born to her on said date a female child; that said child is now living and is said to have been named Sophia Charles

                                     her
                                 Ivy x Abbot
Witnesses to mark.   mark
  Shirly Wofford
  Eliza Childers

Subscribed and sworn to before me this 23rd day of March, 1905.

                                      B.J. Beavers
                                             Notary Public.
My commission expires Dec. 19th. 1908.

Applications for Enrollment of Creek Newborn
Act of 1905   Volume V

Birth Affidavit.
>Department of the Interior,
>Commission to the Five Civilized Tribes.

---------------O---------------

In re application for enrollment, as a citizen of the Creek Nation of Ellis Buffington Charles , born on the 8th day of August , 1902. Name of father Nero Charles , a citizen of the ~~Cherokee~~ Creek Nation. Name of mother: Ellen Charles a citizen of the Creek Nation.

>Coweta Ind. Ter.
>Postoffice.

Affidavit of Mother.

United States of America,, Indian Territory, : ss.
Western District.   :

I, Ellen Charles , on my oath state that I am thirty years of age and a citizen by blood of the Creek Nation; that I am the lawful wife of Nero Charles , who is a citizen by blood of the Creek Nation and a Freedman; that a male child was born to me on 8th day of August, 1902; that said child was named Ellis Buffington Charles, and is now living.

>her
>Ellen x Charles
>mark

Witnesses to mark.
Shirly Wofford
Lizzie Wofford

Subscribed and sworn to before me this 23rd day of March, 1905.

>B.J. Beavers
>Notary Public.

My commission expires Dec. 19th. 1908.

Affidavit of attending Physician or Midwife.

United States of America,, Indian Territory, : ss.
Western District.   :

I, Rose Childers ,a midwife on my oath state that I attended on Mrs. Ellen Charles wife of Nero Charles on the 8th day of August, 1902, that there was born to her on said date a male child; that said child is now living and is said to have been named Ellis Buffington Charles

>her
>Rose x Charles[sic]

Witnesses to mark.
Shirly Wofford
Lizzie Wofford

Subscribed and sworn to before me this 23rd day of March, 1905.

Applications for Enrollment of Creek Newborn
Act of 1905   Volume V

B.J. Beavers
Notary Public.

My commission expires Dec. 19th, 1908.

COMMISSIONERS:
TAMS BIXBY,
THOMAS B. NEEDLES,
C.R. BRECKINRIDGE.

WM. O. BEALL
Secretary

ADDRESS ONLY THE
COMMISSION TO THE FIVE CIVILIZED TRIBES.

**DEPARTMENT OF THE INTERIOR,
COMMISSIONER TO THE FIVE CIVILIZED TRIBES.**

HGH
REFER IN REPLY TO THE FOLLOWING:

NC 416.

Muskogee, Indian Territory, June 5, 1905.

Henry Micco,
   Creek, Indian Territory.

Dear Sir:

    In the matter of the application for the enrollment of your minor child, Lucy Micco as a citizen of the Creek Nation, you are advised that the Commission requires an affidavit relative to the death of your wife, Dechee Micco, and the affidavits of two disinterested witnesses as to the birth of your said minor child.

    There are herewith enclosed two blank forms of birth affidavit and a blank form of death affidavit, and you are requested to fill out and execute before an officer authorized to administer oaths, and return it to the Commission in the enclosed envelope affidavit, which you are requested to have filled out and properly executed before an officer authorized to administer oaths, taking care to see that all blanks are properly filled, all names written in full and in the event that either of the persons signing the affidavits is unable to write, signatures by mark must be attested by two witnesses. Each affidavit must be executed before a Notary Public and the notarial seal and signature of the officer must be attached to each separate affidavit.

Respectfully,
(Name Illegible)
Commissioner in Charge.

2 BA
1 DA

Applications for Enrollment of Creek Newborn
Act of 1905   Volume V

BIRTH AFFIDAVIT.

DEPARTMENT OF THE INTERIOR.
COMMISSION TO THE FIVE CIVILIZED TRIBES.

IN RE APPLICATION FOR ENROLLMENT, as a citizen of the Creek Nation, of Lucy Micco, born on the   22th[sic] day of June , 1904

Name of Father: Henry Micco   a citizen of the   Creek   Nation.
Name of Mother: Dochee Knight nee Micco   a citizen of the   Creek   Nation.

Postoffice   Creek, I.T.

Father
AFFIDAVIT OF ~~MOTHER~~.

UNITED STATES OF AMERICA, Indian Territory, ⎫
   Western Judicial   DISTRICT. ⎭

I, Henry Micco , on oath state that I am 31 years of age and a citizen by Blood, of the Muskokee[sic] or Creek Nation; that I am the lawful ~~wife of~~ Husband of Dochee Knight nee Micco (Deceased) , who is a citizen, by   Blood of the   Muskokee[sic] or Creek Nation; that a Female   child was born to me on 22th[sic] day of   June   , 1904 , that said child has been named   Lucy Micco , and was living March 4, 1905.

Henry Micco

Witnesses To Mark:
{

Subscribed and sworn to before me this 21th[sic] day of March, 1905.

John H. Phillips

My Commission Expires Sept 6th 1906.   Notary Public.

AFFIDAVIT OF ATTENDING PHYSICIAN OR MID-WIFE.

UNITED STATES OF AMERICA, Indian Territory, ⎫
   Western Judicial   DISTRICT. ⎭

I, Jennie Martin , a Mid- Wife , on oath state that I attended on Mrs. Dochee Knight nee Micco, (Deceased) , wife of Henry Micco on the 22th[sic] day of June , 1904 ; that there was born to her on said date a Female child; that said child was living March 4, 1905, and is said to have been named   Lucy Micco

her
Jennie x Martin
mark

Applications for Enrollment of Creek Newborn
Act of 1905   Volume V

Witnesses To Mark:
- Tupper Dunn
- Jno. H. Phillips

Subscribed and sworn to before me this 21th[sic] day of March, 1905.

My Commission Expires Sept 6th 1906.

John H. Phillips
Notary Public.

BIRTH AFFIDAVIT.

DEPARTMENT OF THE INTERIOR.
COMMISSION TO THE FIVE CIVILIZED TRIBES.

IN RE APPLICATION FOR ENROLLMENT, as a citizen of the Creek Nation, of Alabama Kelly, born on the 1st day of August, 1904

Name of Father: Wadley Kelly	a citizen of the	Creek Nation.
Name of Mother: Mahala Kelly	a citizen of the	Creek Nation.

Postoffice   Sonora, I. T.

AFFIDAVIT OF MOTHER.

UNITED STATES OF AMERICA, Indian Territory,
Western   DISTRICT.

I, Mahala Kelly, on oath state that I am Twenty Four years of age and a citizen by Blood, of the Creek Nation; that I am the lawful wife of Wadley Kelly, who is a citizen, by Blood of the Creek Nation; that a Female child was born to me on 1st day of August, 1904, that said child has been named Alabama Kelly, and was living March 4, 1905.

Mahala Kelly

Witnesses To Mark:
- Senora Likowski
- E. C. *(Illegible)*

Subscribed and sworn to before me this 21st day of March, 1905.

MY COMMISSION EXPIRES JULY 13th, 1905.   J. W. Fowler
Notary Public.

Applications for Enrollment of Creek Newborn
Act of 1905 Volume V

AFFIDAVIT OF ATTENDING PHYSICIAN OR MID-WIFE.

UNITED STATES OF AMERICA, Indian Territory, }
Western DISTRICT.

  I, Polly Starr , a Mid Wife , on oath state that I attended on Mrs. Mahala Kelly, wife of Wadley Kelly on the 1st day of August , 1904 ; that there was born to her on said date a Female child; that said child was living March 4, 1905, and is said to have been named Alabama Kelly

              her
            Polly x Starr
Witnesses To Mark: mark
 { J. N. Willhite
  (Name Illegible)

  Subscribed and sworn to before me this 21st day of March , 1905.

  MY COMMISSION EXPIRES JULY 13th, 1905. J. W. Fowler
               Notary Public.

BIRTH AFFIDAVIT.

DEPARTMENT OF THE INTERIOR.
COMMISSION TO THE FIVE CIVILIZED TRIBES.

  IN RE APPLICATION FOR ENROLLMENT, as a citizen of the Creek Nation, of Roman Kelly, born on the 22 day of March , 1902

Name of Father: Wadly Kelly   a citizen of the Creek Nation.
Name of Mother: Mahala Kelly   a citizen of the Creek Nation.

        Postoffice Sonora, I. T.

AFFIDAVIT OF MOTHER.

UNITED STATES OF AMERICA, Indian Territory, }
Western DISTRICT.

  I, Mahala Kelly , on oath state that I am twenty four years of age and a citizen by Blood , of the Creek Nation; that I am the lawful wife of Wadly[sic] Kelly , who is a citizen, by Blood of the Creek Nation; that a Male child was born to me on 22nd day of March , 1902 , that said child has been named Roman Kelly , and was living March 4, 1905.

            Mahala Kelly
Witnesses To Mark:
 { Senora Likowski
  E. C. *(Illegible)*

Applications for Enrollment of Creek Newborn
Act of 1905   Volume V

Subscribed and sworn to before me this 21st day of March, 1905.

MY COMMISSION EXPIRES JULY 13th, 1905.   J. W. Fowler
Notary Public.

AFFIDAVIT OF ATTENDING PHYSICIAN OR MID-WIFE.

UNITED STATES OF AMERICA, Indian Territory, }
Western   DISTRICT.

I, Polly Starr, a Mid wife, on oath state that I attended on Mrs. Mahala Kelly, wife of Wadley Kelly on the 22nd day of March, 1902 : that there was born to her on said date a Male child; that said child was living March 4, 1905, and is said to have been named Roman Kelly

                                        her
                                Polly x Starr
Witnesses To Mark: mark
{ J. N. Willhite
{ *(Name Illegible)*

Subscribed and sworn to before me this 21st day of March, 1905.

MY COMMISSION EXPIRES JULY 13th, 1905.   J. W. Fowler
Notary Public.

BIRTH AFFIDAVIT.
DEPARTMENT OF THE INTERIOR.
COMMISSION TO THE FIVE CIVILIZED TRIBES.

IN RE APPLICATION FOR ENROLLMENT, as a citizen of the Creek Nation, of Hettie Yardy, born on the 28 day of June, 1902

Name of Father: Thomas Yardy   a citizen of the   Creek   Nation.
Name of Mother: Armer Yardy   a citizen of the   Creek   Nation.

                          Postoffice   Morris I.T.

Applications for Enrollment of Creek Newborn
Act of 1905   Volume V

AFFIDAVIT OF MOTHER.

UNITED STATES OF AMERICA, Indian Territory, ⎫
    Western   DISTRICT. ⎬
                                    ⎭

I, Armer Yardy, on oath state that I am 32 years of age and a citizen by birth, of the Creek Nation; that I am the lawful wife of Thomas Yardy, who is a citizen, by birth of the Creek Nation; that a female child was born to me on 28 day of June, 1902, that said child has been named Hettie Yardy, and was living March 4, 1905.

                                                Armer Yardy

Witnesses To Mark:
{

Subscribed and sworn to before me this 23 day of March, 1905.

                                                A.N. Milam
My Commission expires July 2, 1906.   Notary Public.

AFFIDAVIT OF ATTENDING PHYSICIAN OR MID-WIFE.

UNITED STATES OF AMERICA, Indian Territory, ⎫
    Western   DISTRICT. ⎬

I, Nicey Scott, a Midwife, on oath state that I attended on Mrs. Armer Yardy, wife of Thomas Yardy on the 28 day of June, 1902 ; that there was born to her on said date a female child; that said child was living March 4, 1905, and is said to have been named Hettie Yardy

                                                her
                                       Nicey x Scott
Witnesses To Mark: mark
{ R. G. Gordon
  J M Mitchell

Subscribed and sworn to before me this 23 day of March, 1905.

                                                A.N. Milam
My Commission expires July 2, 1906.   Notary Public.

BIRTH AFFIDAVIT.
DEPARTMENT OF THE INTERIOR.
COMMISSION TO THE FIVE CIVILIZED TRIBES.

    IN RE APPLICATION FOR ENROLLMENT, as a citizen of the Creek Nation, of Dock Yardy, born on the 21 day of Nov, 1904

Applications for Enrollment of Creek Newborn
Act of 1905   Volume V

Name of Father: Thomas Yardy   a citizen of the   Creek   Nation.
Name of Mother: Armer Yardy   a citizen of the   Creek   Nation.

Postoffice   Morris I.T.

AFFIDAVIT OF MOTHER.

UNITED STATES OF AMERICA, Indian Territory, }
Western   DISTRICT.

I. Armer Yardy , on oath state that I am 32 years of age and a citizen by birth , of the Creek   Nation; that I am the lawful wife of Thomas Yardy , who is a citizen, by birth of the Creek   Nation; that a male child was born to me on 21   day of November , 1904, that said child has been named Dock Yardy , and was living March 4, 1905.

Armer Yardy

Witnesses To Mark:

Subscribed and sworn to before me this 23 day of March , 1905.

A.N. Milam
My Commission expires July 2, 1906.   Notary Public.

AFFIDAVIT OF ATTENDING PHYSICIAN OR MID-WIFE.

UNITED STATES OF AMERICA, Indian Territory, }
Western   DISTRICT.

I. Nicey Scott , a Midwife , on oath state that I attended on Mrs. Armer Yardy , wife of Thomas Yardy on the 21 day of November , 1904 ; that there was born to her on said date a male child; that said child was living March 4, 1905, and is said to have been named Dock Yardy

Nicey Scott x her mark

Witnesses To Mark:
{ E.J. Ayers
{ (Name Illegible)

Subscribed and sworn to before me this 23 day of March , 1905.

A.N. Milam
My Commission expires July 2, 1906.   Notary Public.

Applications for Enrollment of Creek Newborn
Act of 1905 Volume V

BIRTH AFFIDAVIT.

DEPARTMENT OF THE INTERIOR.
COMMISSION TO THE FIVE CIVILIZED TRIBES.

IN RE APPLICATION FOR ENROLLMENT, as a citizen of the Creek Nation, of Maria Childers, born on the 16th day of February, 1903

Name of Father:	William Childers	a citizen of the	Creek	Nation.
Name of Mother:	Annie Childers	a citizen of the	Creek	Nation.

Postoffice   Coweta, Ind. Ter.

AFFIDAVIT OF MOTHER.

UNITED STATES OF AMERICA, Indian Territory,
Western   DISTRICT.

I, Annie Childers, on oath state that I am 29 years of age and a citizen by blood, of the Creek Nation; that I am the lawful wife of William Childers, who is a citizen, by blood of the Creek Nation; that a female child was born to me on 16th day of February, 1903, that said child has been named Maria Childers, and was living March 4, 1905.

Annie Childers

Witnesses To Mark:
{

Subscribed and sworn to before me this 19th day of April, 1905.

B.J. Beavers
Notary Public.

My Commission expires Dec 19-1908.

AFFIDAVIT OF ATTENDING PHYSICIAN OR MID-WIFE.

UNITED STATES OF AMERICA, Indian Territory,
Western   DISTRICT.

I, Mary Williams, a, midwife, on oath state that I attended on Mrs. Annie Childers, wife of William Childers on the 16th day of February, 1903; that there was born to her on said date a female child; that said child was living March 4, 1905, and is said to have been named Maria Childers

Mary Williams

Witnesses To Mark:
{

Applications for Enrollment of Creek Newborn
Act of 1905 Volume V

Subscribed and sworn to before me this 19th day of April, 1905.

My Commission expires Dec 19-1908.

B.J. Beavers
Notary Public.

BIRTH AFFIDAVIT.

DEPARTMENT OF THE INTERIOR.
COMMISSION TO THE FIVE CIVILIZED TRIBES.

IN RE APPLICATION FOR ENROLLMENT, as a citizen of the CREEK Nation, of Maria Childers, born on the 16 day of Feb., 1903

Name of Father:	Wm Childers	a citizen of the	Creek	Nation.
Name of Mother:	Annie "	a citizen of the	"	Nation.

Postoffice   Coweta

(Child present)

AFFIDAVIT OF MOTHER.

UNITED STATES OF AMERICA, Indian Territory,
Western   DISTRICT.

I, Annie Childers, on oath state that I am 29 years of age and a citizen by blood, of the Creek Nation; that I am the lawful wife of Wm Childers, who is a citizen, by blood of the Creek Nation; that a female child was born to me on 16 day of Feb., 1903, that said child has been named Maria Childers, and is now living. & dont[sic] know where the midwife has moved to

Annie Childers

Witnesses To Mark:
{

Subscribed and sworn to before me this 24" day of March, 1905.

Edw C Griesel
Notary Public.

324

Applications for Enrollment of Creek Newborn
Act of 1905   Volume V

AFFIDAVIT OF ATTENDING ~~PHYSICIAN OR MID-WIFE~~.
Father

UNITED STATES OF AMERICA, Indian Territory, }
  Western   DISTRICT.

I,   Wm Childers , a   Father , on oath state that I attended on Mrs. Annie Childers , wife of myself on the 16 day of Feb , 1903 ; that there was born to her on said date a female child; that said child is now living and is said to have been named Maria Childers

William Childers

Witnesses To Mark:
{

Subscribed and sworn to before me this 24 day of Mar, 1905.

Edw C Griesel
Notary Public.

Index

[ILLEGIBLE]
  C E 308
  E C 318,319
  Hazel 143
  J H 125
  John 47
  Philip C 127
ABBOT, Ivy 314
AFONOSKA 49,51
AHFONOKA 22
ALEX 162
ALEXANDER, J H 233,234
ALLAN, Robert 212,213
ALLEN, George 290
ANDERSON
  B T 23
  Bennie 27,28,29,30,31
  Bennie T 24
  Bessie 27,30,31
  Wicey 27
  Winey 27,28,29,30,31,32
  Wisey 28,29
ANNIE 162
ARTARKINNAY 60
AYERS, E J 322
BAKER
  Anna 266,267
  Dan M 71,72
  George 266,267
  Lasley 267
  Leslie 266,267
BANNATT, Katie 113,116
BANTOR, R 157
BARD
  Daniel 5
  Daniel N 3
BARNETT
  Austin 187,188
  Betsey 225
  Betsy 163,164
  Dick 114,284
  Dock 285,287,291
  Elizabeth 184,187,221,285
  Herford

283,284,285,286,287,288,289,290,291,292
Jeff 284
Johnson 227
Kate 110
Katie 112,116,270,271,272
Phoeba 228
Polly 220,221
Rachel 283,285,287,288
Rachell 221
Rosanna 270,271,272,273
Ru Dick 114
Scipio 221
Tucker 114,270,271,272
BASHAW, Nancy S 121
BASTABLE, John 179,180,181
BEALL, Wm O 11
BEAR, Lotty 1,3
BEAVER
  Dinah 76,85
  Eliza 252,253
  Lelah 197
BEAVERS, B J 314,315,316,323,324
BELL
  Eli 201,202,203
  Joseph 34,35,36,38
  Josie 35,36,37,38
  Lizzie 36
  Lizzie Marshall 38
  Nellie 34,35,36,38
  Silby 201,202,203
  Suthie 201,202
  Thompson 202,203
BELLE
  Joseph 37
  Lizzie 37
  Lizzie Marshall 38
  Nellie 37
BENHAM
  C A 119,120,121
  Claude 119,122
  James Albert 119,120,121
  Lucy Etta 122
  Malinda 120,121

Index

Melinda 118,119,120,122
BERRY
  J D 8
  Virgil, MD 135,138
BERRYHILL
  Clent 273,274
  J E 173
  Sam 273,274
  Sophia 273,274
BIRD, Louisa 225
BIXBY
  Hon Tams 55,64
  Tams
    2,4,6,14,35,78,80,87,88,89,91,103,11
    7,132,134,136,166,167,175,182,194,
    205,214,245,247,264,282,286
BLACKMAN
  E L 112,115
  T W 227,228
BLACKSTONE, Albert 301
BLAKE, W R 271
BOLEY 236
BOSHAW, Mrs 119
BOYLE, J P 85,86
BROWH
  Jeff 132
  Lueree 132
BROWN
  Betsy 163,166
  F J 134
  Hettie 162,163,164,165,166,167
  Jeff
    131,132,133,135,136,137,138,139,14
    0
  Joe . 83,84,162,163,164,165,167,225
  Josiah 162
  Julia
    131,132,133,134,135,136,137,138,13
    9,140
  Lizzie 162
  Lueree 131,132,133,134,137
  Malinda 121
  McKinley
    131,134,135,136,137,138,139,140

Nancy 165
BRUNER
  Dave 256,257,258,259
  David 254,257,258
  Elsie 254,258,259
  Ilsey 253,254,255,256,257,258
  Paul 291
  Pauline 291
  Robert
    232,234,235,239,240,241,242,254,25
    6
  Willie
    253,254,255,256,257,258,259,260
BUCK, Sarah 291
BUFORD, Charles 3,4
BUTCHER
  Cheparney 48
  Cheparny 50
  Lela 48,49,50,51,52
  Mildred 48
  Millie 50
  Missie 49
  Musser 48
  Mussey 50,52
  Mussie 50,51
  Mussy 49
  Nafa 48,52
  Nofa 50,51
  Norfer 48,49,50
CAHCOHETHLON 60
CAH-CO-KE-THLON 62,64
CAIN, W A 302,304,306
CALDWELL, L P 274
CALLAHAN, Benton 24,28,30,51
CANARD
  Billy
    110,111,112,113,114,115,116,271
  Geo 68
  Katie 271,272
  Kizzie
    109,110,111,112,113,114,115,116,11
    7,118,272,273
  Louisa
    109,110,113,114,115,116,117,118

Index

Millie 111,112,113,115,116,117
Rosanna 271
CANE, Jennie 144
CAROLINA, Charley 284,288
CARPENTER, E 83,84
CARR, Lotty 1
CATCH, Willie 170
CAVES, T T 108,109
CEASAR, Calley 291
CHARLES
   Ellen 313,314,315
   Ellis Buffington 315
   Nero 313,314,315
   Sophia 313,314
CHECOTE, M L 195
CHEPARNEY 22
CHILDERS
   Annie 323,324,325
   Daniel 141,142
   Eliza 314
   Ellen 315
   Ellis Buffington 315
   Maria 323,324,325
   Mildred 141,142
   Nero 315
   Rose 315
   Ruby Mildred 141,142
   William 323,325
   Wm 324,325
CHITWOOD, B B 139
CHUPCO
   Heneha 42
   John 162,227
CLEMENTS, J W 9
COACHMAN
   Anna 267
   Chas 266,267,268
COASHMAN, Charles 8
COH-CO-KE-THLON 63
COONHEAD
   John 1,2,3,4,5,6
   Susana 2,3
   Susanna 2,4,5,6
   Susannah 1

Wiley 1,3,4,5,6
Willie 2,5
COTCHOCHE 225
COTT
   W M 211
   W M, MD 211
COWANS
   Katie 124,125
   Myrtle Hewlett 125
COWE, Anne 255
CRAIG, Inez 142
DARLING
   A M 303
   R M 172,173
DAVIDSON
   Charles A 144,209
   Chas A 144,208,209
DAVIS
   Alice 292,293,294,295
   Annie 174,175,176,177
   Cogee 292,293,294,295
   Ella 65
   Georgia 291
   Joe 292,293,294,295
   John 174,175,176,177
   John M 174
   Lewis 290
   Martha 177
DEAN, Josie A 208
DEERE
   Lucy 19,20,21
   Raymond 19,20,21
   Thompson 19,20,21
DEMPSEY, R G 92,93
DEPUE, J A 108
DEPUT, J A 109
DICKSON, Lottie 291
DILL
   R A 274
   W H 210,276,277
DIXICO, Dela 282
DODGE, Emma 291
DONOVAN, Irwin176,177,251,252,253
DUNN, Tupper

Index

37,45,46,65,66,144,154,155,274,275,27
6,277,279,318
DUNZY, J R 133,140,141
DYSON, Wesley M 294
EASTMAN, J E 278,281
EDWARDS, Henry 290
ELAM, Jas T 308
ELLIE, Sallie 58
ELLIS
   Anne 14,15,18
   Annie 12,13,15,17,18,19
   Dabe 15
   Dave 15
   Fannie 15,19
   Fanny 12,14,16,17,18
   Marry 18
   Mary 13,14,15,16,17,18,19
   Sally 62
   Sargent 12,13,14,18
   Sargis 15
   Wally 12,13,14
ENRIQUES
   Jesus 203
   Lizzy 202
ESKRIDGE, C C 24,28,29,30,31,51
EVANS
   Della A 305,306,307
   Nettie 305,306,307
   Richard 305,306,307,308
EVERT, L H 74,75
FARNOSKE 22
FAULKNER, J D 2
FIELD
   Foster 273,274
   William 273,274
FIELDS, D W 224
FIFE
   Andrew 194
   James 67,68,69,70
   Louisa 67,68,69,70
   Sam 194,195
   Sandy 69,70
   Sarah 194
   Sinda 68

Sundy 68
FISH, Peter 250
FIXICO
   Cinda 296,297
   Cotcha 296
   Daley 276,279,280,281
   Dela 279
   Fela 278
   Katcher 296,297
   M H 278,281
   Rhoda 38
   Sallie 277,278,279,280,281,282
   Upsie 151
   Willie 296,297
FOSTER
   George Cameron 142,143,144,146
   Jennie May 142,143,144,146
   W C 146
   William C 142,143,144,146
   Wm C 144
FOWLER, J W 318,319,320
FOX
   Kate 156,159,160
   Katie 155,156,158,159,161
   Katy 156,157,158
   Luke .. 155,156,157,158,159,160,161
   Maggi 157
   Maggie155,156,157,158,159,160,161
   Sukey 157,160
   Sukie 156
   Ta sa la 159
   Willie 155,156,157,160
FRANK
   Amanda J 65,66
   Betty 251,252,253
   Mahala 251,252
   Neddie 252,253
   Short 251,252,253
   Tingo 65,66
   William 65,66
FREEMAN, John 180
GAMMILL, L C 206
GARRIGUES, Anna
   23,60,61,63,131,156,162,223

Index

GENTRY, Joshua 291
GIBSON, Thelma Maud 291
GOODEN, Sordie 203
GOODMAN
   Ah.ha.co.nan.ney 153
   Ah-ha co.nan.ney 154
GORDON, R G 321
GRAHAM, M F 217,220
GRAY, Sarah 195
GRAYSON, John 284
GREENLEAF
   Annie 229
   Sarah 230
GRIESEL
   E C 176
   E D 177
   Edw C
      23,61,111,131,139,158,159,172,177,
      185,209,237,238,239,261,324,325
   Edw E 76
GRIESELE, Edw C 243
GROSS, Ben D 298,299
GUILFOYLE, M D 124
HAINS
   H G 63
   Henry G 45,63,137,237,293
HAMIL5TON, J O 180
HAMILTON
   J O 178
   James O 179
HANNIGAN, Saml E 144
HARJAGE
   Daley 275,279,280
   Frank 275,279,280
   Nora 275,279,280
   Roller 275
HARJO
   Dailey 282,283
   Daley 276,277,278,281,282
   Dinaer 206
   Frank 276,277,282,283
   Lucy 206
   Pin 276,277,278,281,282,283
   Roler 283
   Roller 276,277,278,280,281,282,283
   Sar-woch-koch-kah 206
   Tubus 206
HARJO CHEE, Roller 279
HARJOCHEE
   Dela 278,279,282
   Pin 278,282
   Roller 278
HARJOGE
   Dailey 283
   Frank 283
   Roller 283
HARLAN, John 196
HARLINGS, Tony 290
HARNEY 22
HARRIS
   Charley 221,285
   Cora 220,221
   Polly 220,221,285
HARRISON
   Luke 105
   M H 268,269,270
   R P 195,196,307,308
   Robert P 195,307
HARTMAN, Mattie 74,75
HARVISON, Geo A ... 128,193,197,210
HAVRISON, Geo A 126
HAWKINS, Gabriel 291
HAYNES, S J 297
HELTON
   Nellie 39,40,41
   Romie Robert 40,41
   Ruthia Ellen 39,40
   William B 39,40,41
HEN
   Betsey 162
   Betsy 163,164
   Eblow 162
HENEHA, Eli 293,294
HENKINS, A C 124
HENRY
   Eugene Rolley 33
   Hugh 46,47
   J S 33,129,130

James Pier 128,129
James S 128,130
Lucy 128,129,130
Lula 32,33,34,130
Mintie 46,47
Tchinina 46,47
Viola Velmer 129,130
W A 32,33,34
Wilhe Jackson 32,33
HERROD, Cindy 97
HEWLETT
  Myrtle 124
  Will 124
HILL
  Arney 154,155
  A B 92,93
  Elmer 154,155
  Lottie Buck 154,155
  Lucy 70,73
HOKTOCHE 22
HOLT
  Cebern 291
  Z I J 141,142
HOOD
  Reid Lee 103,104
  Sarah Malinda 103,104
  Sterling P 103,104
HUDDLESTON, Creed T 144,210
HUDSON
  H J 143
  J H, MD 143
HULLIE
  Dave 236
  Eliza 236
  Tarpie 236
HUNDLEY, Mrs Mal 142
HURD, F S 142
HUTTON, Amelia 230,231
JACKSON
  Joe 1
  Susanna 2
  Susannah 1
  Walker 139
JAMES, E W 227,228

JEFFRIES
  Mattie 291
  Tom 291
JENNINGS, Robwrt 97
JOHNSON
  Arlie 225
  Carr Raymond 52,53,56,58
  Ceasar 236
  Eliza 236
  Ellie 225
  Hiram 97
  Hotulke 236
  J C 245,246
  Little Tom 225
  Little Tommy 225
  Mahala 193
  Mahalla 193
  Minnie
    52,53,54,55,56,57,58,59,60,61,62,63,
    64
  Wesley 236
JOHNSTON
  Emma 94
  Hiram 94
JONES
  Hannah 234,238,239
  Polly 233,234
KANARD
  Geo 83
  George 83
KELLEY, Caesar 108,109
KELLY
  Alabama 318,319
  Mahala 318,319,320
  Roman 319,320
  Wadley 318,319,320
  Wadly 319
KING, Cogee 255
KIZZIE 236
KNIGHT
  Amy 150,151
  To-che 99
  Dochee 317
  Fuller 44

Index

Jackson 70
Jenetta..192
Leaster 150,151
London 193,197,293,294
Ramsey 150,151
Susan 193
Wilson 98,100
LADD, W J..................................153,154
LARNEY
   Billy..223
   Mina 222
   Minnie 223,226,228,229
   William..................................222,223
LARRABEE, C F 18,290
LAVAL, Julia C 196
LAW, Sinda..68
LEVI, Eddie....................................291
LEWIS
   E E32,33,34,129,130,148,150,200,201
   Ellen 87,88,89,90,91,92,93
   Frank Turner........87,88,89,90,91,92
   John David...........87,88,89,90,92,93
   John Davis 91
   Oskar 90,91,92,93,104
LIETKA
   Martha 243
   Newman 242,243
   Richard 242,243
LIKOWSKI, Senora 318,319
LILLEY, John 65
LILLY, John 65
LINTON, W H..........................278,281
LITKA
   Dick 245
   Malinda..245
   Martha 244,245,246,247,248
   Newman 245,246,247,248
   Richard 244,245,246,247,248
LIYERWINEY 275
LOONEY
   Della 199,200
   Della May 197,198,199,200
   Ella 149,150,199,200
   Eller 147,148,150,197,198,200

Forest Leonard....... 147,148,149,150
N W 147,148,149,150,198,200
Newton 149,199
LOTT
   Jennie..236
   Lucy..236
   Tena..236
   Tommie 236,250
LOWE
   Ales..115
   Alex 110,112
   Cindy 68,70
   Con Nar Ky 67
   Lena..67
   Louisa...67
   Sam..226
LUCAS, J B....................................104
LUCUS
   Emerline 269,270
   Frank.....................................190,191
   Josephine 189,190
   Lucy...............203,204,205,206,207
   Martha 189,190,191,192,204
   Mary 188,189,190,191
   Mary A 191,192
   Nanie 205
   Nannie 206
   Nenie 203,204,205,206
   Rufus 188,189
   Rufus James..........................191,192
   Thomas 188,189,190,191,192
   Thos...191
   Toney..............................205,206,207
   Tony 203,204,206
LUSK, A M 208,209
LYFORD, Dr Harry O..................40,41
MADAWEE, Betsey 164
MAELOT, H G.................................39
MAHADY, Billie 52
MAHARDY, Billi 58
MALLEY 22
MALOT, H G 38,45,46,275,279
MANAWEE
   Betsey 165

Index

Betsy 163,166
MANER 223
MARCUM
  Ros. 301
  Rose 301
  Sarah 301
MARS, F L 39,40,41
MARSHALL, Lizzie 34,35,36,37
MARTIN
  Jennie 317
  William T 8
MASON, Henry 74,75
MAYES
  Marry 74
  Martha 74,75
  Wyatt 74
MCDERMOTT
  J
    1,9,20,52,58,98,156,163,223,244,246
    ,251,252,253,280,295
  Jesse
    1,22,53,75,76,95,96,109,159,183,222
    ,251,252,253,261,275,276,280,284
MCGILBRA, Sinda 267
MCGIRT
  Eli 97
  Loney 254,257
MCINTOSH
  F A 3
  Josiah 290
  Nelson 291
  Susan D 177
MCNAC
  Annie 229,230
  Flossie 229,230
  Fred 229,230
MCQUEEN
  W C 82
  W E 68,84,85
MEACHAM, Olin W 47,218,220
MEDLEN, T A 217,220
MERRICK
  Edward 196,226
  Lona 76,185,226

MERRITT, W G 144
MICCO
  Dechee 316
  Dochee 317
  Henry 297,316,317
  Lucy 316,317
MICHILEY 70
  Lucy 70
MILAM, A N 321,322
MILES, E D 274
MILLER
  Cecil 300,302,303,304
  J Y 111,178,237,261
  Lizzie 42,43,44,46
  Louisa 41,42,46
  Lousa 45
  Malvin H 300,301,302
  Quint 302
  Quint H 300,301,302,303,304
  Rose E 301
  Rose Etta 300,301,302,303,304
  Sam 42
MILLS, B H 134,266,267
MINA 223
MITCHELL
  J M 321
  Lucinda 225
  Ralph 70
  Roy 70
MITCHILEY 71,72,73
  Lucy 71,72,73
  Lucy Hill 71,72
  Ralph 72,73
  Roy 71,72,73
MONAHEE, Betsey 162
MONAYEE 297
MOON, Geo G 121
MOONEY, Bernard B 268
MOORE
  Hainey 106,108,109
  Haney 107,108
  Hensy 107
  John 106,107,108,109
  John W 108,109

Index

MORGAN, Della Agnes 308
MORRISON, Louisa 310,312
MORROW
   Alfred 263,265
   Alice 260,261,262,263,264
   Elva 261,265
   J B
      88,92,93,104,105,106,229,230,298,299
   Maercy 261
   Marcy 260,262,263,265
   N L 262
MORTON
   Claude S 207,210,211
   Josie 210
   Josie A 208,210,211,212
   Jossie A 212
   Maude 211,212,213
   Mossid 211
   Mossie 207,210,212,213
   Mossie M 208
MOSQUITO
   Albert 123
   Kattie 123,124
   Polly 123
MOTT, M L 16,288
MUSQUITO
   Albert 123,124
   Kattie 123
   Polly 124
MYERS, J B 77,82,164
NAPIER, Martha 174,175,176
NEEDLES, Hon T B 206
NOBLE, E T 211
NORBE 54,57,58
NORBI 58
NORBIE 53
ORR, J S 179,181
PARRISH
   Zera E 178
   Zera Ellen 243
PATTERSON 111
   J B 115
   John B

112,113,114,115,116,186,187,188,221,227,228,284,285,286
PAUTH, J F 160
PEACOCK, J L 195,307
PERRYMAN
   Legus C 201,202,203
   Martha 178,181
   Silla 179,180,181
   Willie 291
PHILLIPS
   Jno 151
   Jno H 72,318
   John H
      70,72,73,151,262,263,264,265,266,297,317,318
PLACIOS, Estoban 127
POE, Magie Nola 291
PONOSKI, Martha 174
PORTER
   Benjamin 194,196,197
   James 194
   James E 196,197
   Nancy 196,197
POSEY
   Ale 7
   Alex
      12,14,25,29,32,41,42,44,52,53,57,59,61,62,69,76,77,82,86,87,97,98,100,108,111,113,162,163,164,165,169,184,185,189,190,191,204,216,217,218,219,223,224,226,227,229,230,231,232,236,237,238,241,250,253,254,255,258,259,272,273
POWELL
   Charles 177,178,179,180,182
   John 177,178,179,180,181,182
   Martha 178,179,180,181,182
PROCTOR 170
   [Illegible] 170,171
   Jailler 108
   Schoka 170
   Toney E 170
RALSTEN, Scott 143
RANDLETT

Index

Col Jas F 55,64
James F 54,63
RICE
   Benjamin F Rice, Jr 125
   Benjamin F, Jr 125
RICHARDS, John D 70
ROBERSON
   Annie 215,216,218,219
   Bertha 215
   Dave 216,218,219
   Hannah 216,217,219
   Louisa 216,217
   Nelson 218,219
ROBERTS, Mrs S J 33
ROBERTSON
   [Illegible] 129
   Dr 199
   Dr J W 147,148
   J W 148,150,197,198,199,200
   J W, MD 150,200
ROBINSON
   Annie 215,217,218,219,220
   Dave 217,218,219,220
   Dr 149
   Hannah 218,220
   Louisa 215,217,218
   Nelson 215,219,220
ROBISON
   Barney C...120,121,233,234,256,257
   Ida 120
RUCKER
   G R 106
   G R, MD 106
RYAN, J F 151
SANDERS, Gennie 291
SARLS, Jennie 162,164
SAWAKEE 42
SAWYER
   B F 125
   Nancy 125
SAYOCHEE 22
SCHARNAGEL
   Bille C 47
   Charles E 47

Charles E, MD 47
SCOTT
   Bessie 7,8,9,10,11
   Lambert 222,227
   Louisa 197
   Lucinda 7,8,9,10,11
   Marguerite 291
   Martha 122
   Mina 222,227,228
   Nannie 225
   Nicey 321,322
   Pleasant 8,10
   Robert 290
   Turner 7,8,10,11
   Wicey 222
SEMHOYE 76
SENEGEE 42
SHABER, F W 139
SHELBY, David 159
SHIPP, J M 233,234
SIEKA, Sukie 109
SIMHOYA 77
SIMHOYE 79,80
SIMMER 22
SIMMONS
   George 168,169,170
   Martha 168,169,170
   William 168,169,170
SIMMS, E W 123,153,154
SIMON
   Caesar 137
   Charity 137
   Ellen 132,133,140
SIMS, E W 124
SKAGGS
   D C
      7,12,14,25,29,32,42,44,52,57,59,61,6
      2,69,86,87,97,98,100,108,111,113,16
      5,169,185,189,190,191,204,209,216,
      217,218,219,224,227,229,230,231,23
      8,239,250,254,255,258,259,272,273
   Drennan C
      7,12,13,14,21,25,29,44,45,52,57,59,6
      1,62,66,69,70,86,87,98,99,100,101,1

08,112,113,119,122,123,149,165,169,186,188,189,190,191,199,204,211,212,213,216,217,219,231,232,235,237,240,250,251,259,272,273,310,311,312

Mr 22
SKEETER, Albert 153,154
SKELTON
   A ? 34
   A V 192
SMITH
   A A 298,299
   Adeline 268,269,270
   Albert K 268,269
   Amanda 34
   Ella 149,199
   Eller 147
   Frank J 284
   Gladdis G 171,172
   Gladdis Gertrude 171,172,173
   J M 171,172,173
   J W 171
   James R 269,270
   John 85
   Josie 245
   Minnie 269,270
   A O 105
   Rachel 171,172,173
   Rachel A 171
   Stere J 269,270
   Thomas M 268,269,270
SNELSON
   Andrew J, MD 173
   Ea J 300
   A J 171,173,302,303,304,306
   A J, MD 171,302,306
SOLOMAN, Wisey 70
SOMERVILLE, O S 303
SPANIARD, James 236
STAMPER, J B 143
STARR
   Daniel 21
   Polly 319,320
STEPHENSON
   Mr 184
   A P 184,185,186,187
   Polly 182,183,184,185,186,187
   Siney 182,183,184,185,186,187
STEWARD, Chas E 202
STEWART, Chas E 201
STIDHAM
   Liza 236
   Mattie 236
   Timmie 236
STODDARD
   William F 47
   Wm F 50
STORM
   Bertha 297,298
   John 297,298,299
   Lori 297,298,299
   Pocahontas 298,299
SUNARKEY, Sam John 60
SUNTHLOPPA 163
SWOFFORD, J H 276
TARVIN
   Marie Louisa 125,126,127,128
   Patience 125
   Patience F 126,127,128
   Pharauh F 126,127
   Pleasant F 127,128
TAYLOR, Dennis 291
THACKERY, Frank A 55,64
THLATISKE 1
THLOPPA, Sun 225
THOMPSON
   Alice 301
   Ellen 301
   Eva 301
   Patsy 301
   Thomas 21
TIGER
   Ada 152,153,154
   Charles 291
   Jumbo 152,153
   Losanna 44
   Louisa 41,42,43,44,45,46
   Lousa 45

Index

Lousanna 41,42,43,44,45,46
  So.con.thla.ney 153
  So.con-thla-ney 124
  Thomas 42,43,44,45,46
TOWNSEND, W M 134
TURNER
  J M 38,39
  Jno E 134
UNAH
  Barney 23,24,25,26,51
  Mardie 22,23,24,25,26
  Nicey 22,23,24,25,26
  Parnosy 29,31
UNNUSSEE, Barnosee 22
UNUSSEE 22
  Mardie 23
  Nicey 22
UPTON, Dan 68,69,83,84,95,96
VAN COTT, M C 127
VIVERO, Nicolasa 127
WALKER, Rhoda 290
WALLACE
  Chaney 133
  S W 134
  W A 303
WALLAS, Chaney 133,140,141
WARRIOR
  Carr Raymond 52,53,54,55,57,59
  Sam 53,54,55,56,57,59,60
WASHINGTON
  Colbert 232,233,234
  Lillie 232,233,234
  Polly 232,233,234,235
  Sucky 233
WATSON
  Dave 222,223,227,228
  David 223,226,228,229
  Louisa 225
  McDaniel 225
  Sandy 222,223,224,225,226,227,228
  Santy 228
WATTS
  B, MD 264,265
  Dr B 263,265

WEBB, John 186
WELLS, Lydia 92,93,104,298,299
WESLEY
  Charley 9
  To-che 99
  Ida 94,95,96,97,98,99,100,102
  Iva 101
  Matilda 9
  Thomas 94,95,97,99,102
  Toche 97,98,99,100,101,102
  Tochee 94
WEST
  Billy 224
  Emma 225
  Louisa 224
  Lumsey 225,226
WHITE, J T 173
WHITLOW
  Edward 77
  John 75,76,77,78,80,81,85
  Semhoye 78,82,83,84,85,86
  Simhoye 75,76,81,83,84
  Sissie 78,79,80,81,82,83,84,86,87
  Sissy 77
  Wemond 77
  William
    75,76,77,79,80,81,82,83,84,85,86,87
WILDAN, Sam 51
WILDCAT
  Losanna 225
  Sandy 225
WILEY 14,15
WILLHITE, J N 319,320
WILLIAMS
  M R 174
  Mary 323
  Nat 134,266,267
WILLS
  John J 231
  Ollie Ann 231
  William H 230,231
WILSON
  Bennie 249,250
  Bessie 59,60,61,62,63,64,65

Bettie 236,237,238,240,241
Carl 62
Charley 237,238,249,250
Charlie 254
Chlie 257
Clark 60,61,62,63,64
Clarke 63
Hattie 308,309
Hettie 310,311,312,313
Horace 198,199,311,313
Jesse E 18,291
Lizzie 249,250
Minnie236,237,238,239,240,241,242
R B 310,311,312,313
Raymond 309,310,313
Sarah Jane 309,311,312
Thomas 236,237,238,240,242
Wicey 237,238,240
Wisey 236,241,242
WOFFORD
   Lizzie 315
   Shirly 314,315
WOLF 60
WRIGHT
   C J 105,106
   Jane P 105,106
   Olive A 105,106
YAHOLA
   Fushushte 117
   Kizzie 117
   Mary 117
YARDY
   Armer 320,321,322
   Dock 321,322
   Hettie 320,321
   Thomas 320,321,322
YARHOLA
   Fushutche 109
   Hallake 110
   Kizzie 109
   Mar wak kikee 155
   Mary 109

www.ingramcontent.com/pod-product-compliance
Lightning Source LLC
Chambersburg PA
CBHW020243030426
42336CB00010B/595